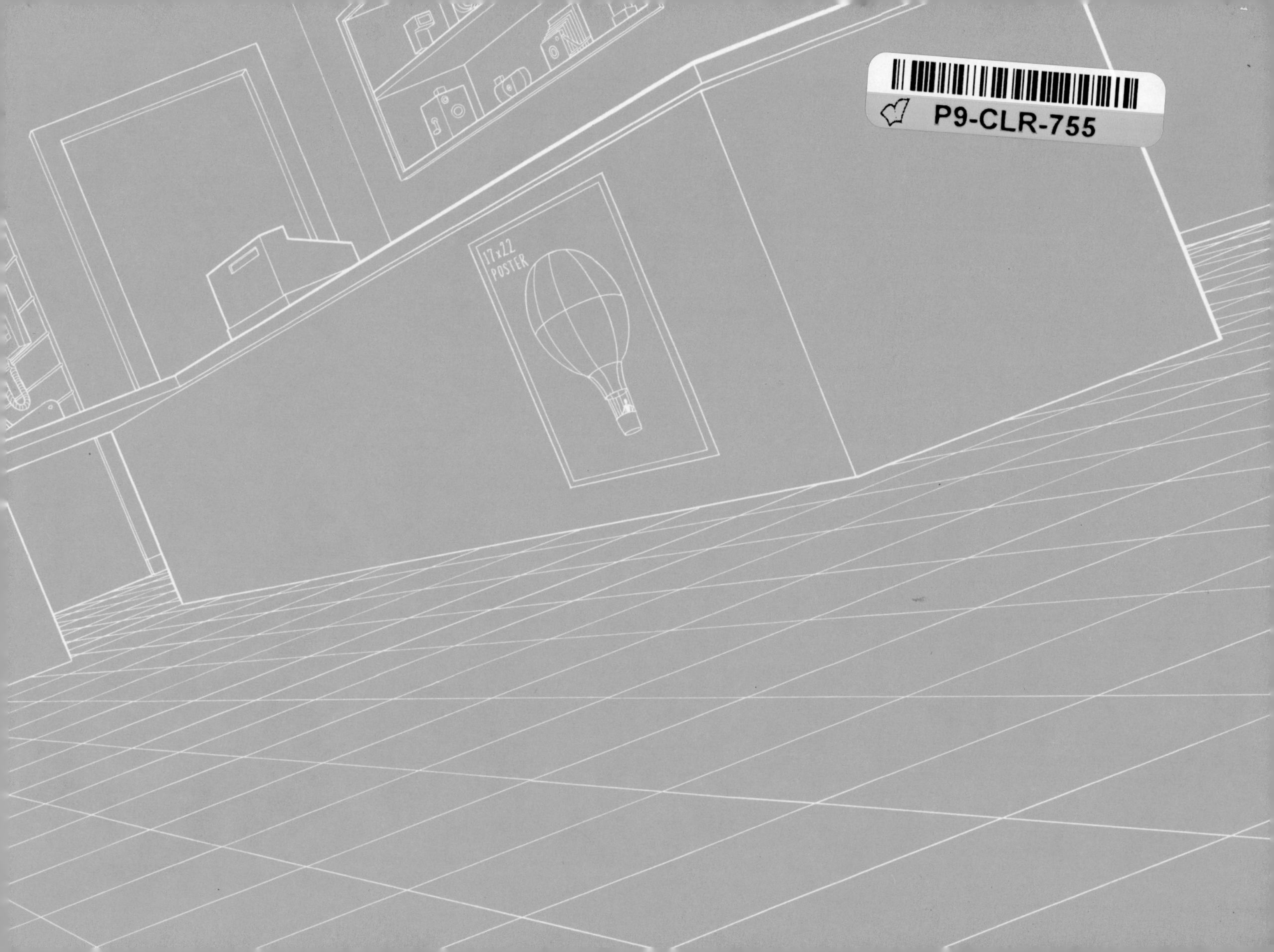
17x22
POSTER

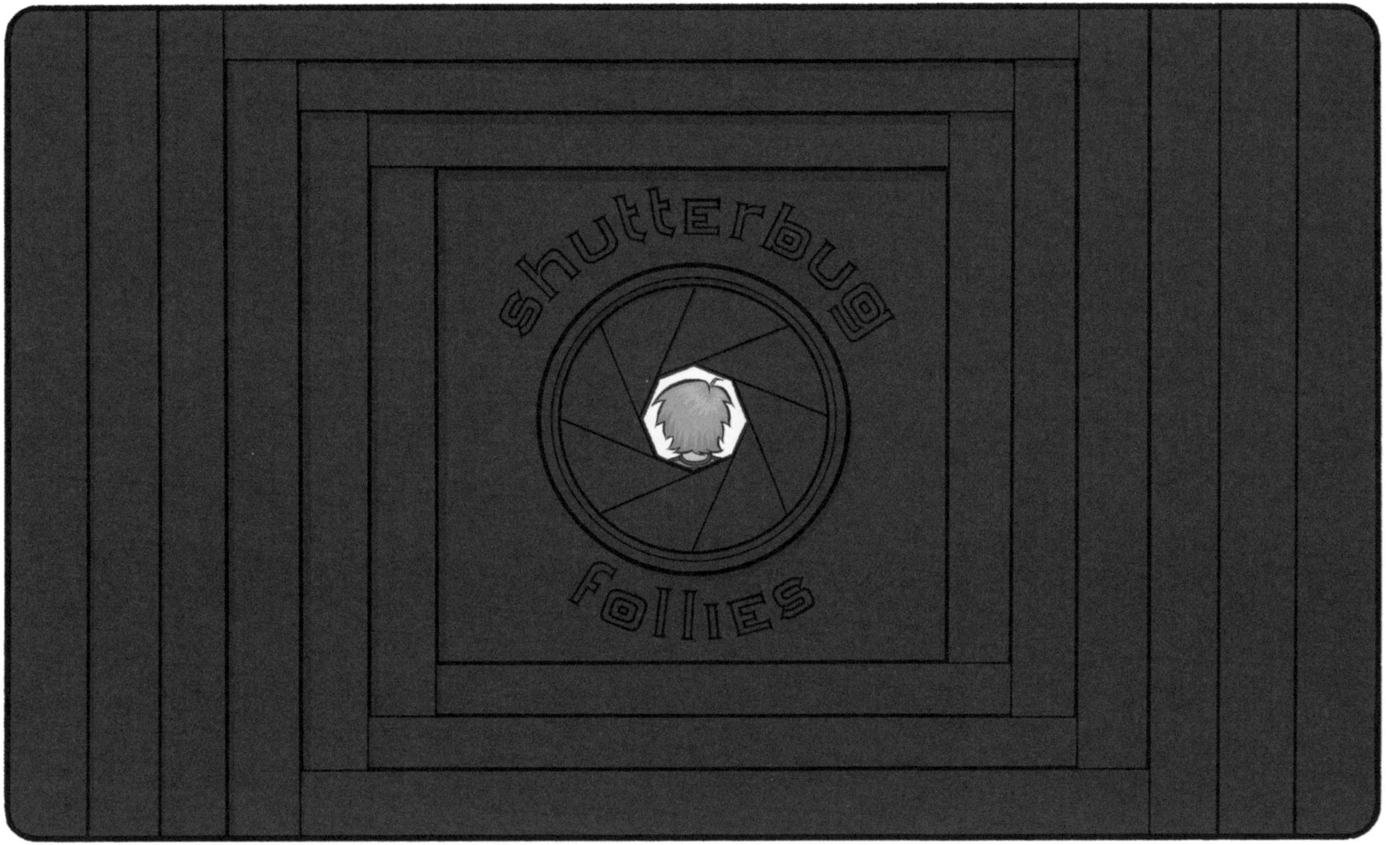
shutterbug
follies

Published by Doubleday Graphic Novels, a division of Random House, Incorporated, 1540 Broadway, New York, New York 10036. Material herein originally appeared in the *New York Press* and the *Ripsaw News*. This graphic novel is a work of fiction. Any references to real persons, events, establishments, organizations, or locales are intended only to give the fiction a sense of reality and authenticity. All other names, characters, and incidents are either derived from the author's imagination or are used fictitiously, as are those fictionalized events that may involve real persons. Book design by the author. Printed in the United States of America.

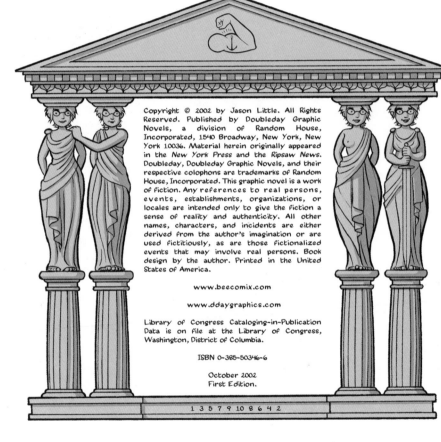

www.beecomix.com

www.ddaygraphics.com

Library of Congress Cataloging-in-Publication Data is on file at the Library of Congress, Washington, District of Columbia.

ISBN 0-385-50346-6

October 2002
First Edition.

1 3 5 7 9 10 8 6 4 2

For Myla

shutterbug follies

jason little

DOUBLEDAY GRAPHIC NOVELS
New York

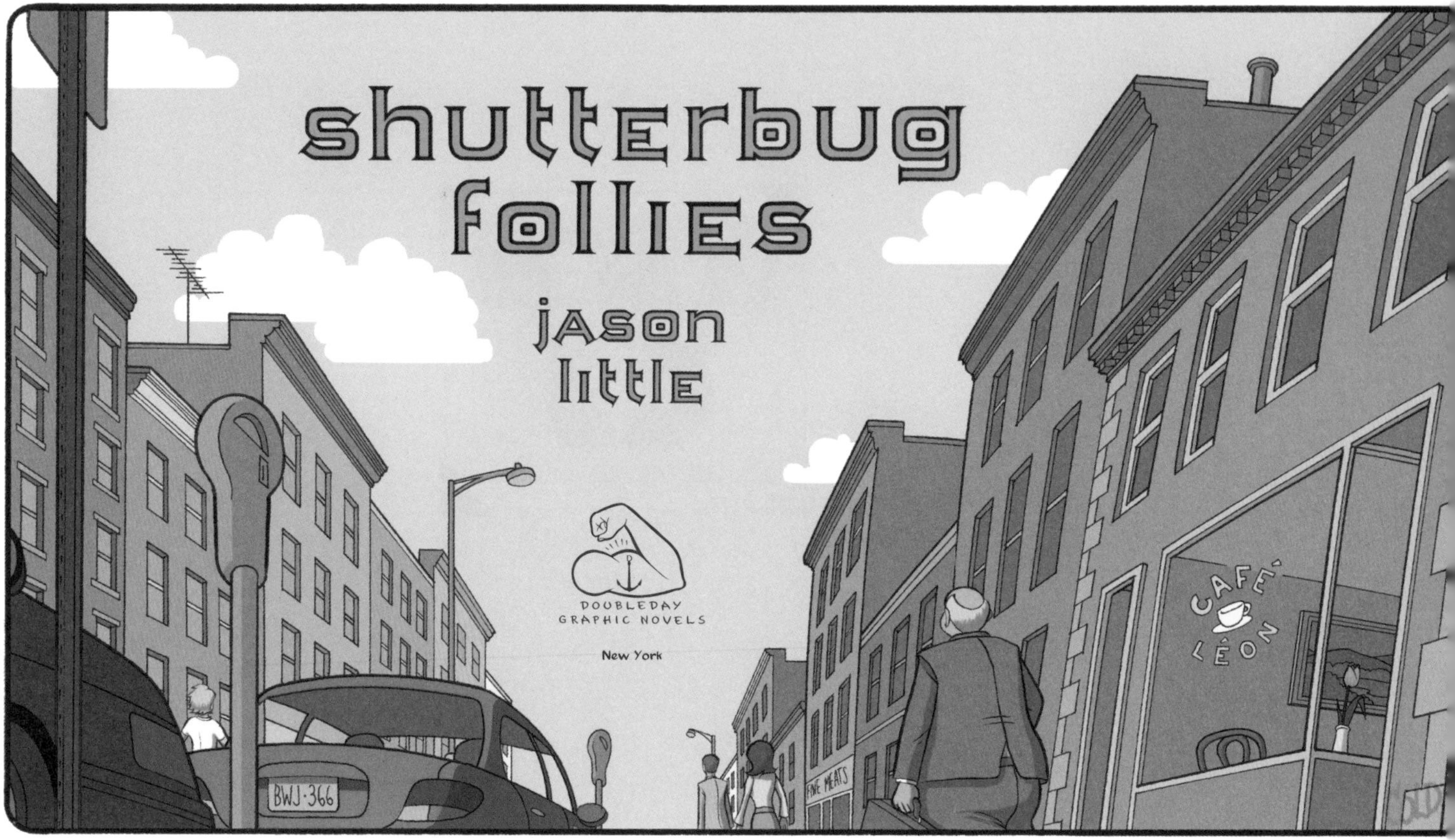
BWJ·366
FINE MEATS
CAFÉ LÉON

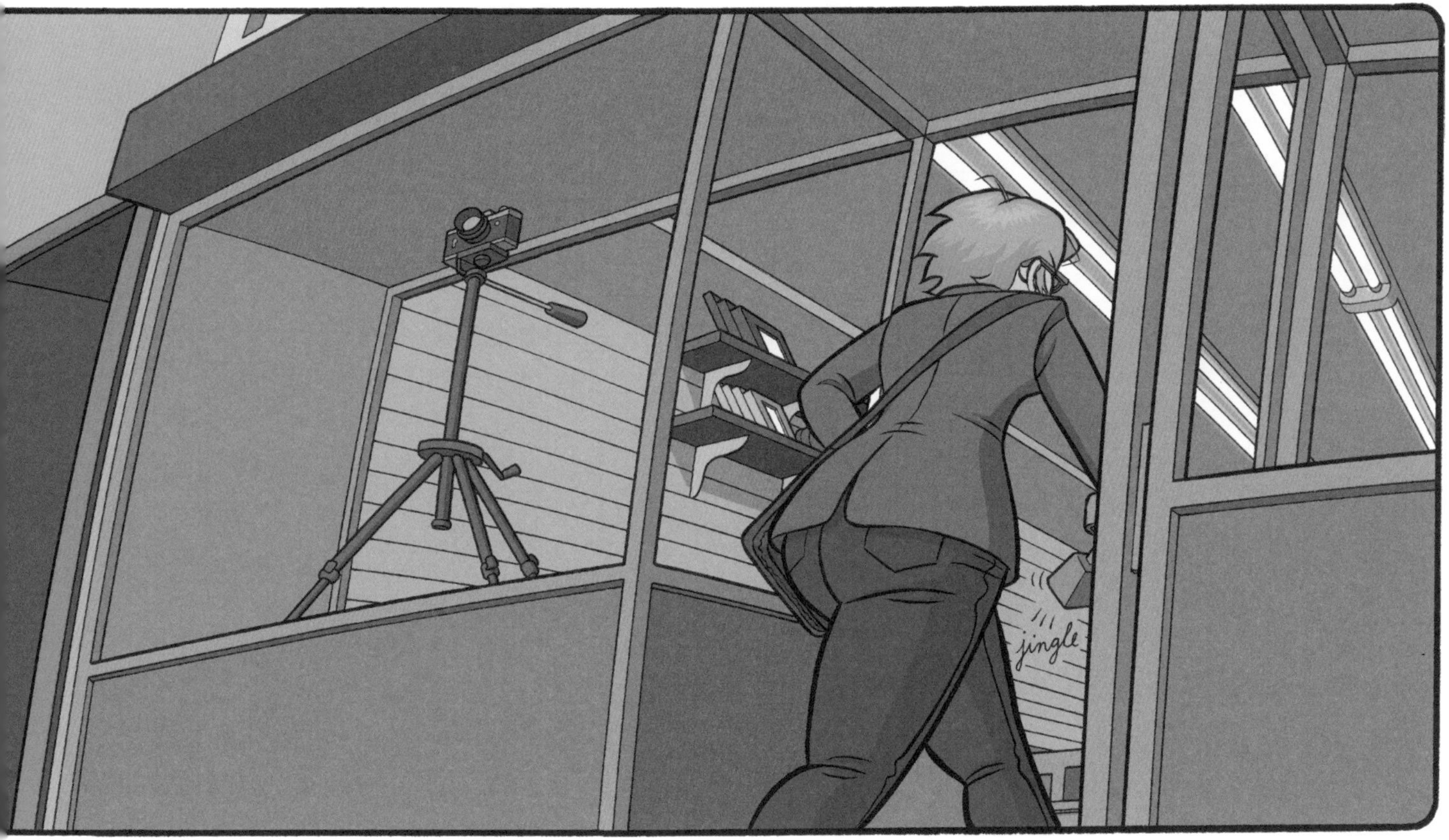
jingle

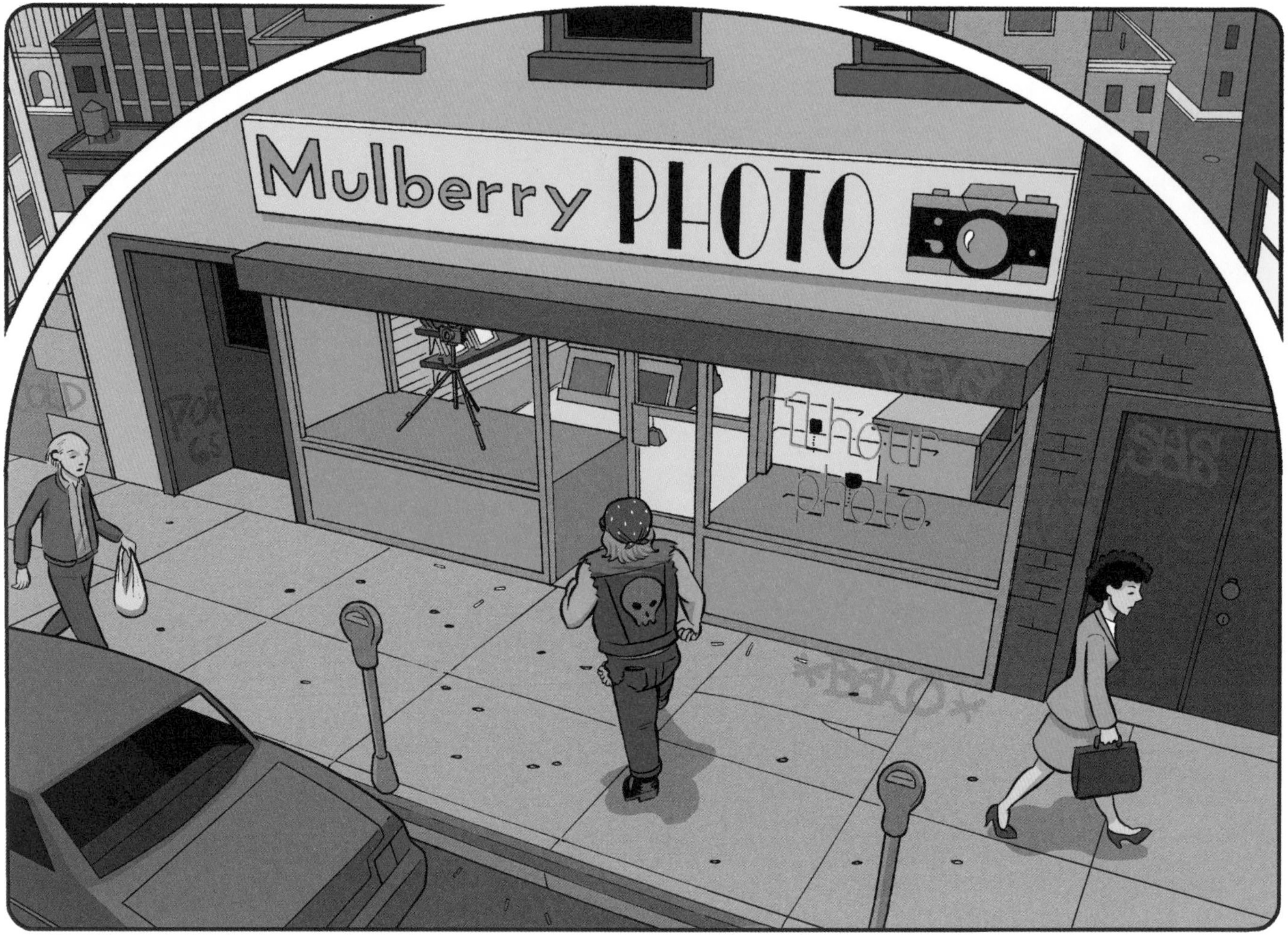
Mulberry PHOTO
1 hour photo

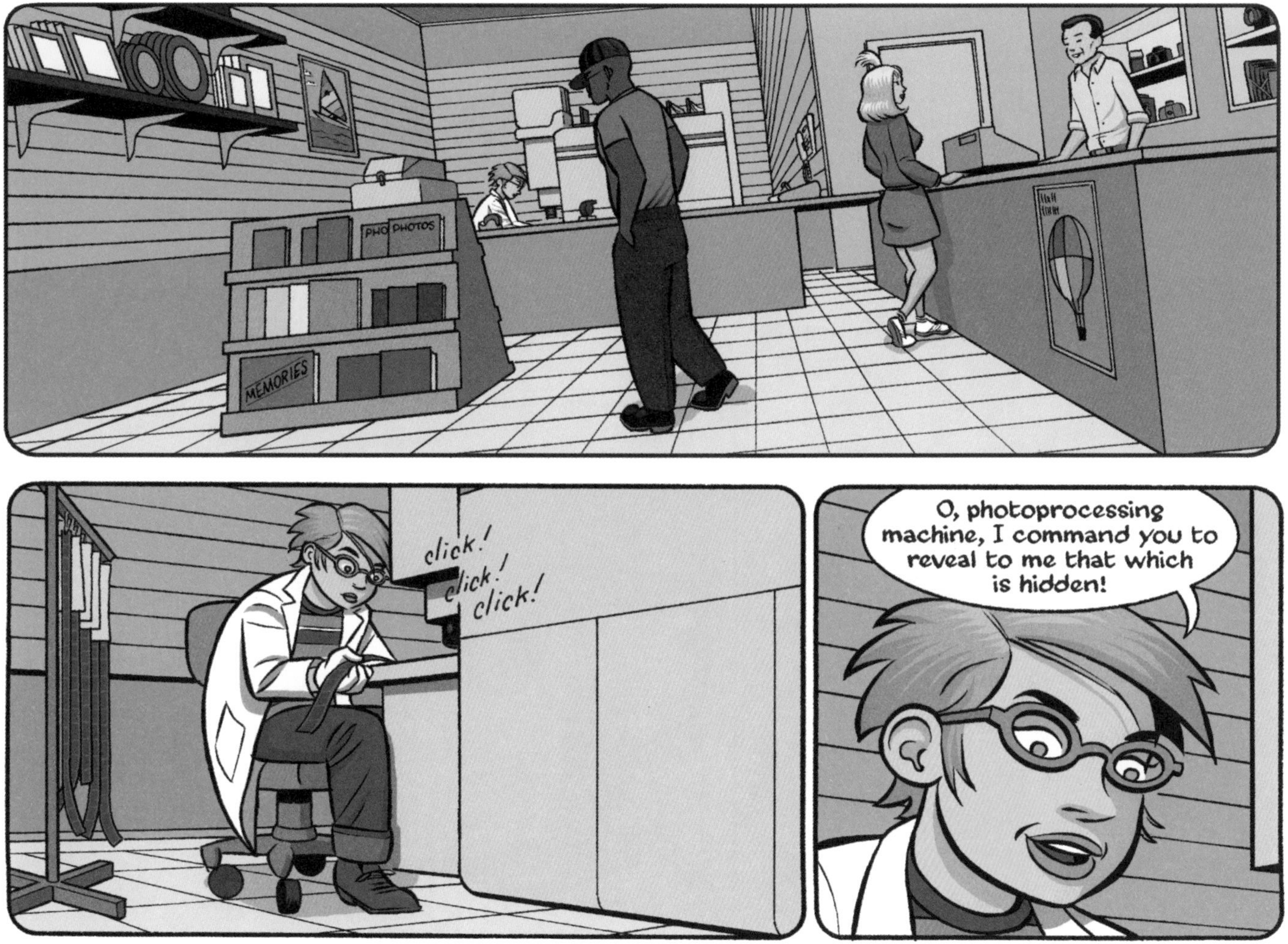
PHO
PHOTOS
MEMORIES
click!
click!
click!
O, photoprocessing machine, I command you to reveal to me that which is hidden!

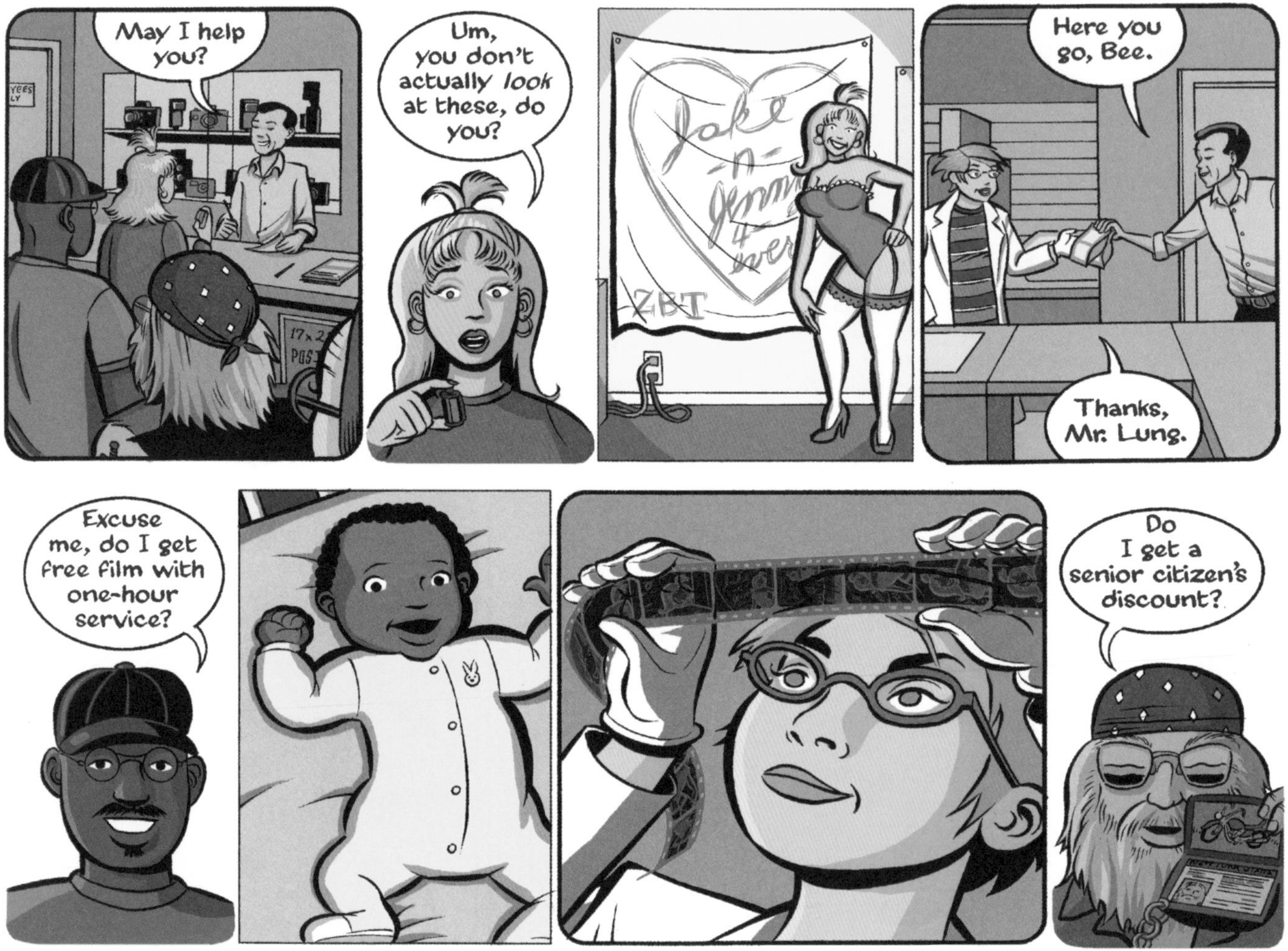
May I help you?
Um, you don't actually *look* at these, do you?
ZBT
Here you go, Bee.
Thanks, Mr. Lung.
Excuse me, do I get free film with one-hour service?
Do I get a senior citizen's discount?

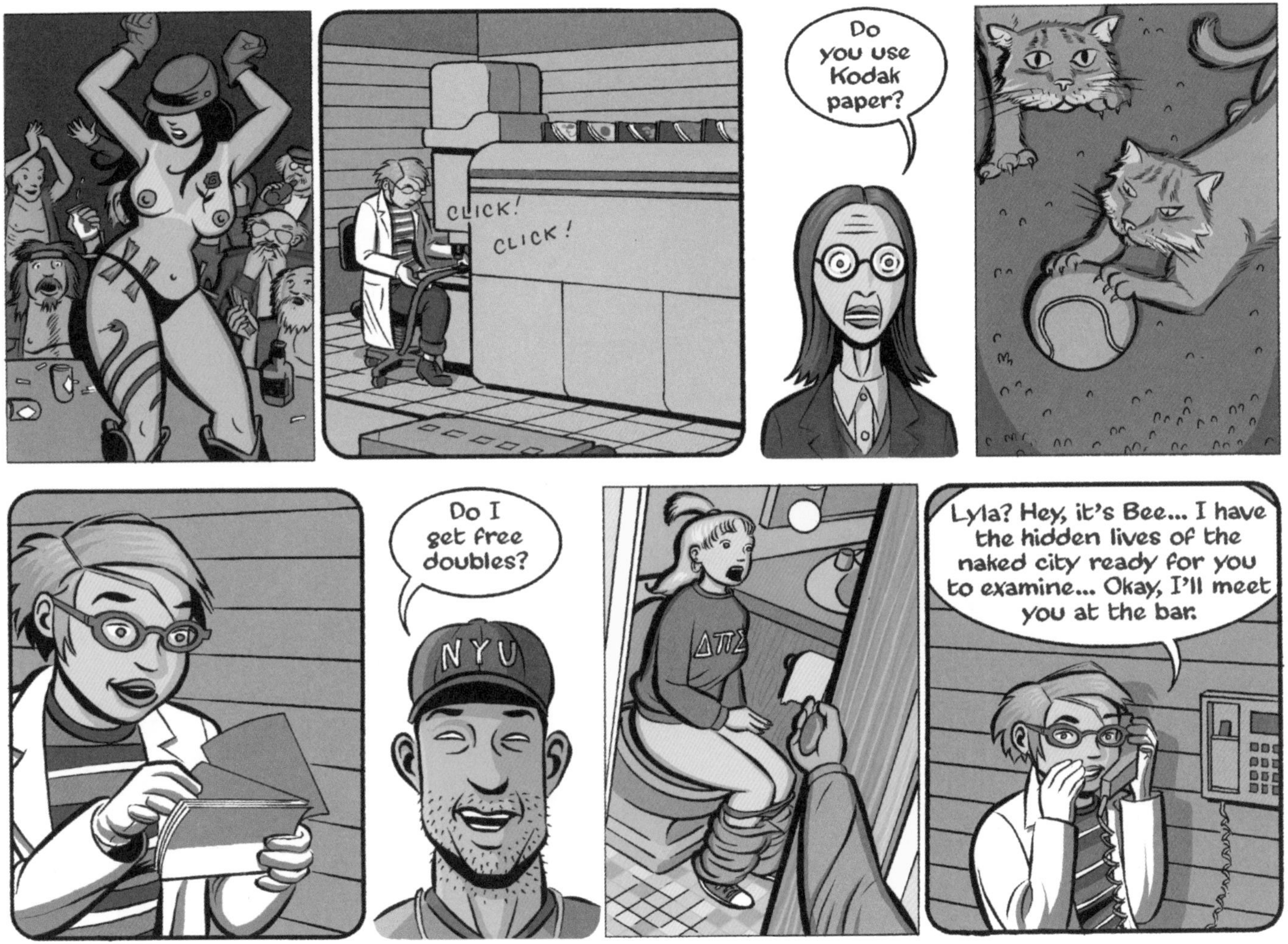
CLICK!
CLICK!
Do you use Kodak paper?
Do I get free doubles?
ΔΠΣ
NYU
Lyla? Hey, it's Bee... I have the hidden lives of the naked city ready for you to examine... Okay, I'll meet you at the bar.

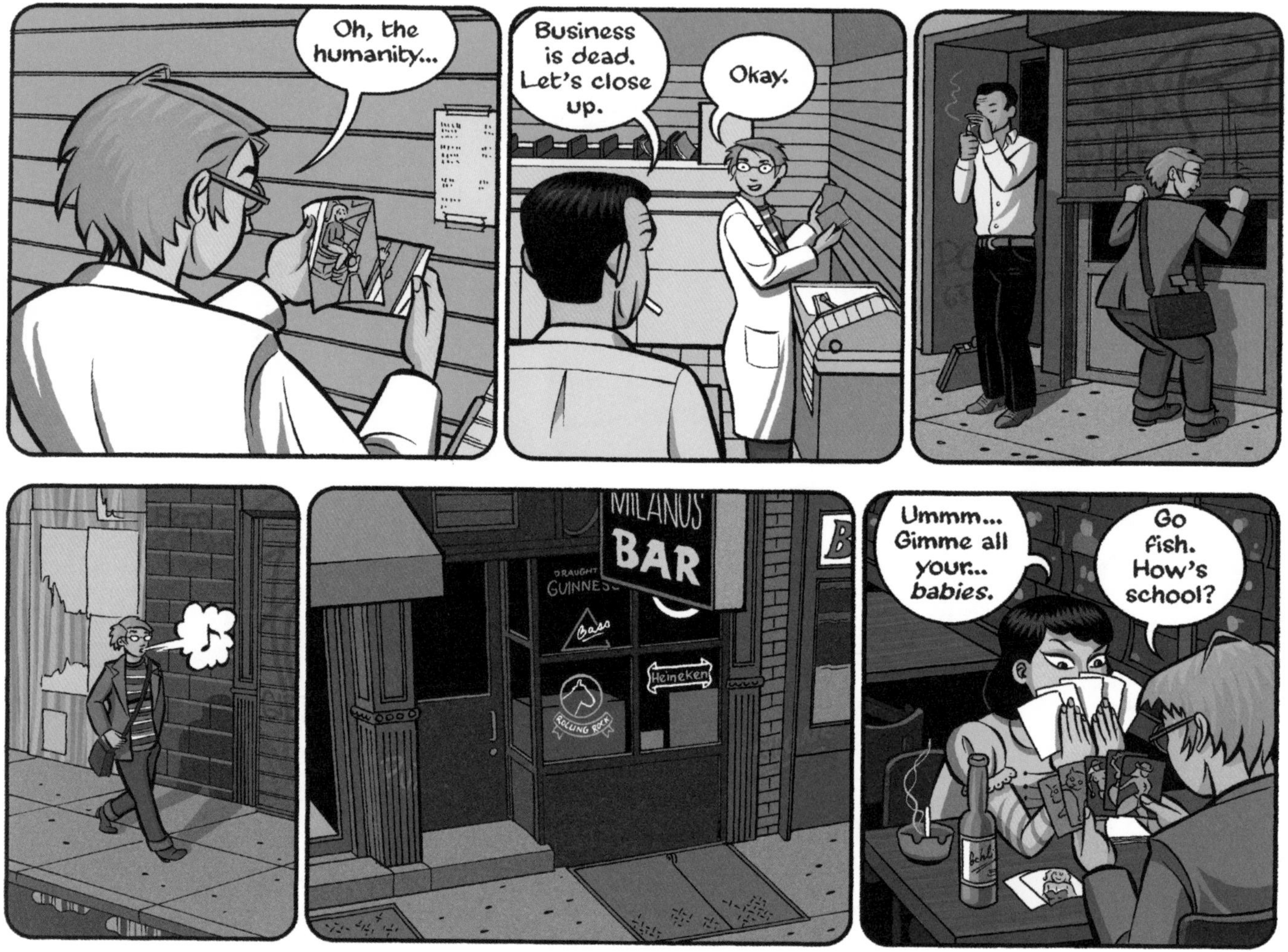
Oh, the humanity...
Business is dead. Let's close up.
Okay.
MILANOS'
BAR
DRAUGHT
Bass
Heineken
ROLLING ROCK
Ummm... Gimme all your... *babies.*
Go fish. How's school?

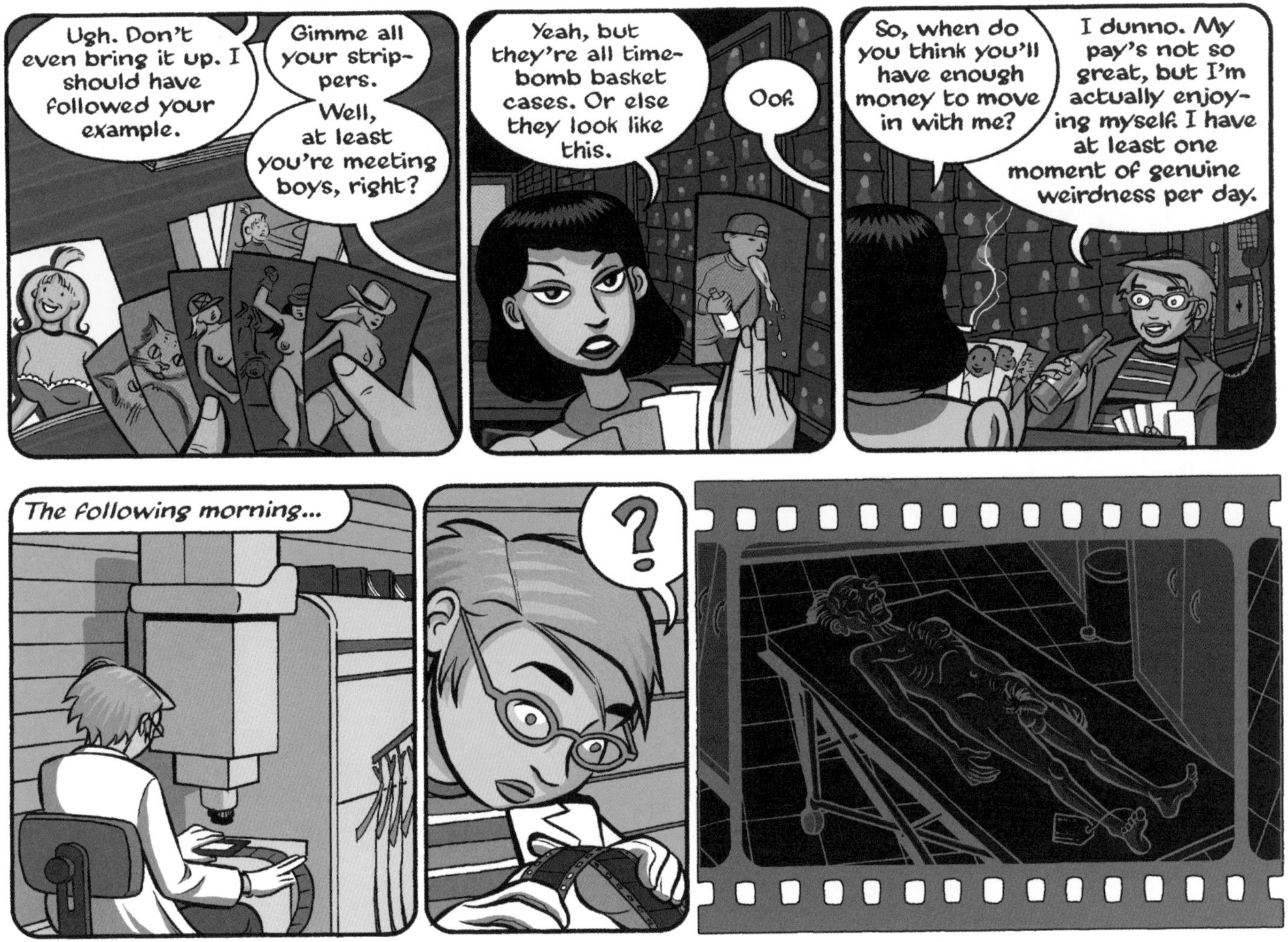
Ugh. Don't even bring it up. I should have followed your example.
Gimme all your strip-pers.
Well, at least you're meeting boys, right?
Yeah, but they're all time-bomb basket cases. Or else they look like this.
Oof.
So, when do you think you'll have enough money to move in with me?
I dunno. My pay's not so great, but I'm actually enjoy-ing myself. I have at least one moment of genuine weirdness per day.
The following morning...
?

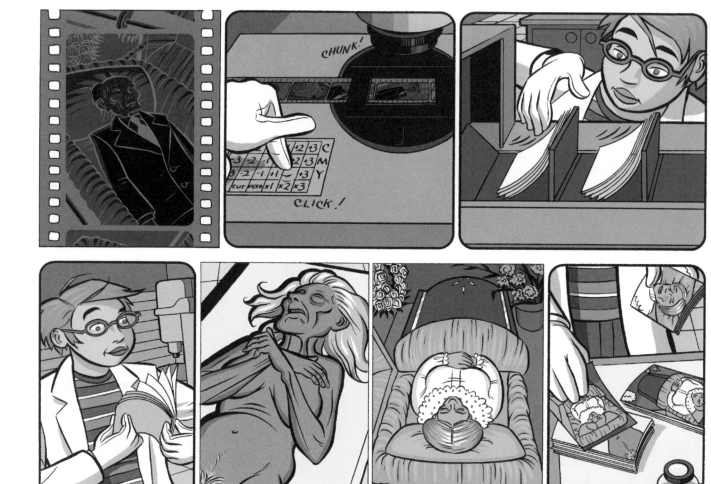

CHUNK!

CLICK!

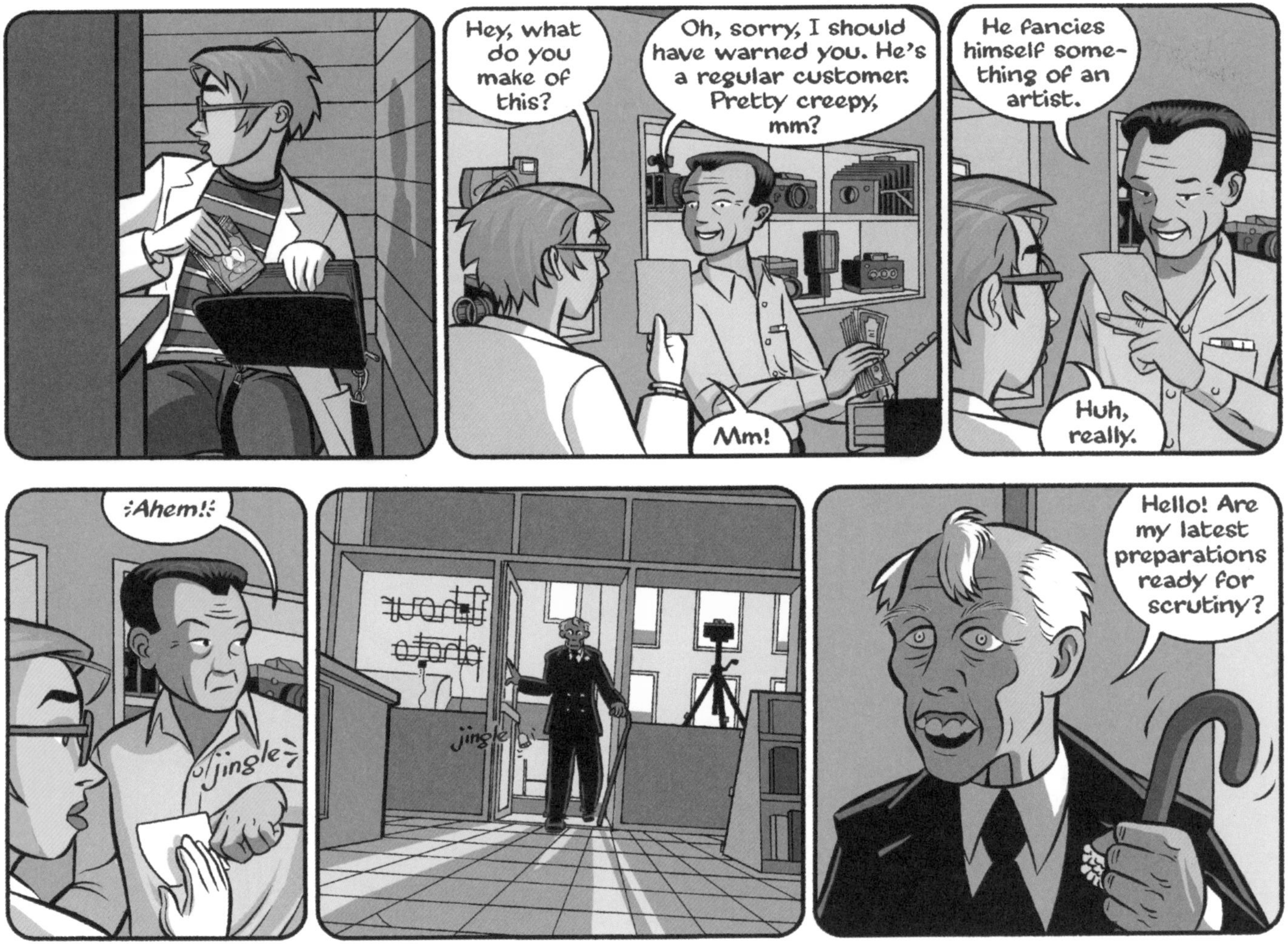
Hey, what do you make of this?
Oh, sorry, I should have warned you. He's a regular customer. Pretty creepy, mm?
Mm!
He fancies himself some-thing of an artist.
Huh, really.
Ahem!
jingle
jingle
Hello! Are my latest preparations ready for scrutiny?

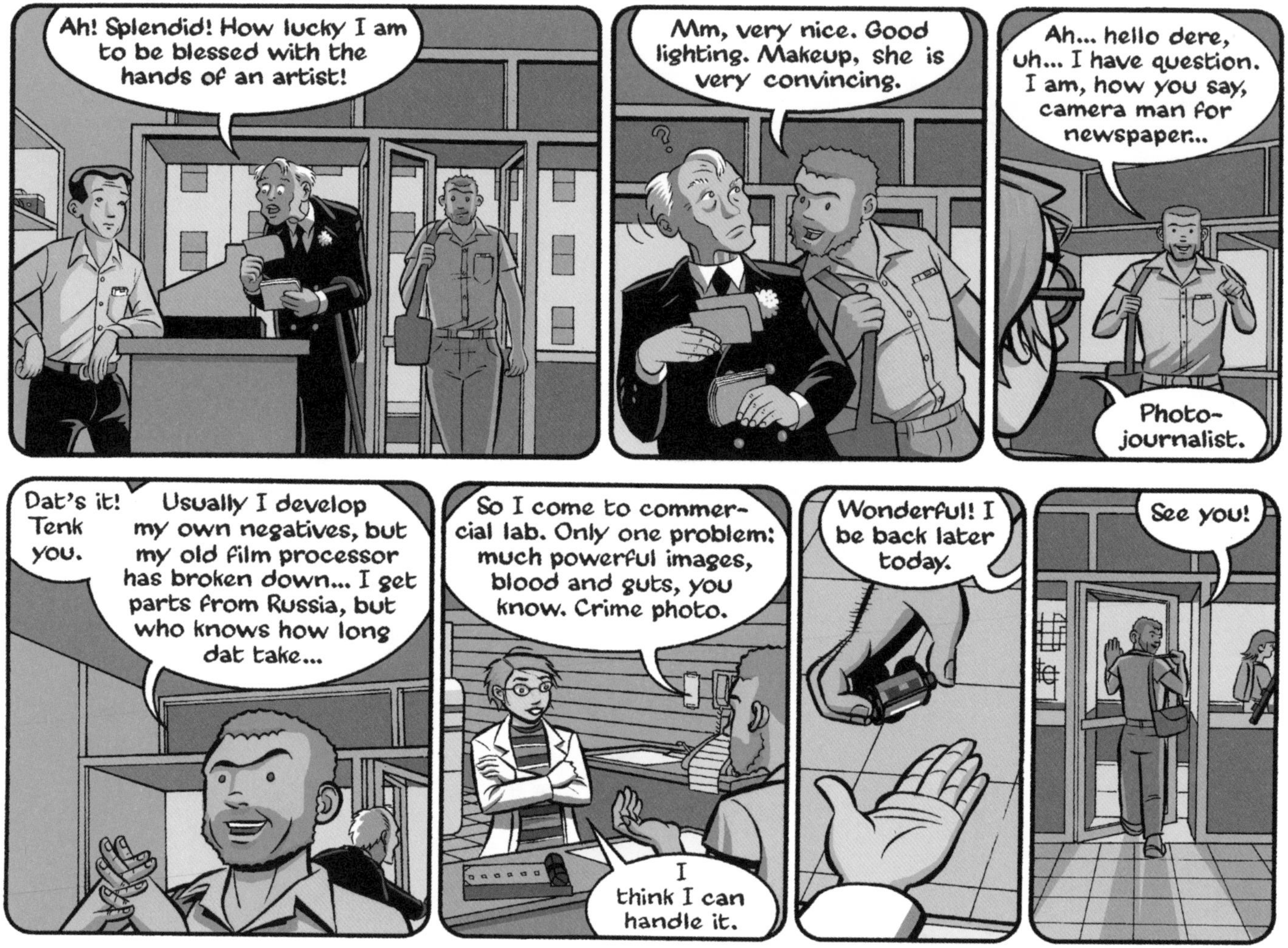
Ah! Splendid! How lucky I am to be blessed with the hands of an artist!
Mm, very nice. Good lighting. Makeup, she is very convincing.
Ah... hello dere, uh... I have question. I am, how you say, camera man for newspaper...
Photo-journalist.
Dat's it! Tenk you.
Usually I develop my own negatives, but my old film processor has broken down... I get parts from Russia, but who knows how long dat take...
So I come to commercial lab. Only one problem: much powerful images, blood and guts, you know. Crime photo.
I think I can handle it.
Wonderful! I be back later today.
See you!

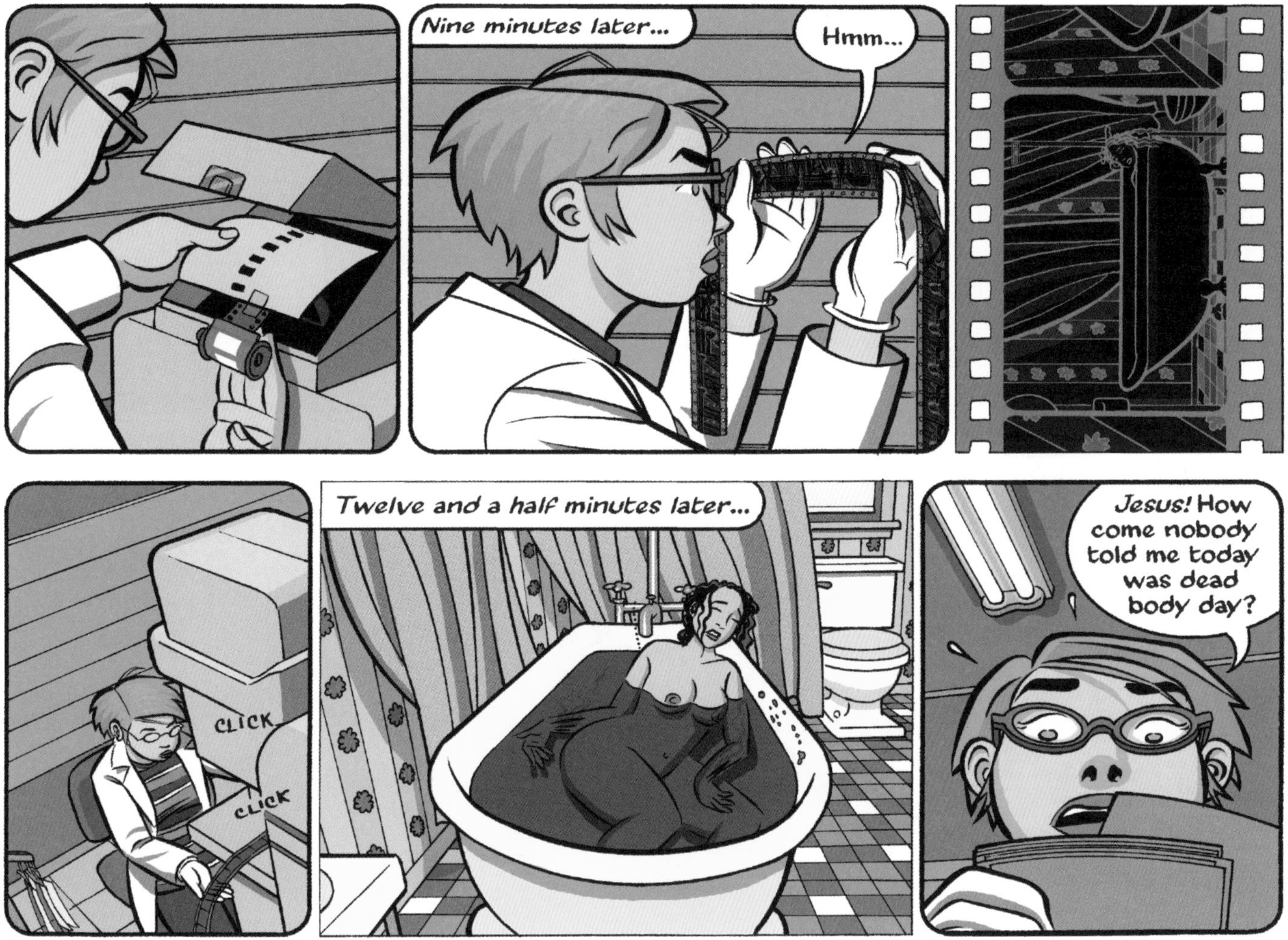
Nine minutes later...
Hmm...
Twelve and a half minutes later...
CLICK
CLICK
Jesus! How come nobody told me today was dead body day?

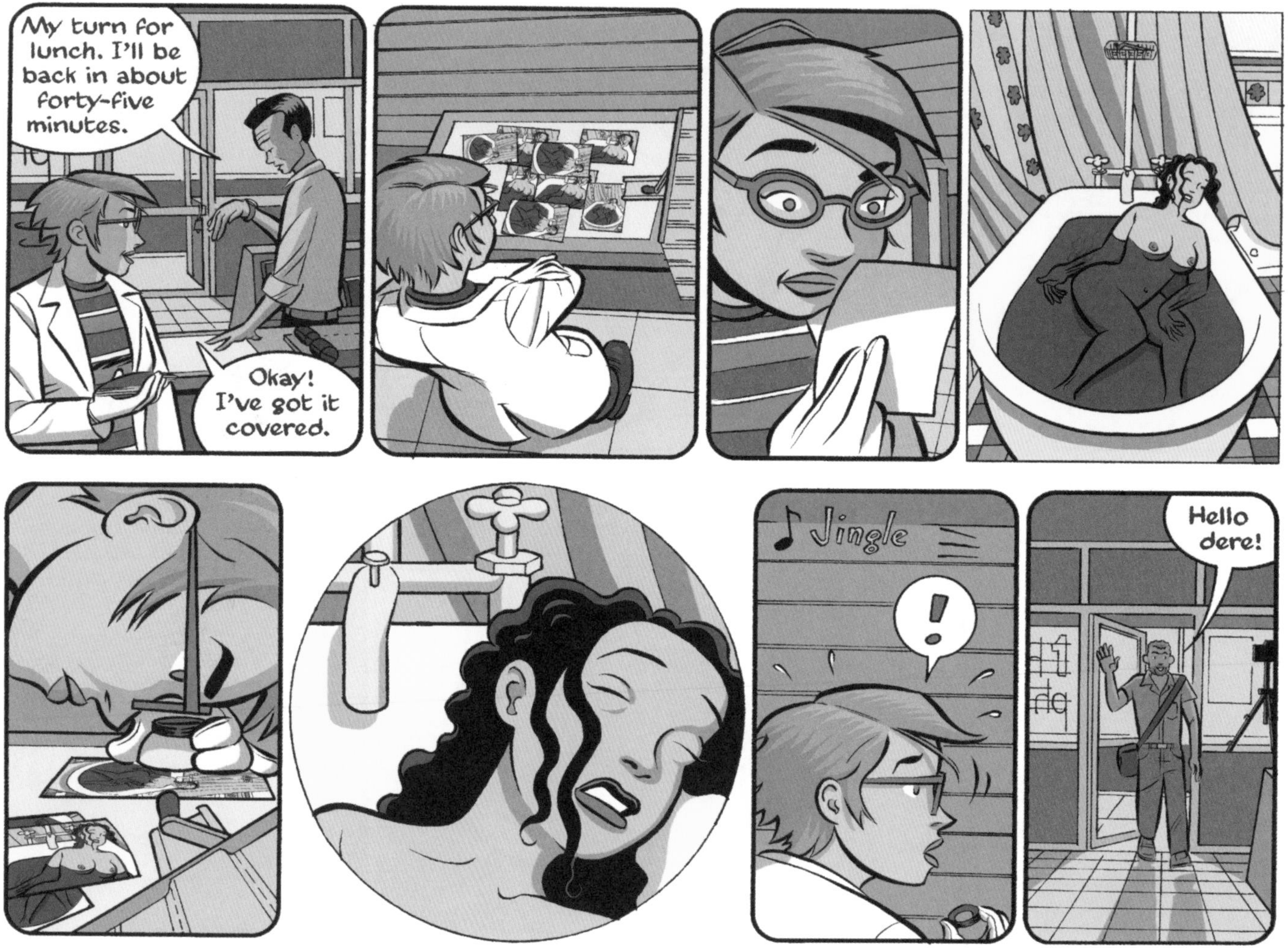
My turn for lunch. I'll be back in about forty-five minutes.
Okay! I've got it covered.
♪ Jingle
!
Hello dere!

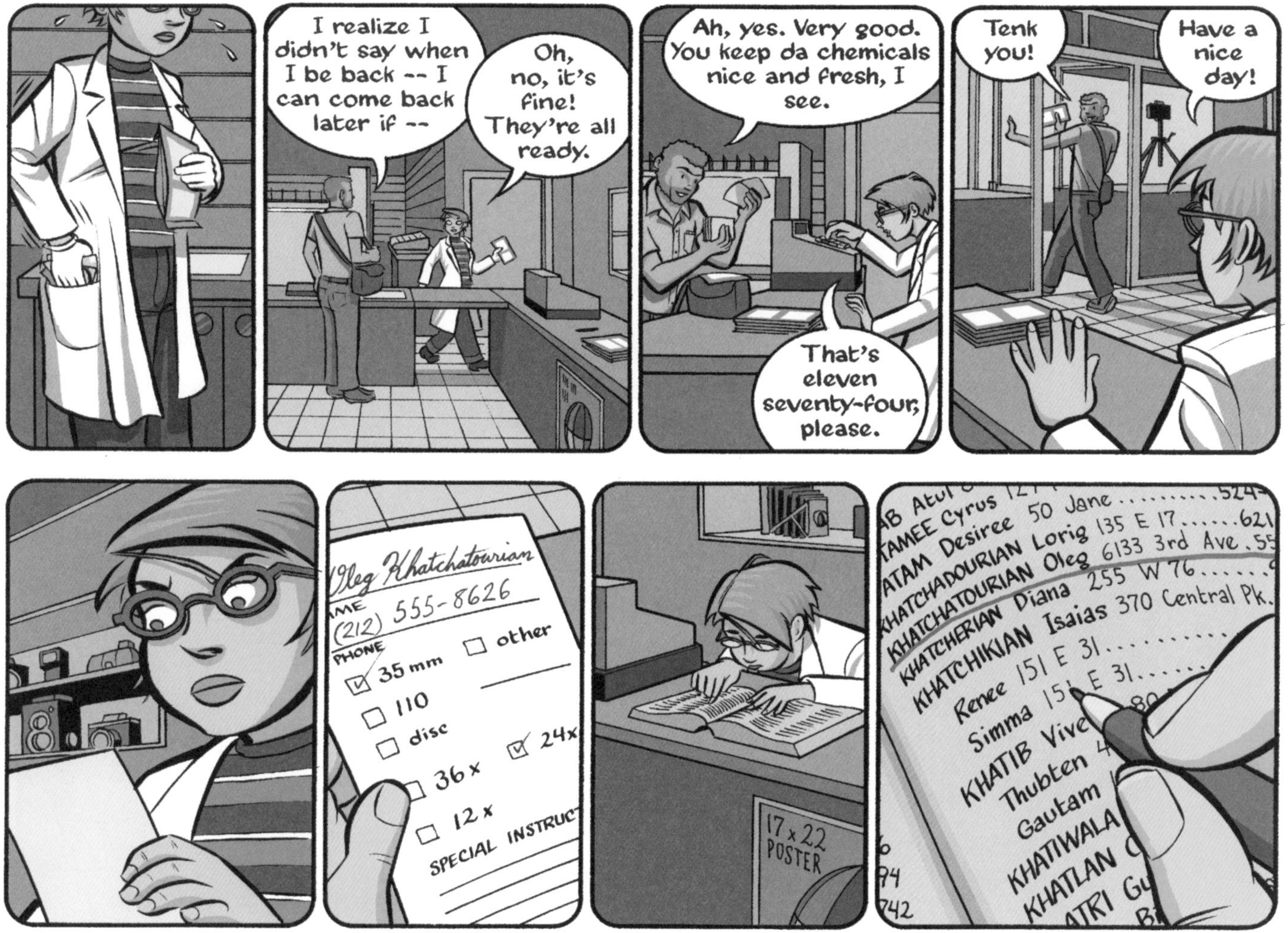
I realize I didn't say when I be back -- I can come back later if --
Oh, no, it's fine! They're all ready.
Ah, yes. Very good. You keep da chemicals nice and fresh, I see.
That's eleven seventy-four, please.
Tenk you!
Have a nice day!
Oleg Khatchatourian
(212) 555-8626
PHONE
35 mm
other
110
disc
24x
36x
12x
SPECIAL INSTRUCT
17 x 22 POSTER
TAMEE Cyrus
TAM Desiree 50 Jane
KHATCHADOURIAN Lorig 135 E 17
KHATCHATOURIAN Oleg 6133 3rd Ave
KHATCHERIAN Diana 255 W 76
KHATCHIKIAN Isaias 370 Central Pk.
Renee 151 E 31
Simma 151 E 31
KHATIB Vive
Thubten
Gautam
KHATIWALA
KHATLAN

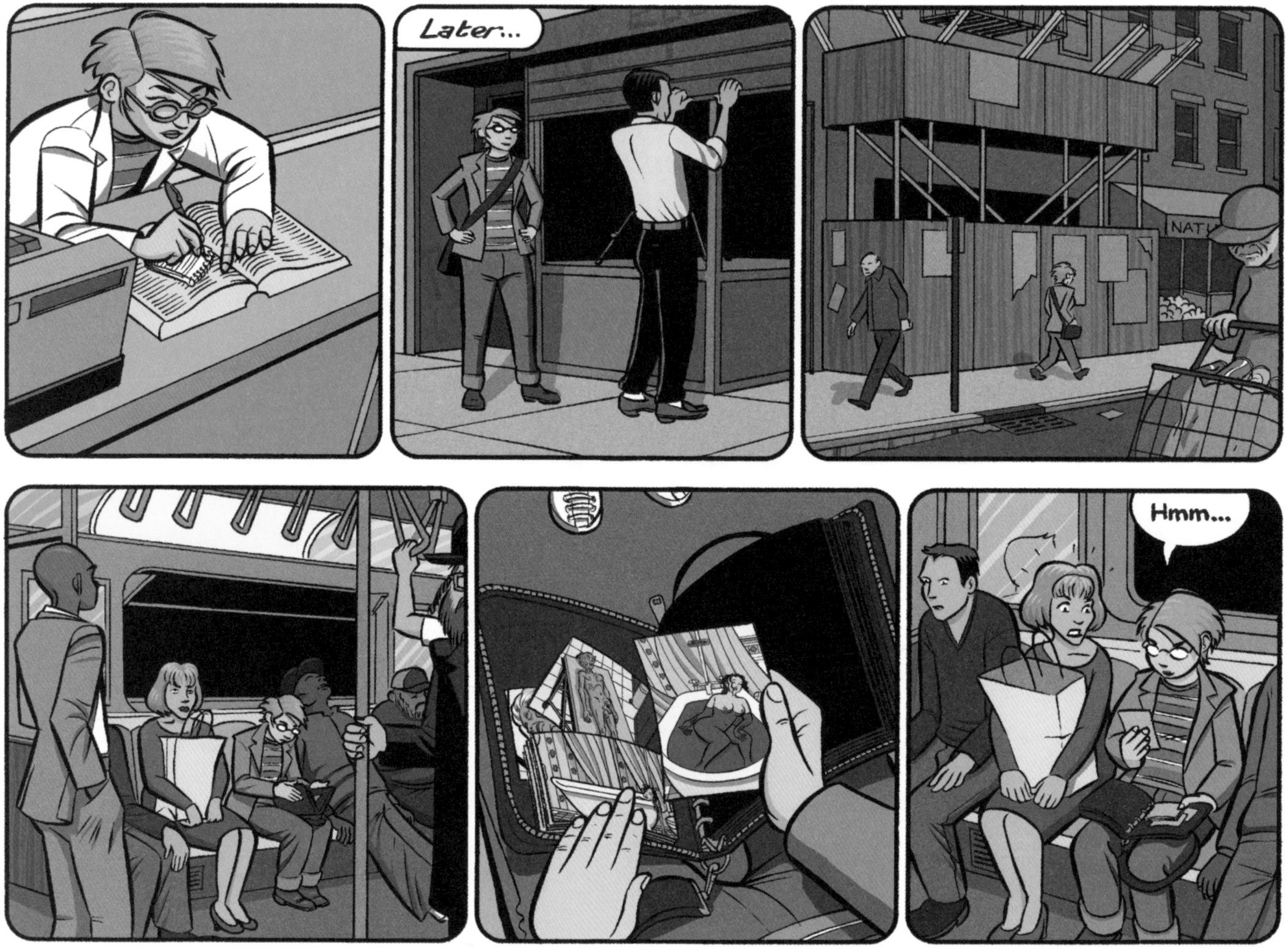
Later...
Hmm...

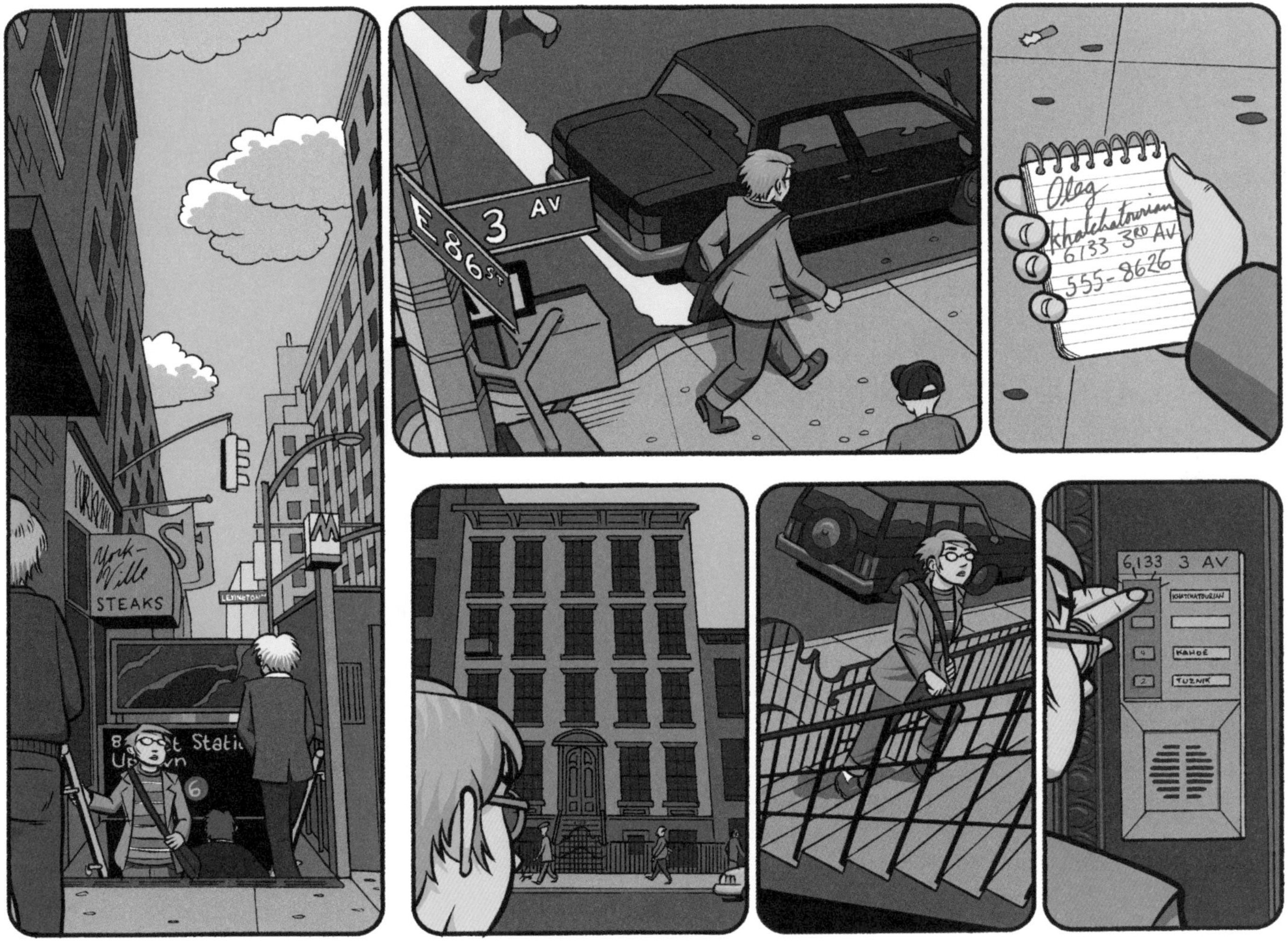
York-Ville
STEAKS
6
E 86 ST
3 AV
Oleg
Khatchatourian
6133 3RD AV
555-8626
6133 3 AV
KHATCHATOURIAN
9
KAHOE
2
TUZNIK

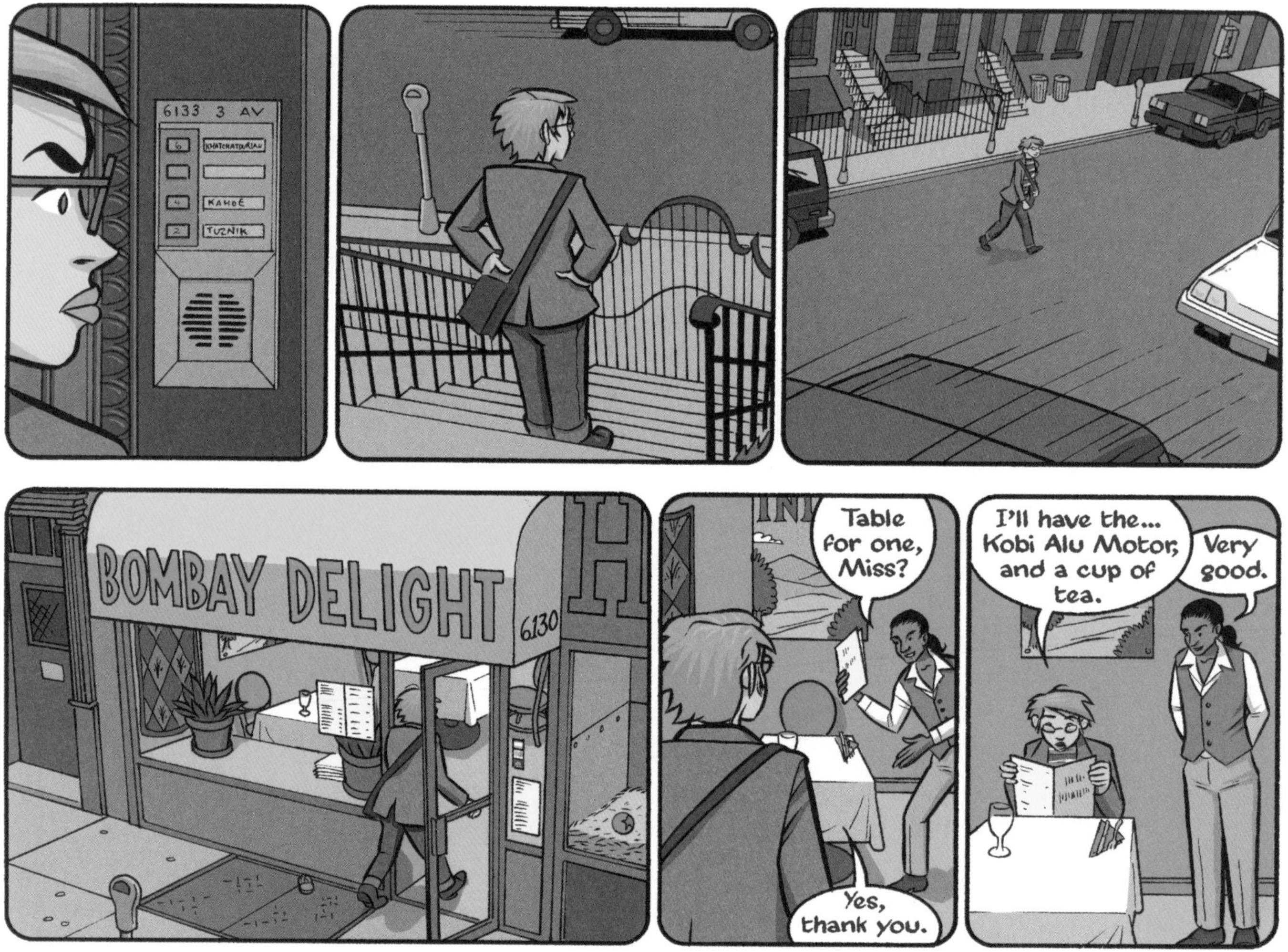
6133 3 AV
6 KHATCHATOURIAN
4 KAHOE
2 TUZNIK
BOMBAY DELIGHT
6130
Table for one, Miss?
Yes, thank you.
I'll have the... Kobi Alu Motor, and a cup of tea.
Very good.

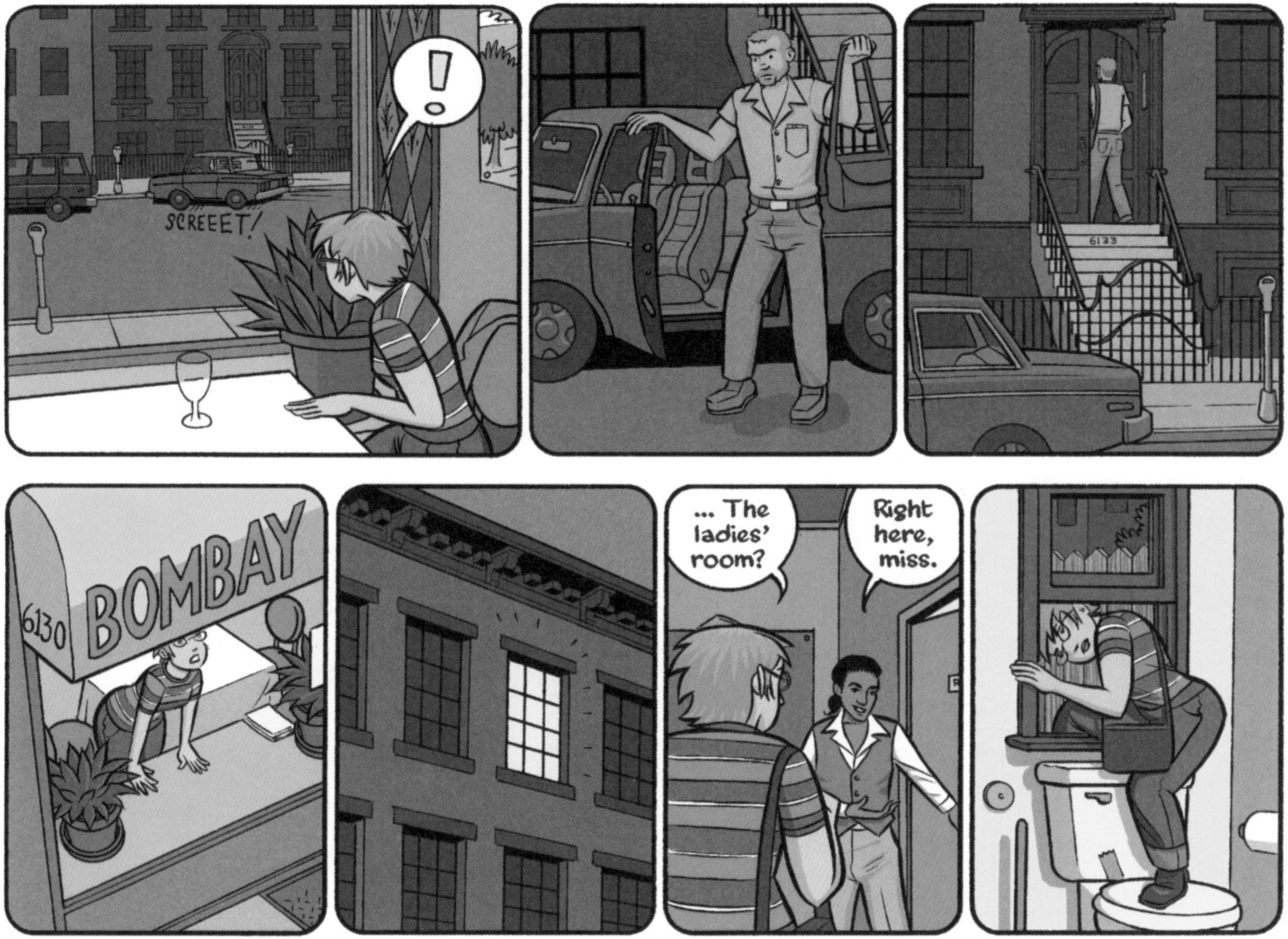
!
SCREEET!
6133
6130
BOMBAY
... The ladies' room?
Right here, miss.

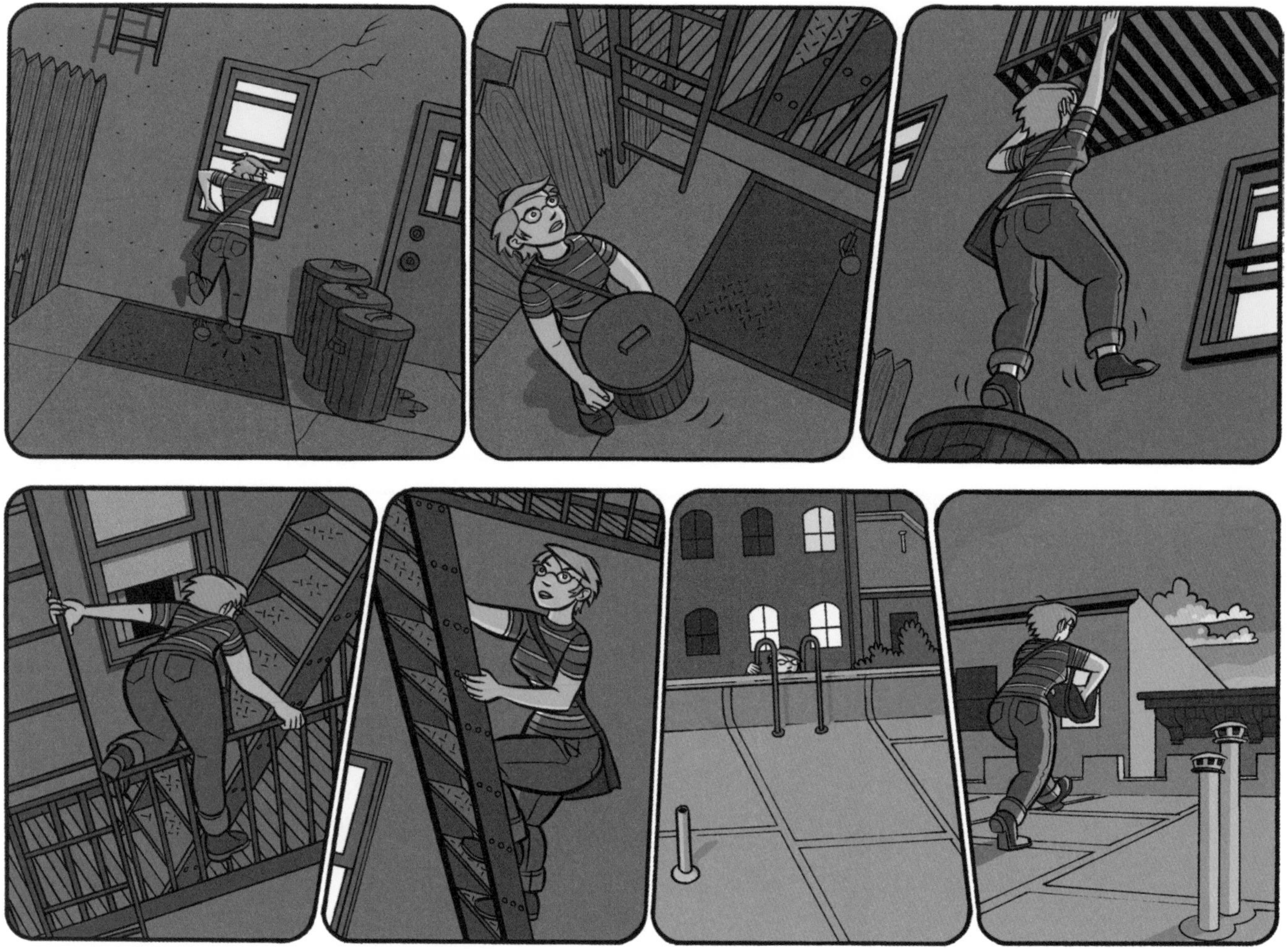

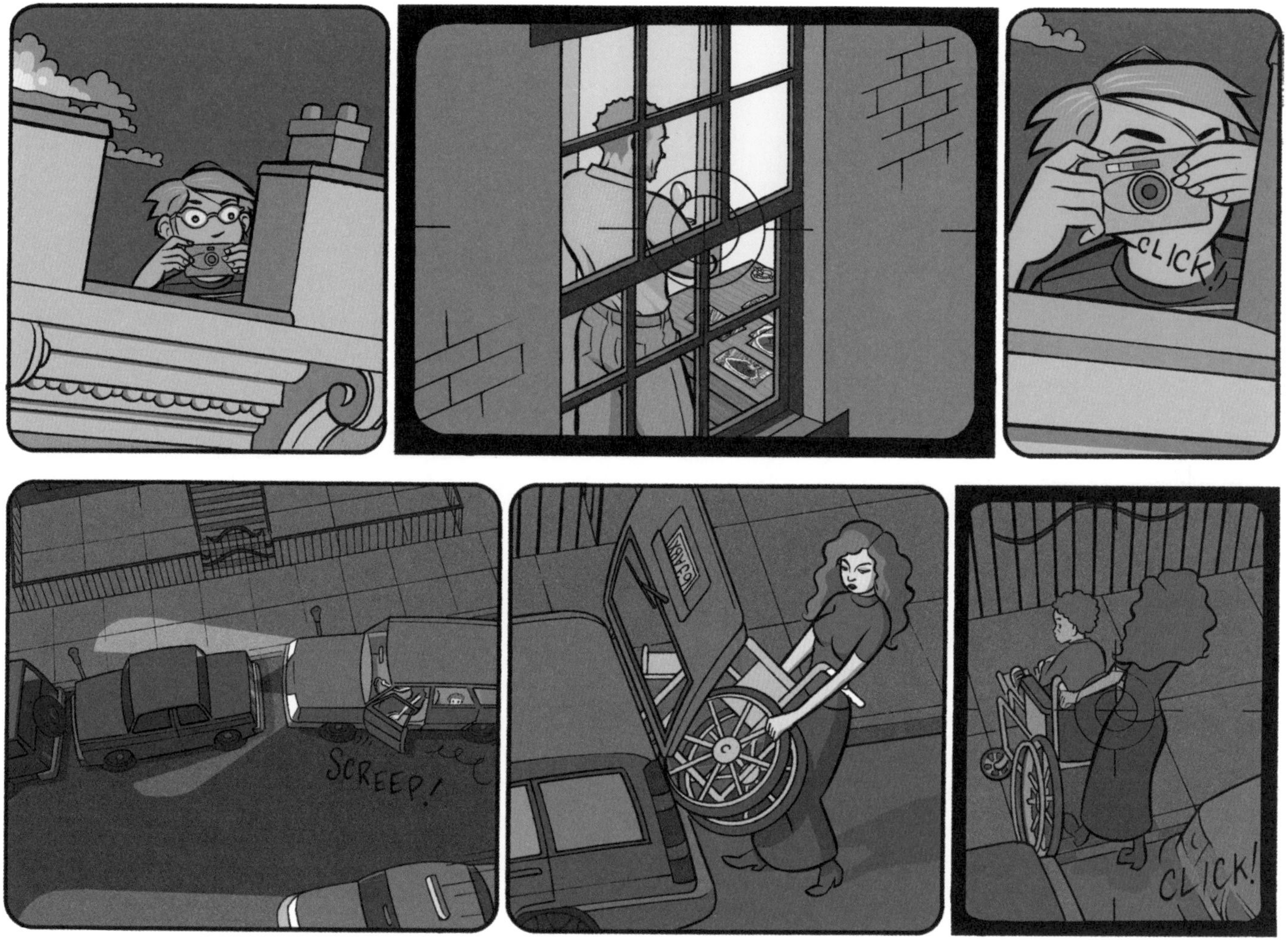
CLICK!
SCREEP!
CLICK!

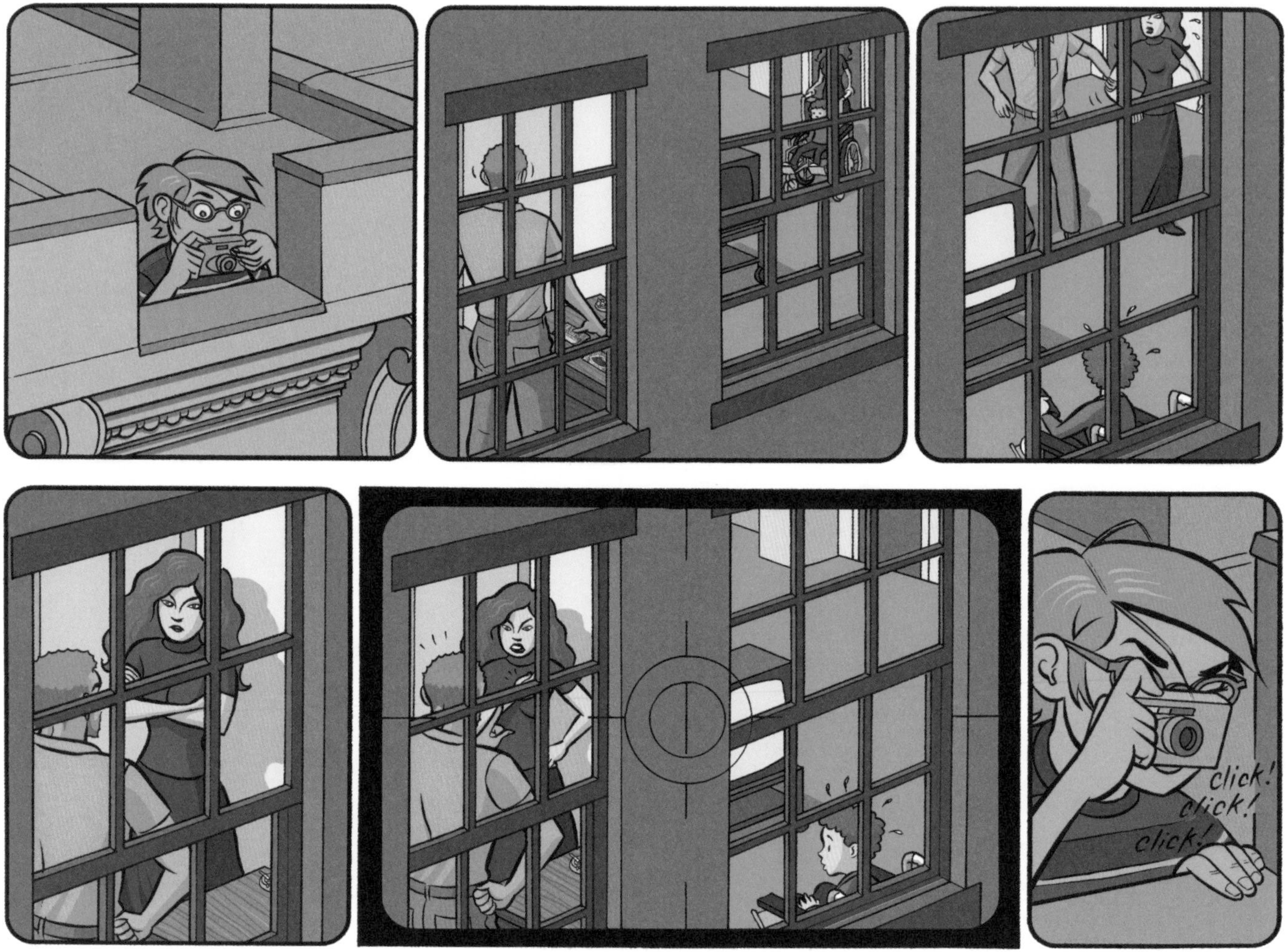
click!
click!
click!

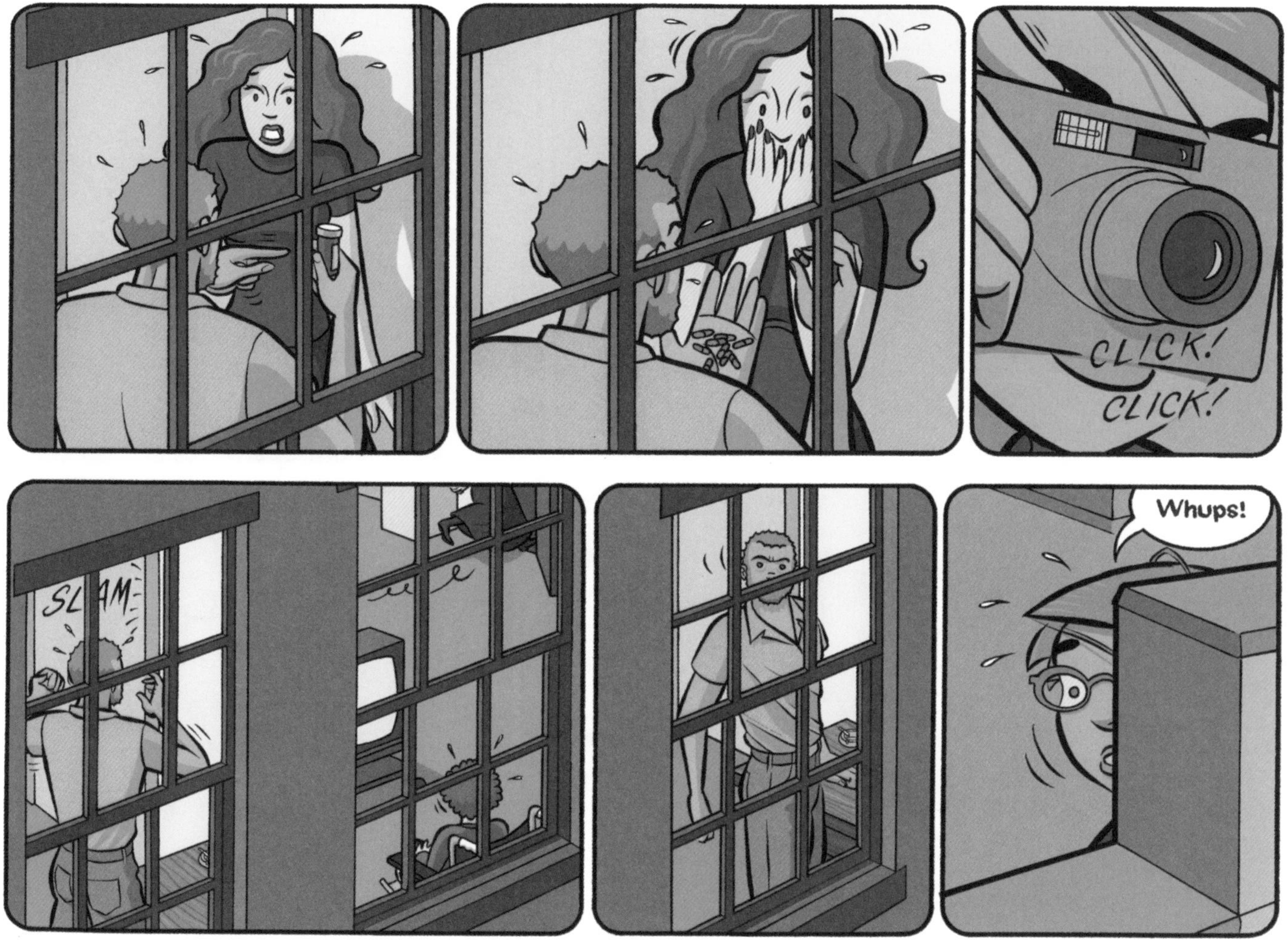
CLICK!
CLICK!
SLAM!
Whups!

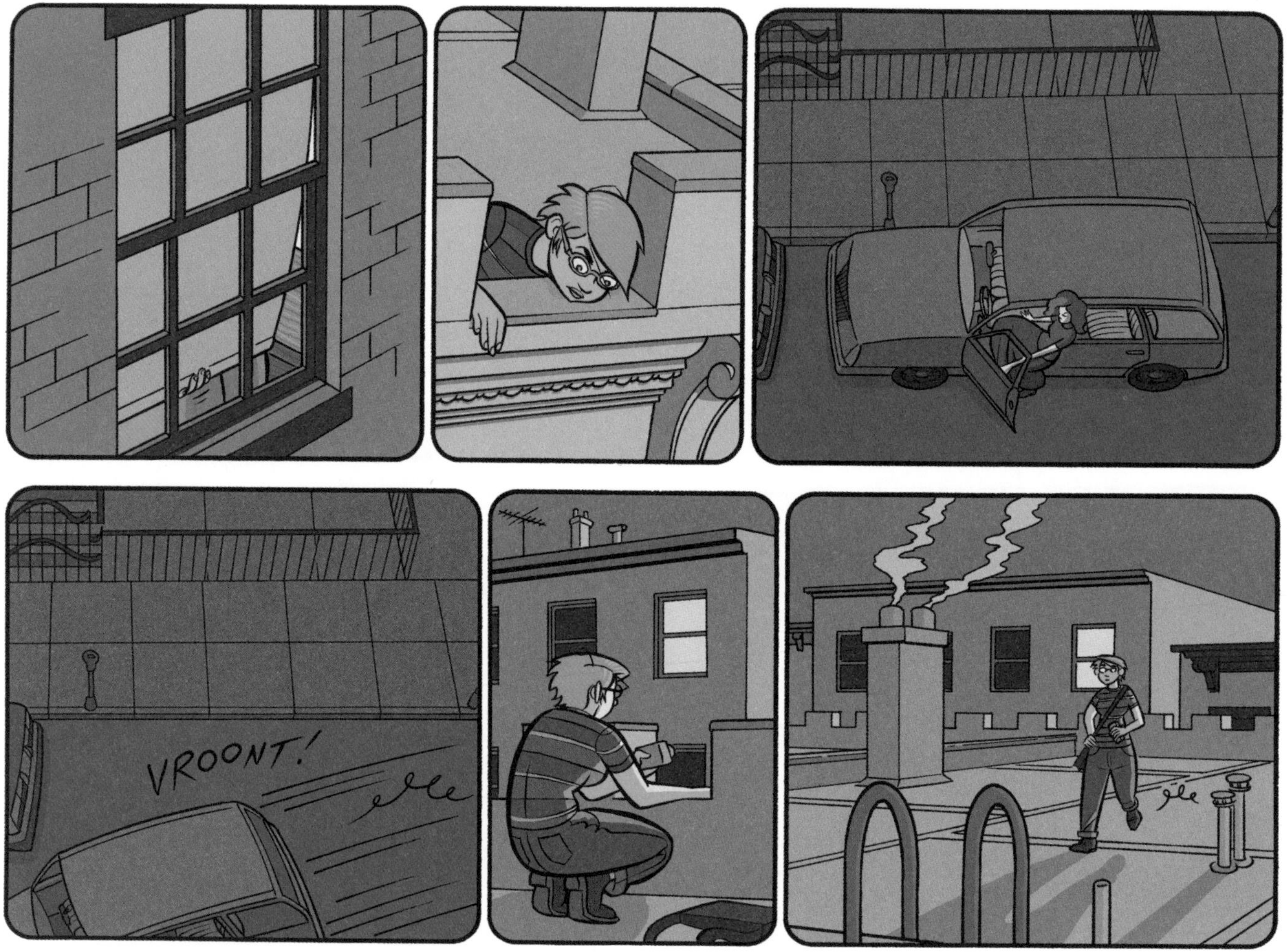
VROONT!

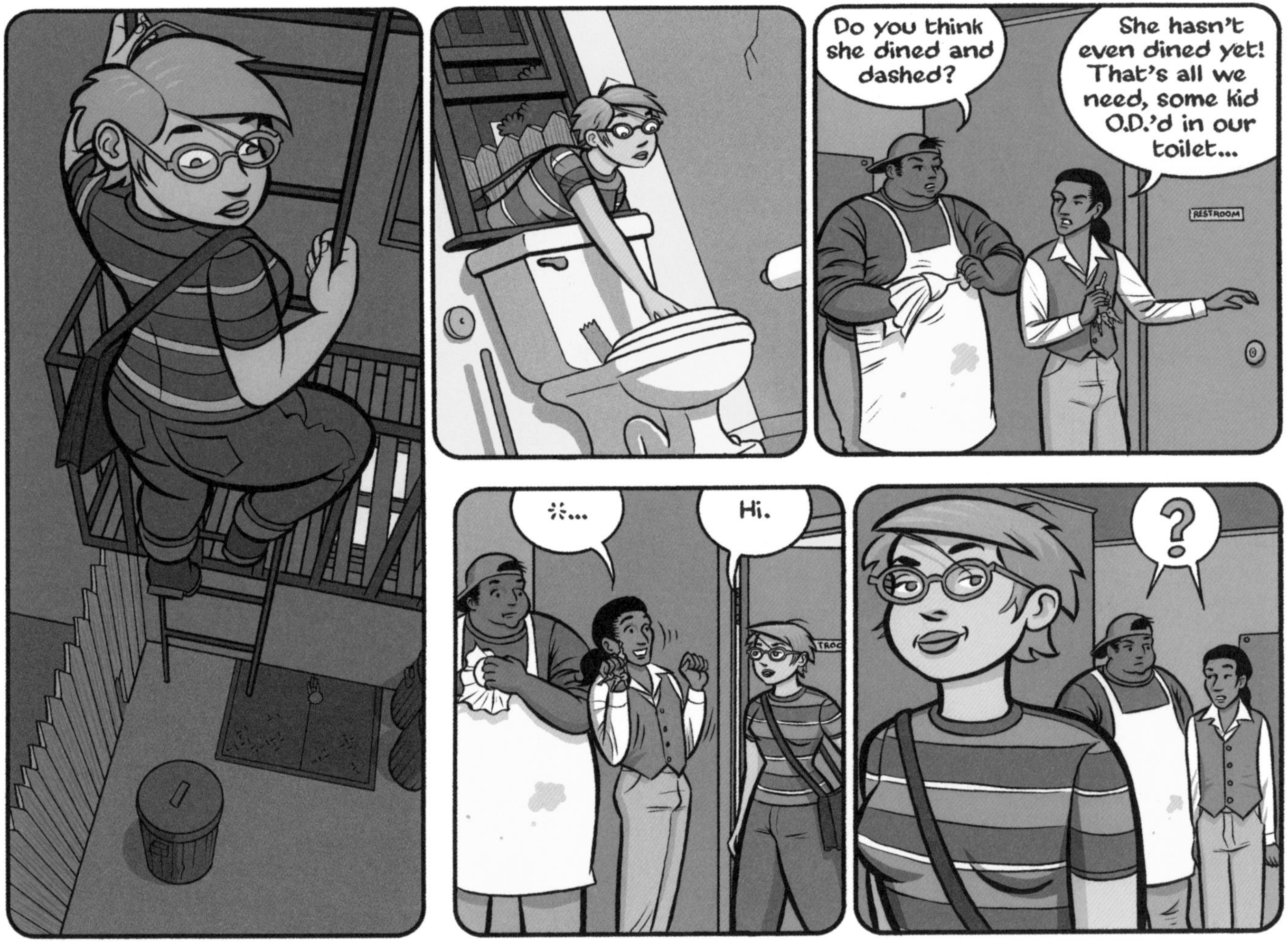
Do you think she dined and dashed?
She hasn't even dined yet! That's all we need, some kid O.D.'d in our toilet...
RESTROOM
Hi.
?

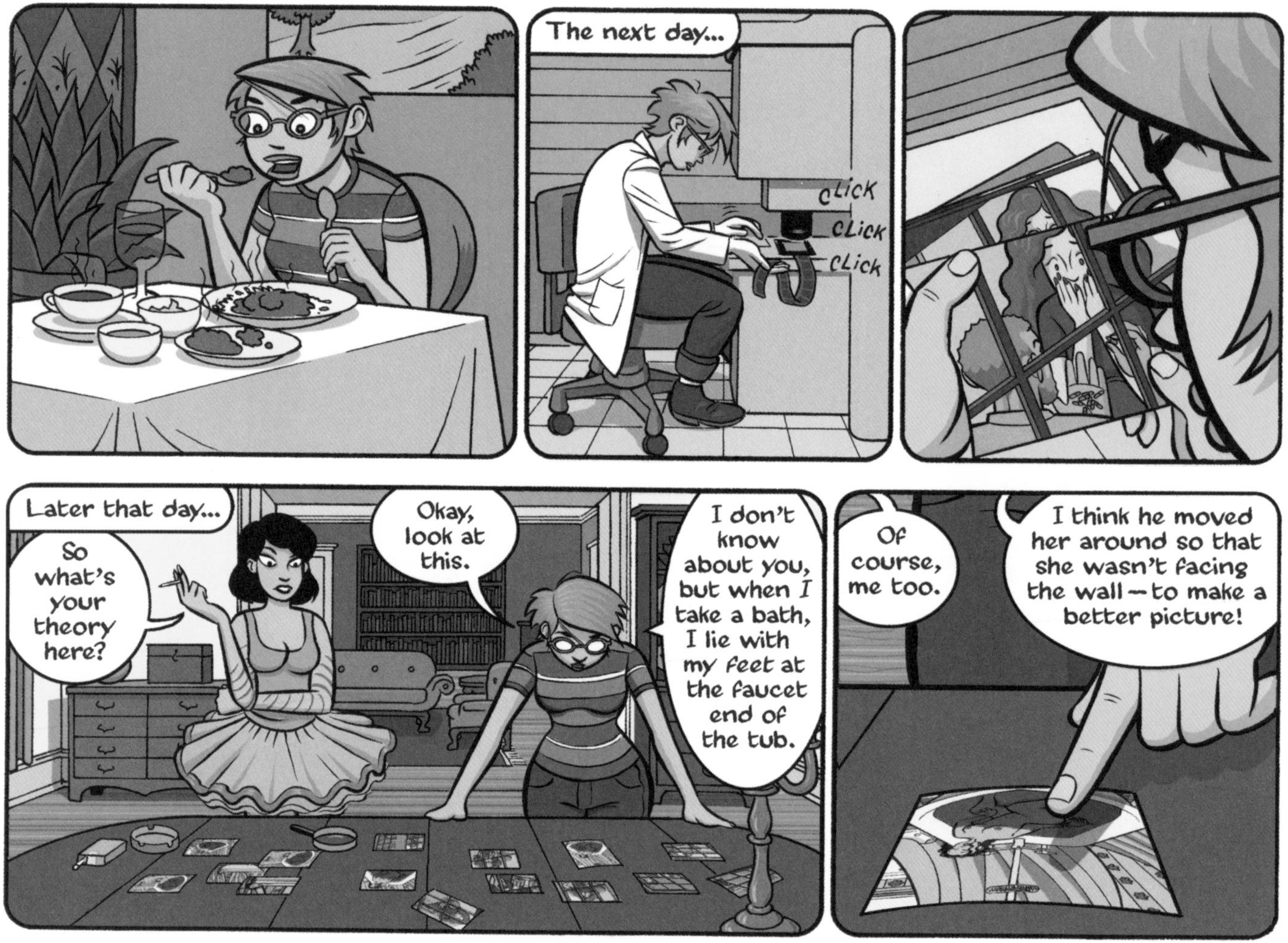
The next day...
CLICK
CLICK
CLICK
Later that day...
So what's your theory here?
Okay, look at this.
I don't know about you, but when *I* take a bath, I lie with my *feet* at the faucet end of the tub.
Of course, me too.
I think he moved her around so that she wasn't facing the wall—to make a better picture!

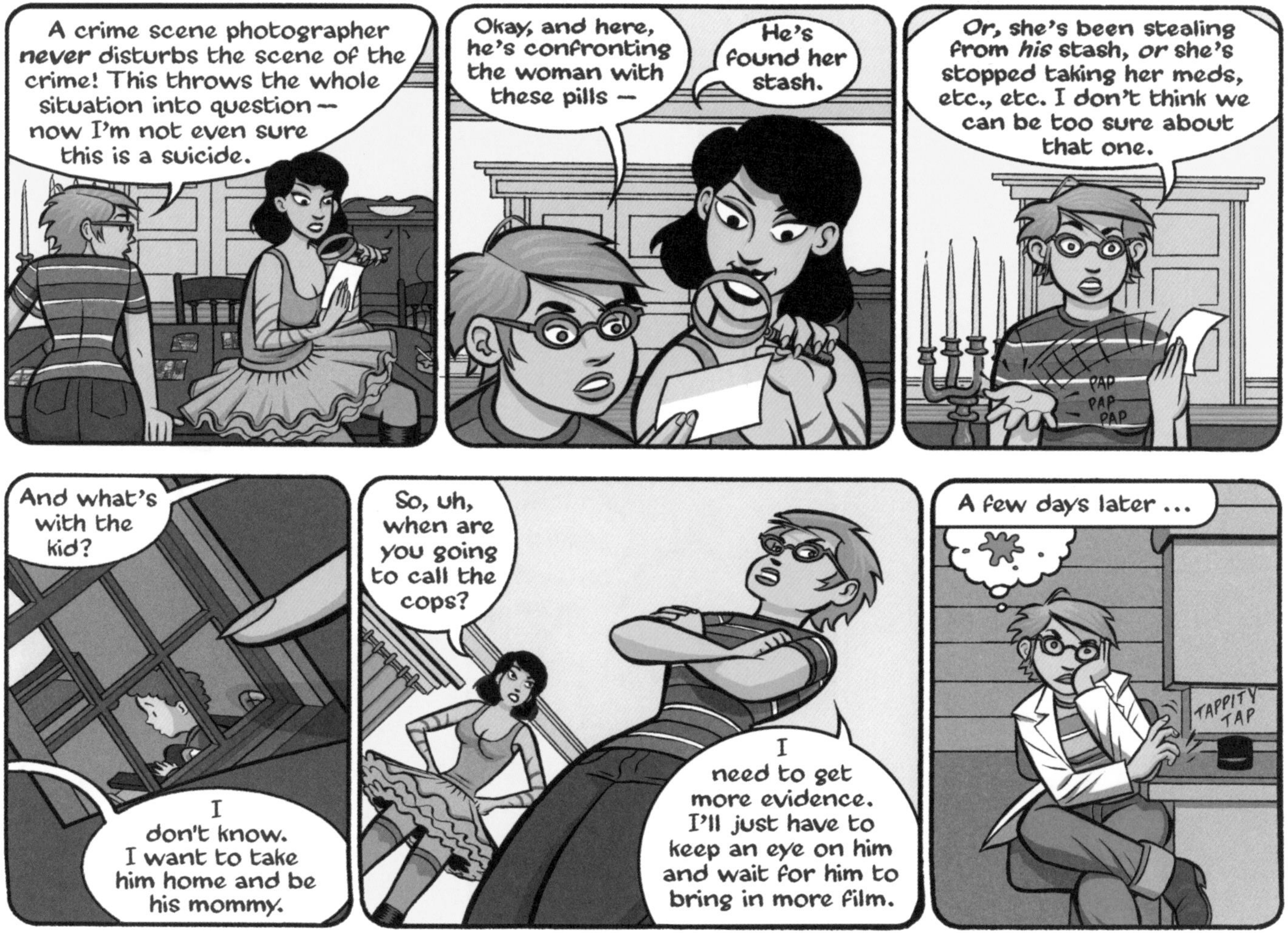
A crime scene photographer *never* disturbs the scene of the crime! This throws the whole situation into question — now I'm not even sure this is a suicide.
Okay, and here, he's confronting the woman with these pills —
He's found her stash.
Or, she's been stealing from *his* stash, *or* she's stopped taking her meds, etc., etc. I don't think we can be too sure about that one.
PAP PAP PAP
And what's with the kid?
I don't know. I want to take him home and be his mommy.
So, uh, when are you going to call the cops?
I need to get more evidence. I'll just have to keep an eye on him and wait for him to bring in more film.
A few days later ...
TAPPITY TAP

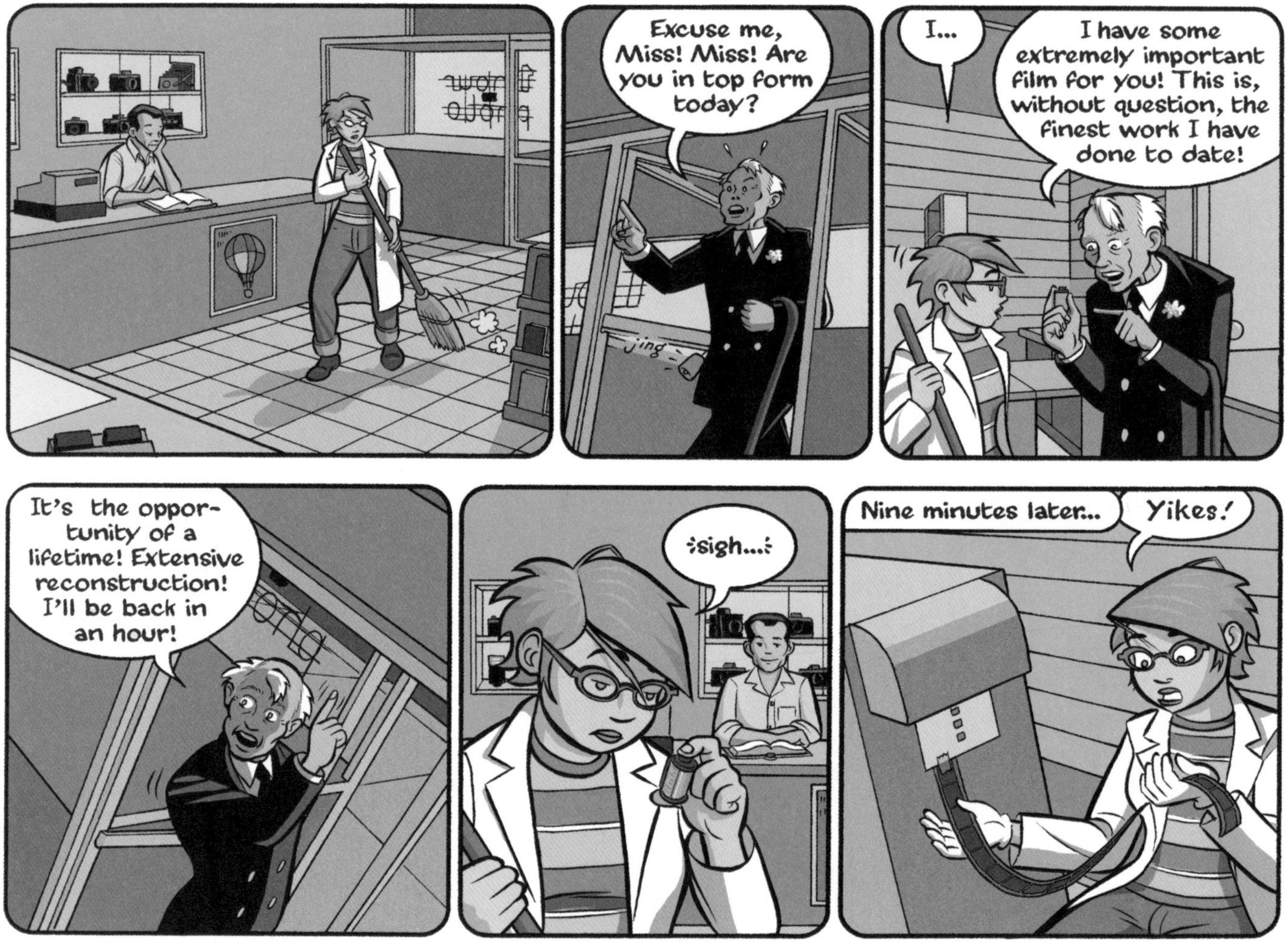
Excuse me, Miss! Miss! Are you in top form today?
jing
I...
I have some extremely important film for you! This is, without question, the finest work I have done to date!
It's the opportunity of a lifetime! Extensive reconstruction! I'll be back in an hour!
sigh...
Nine minutes later...
Yikes!

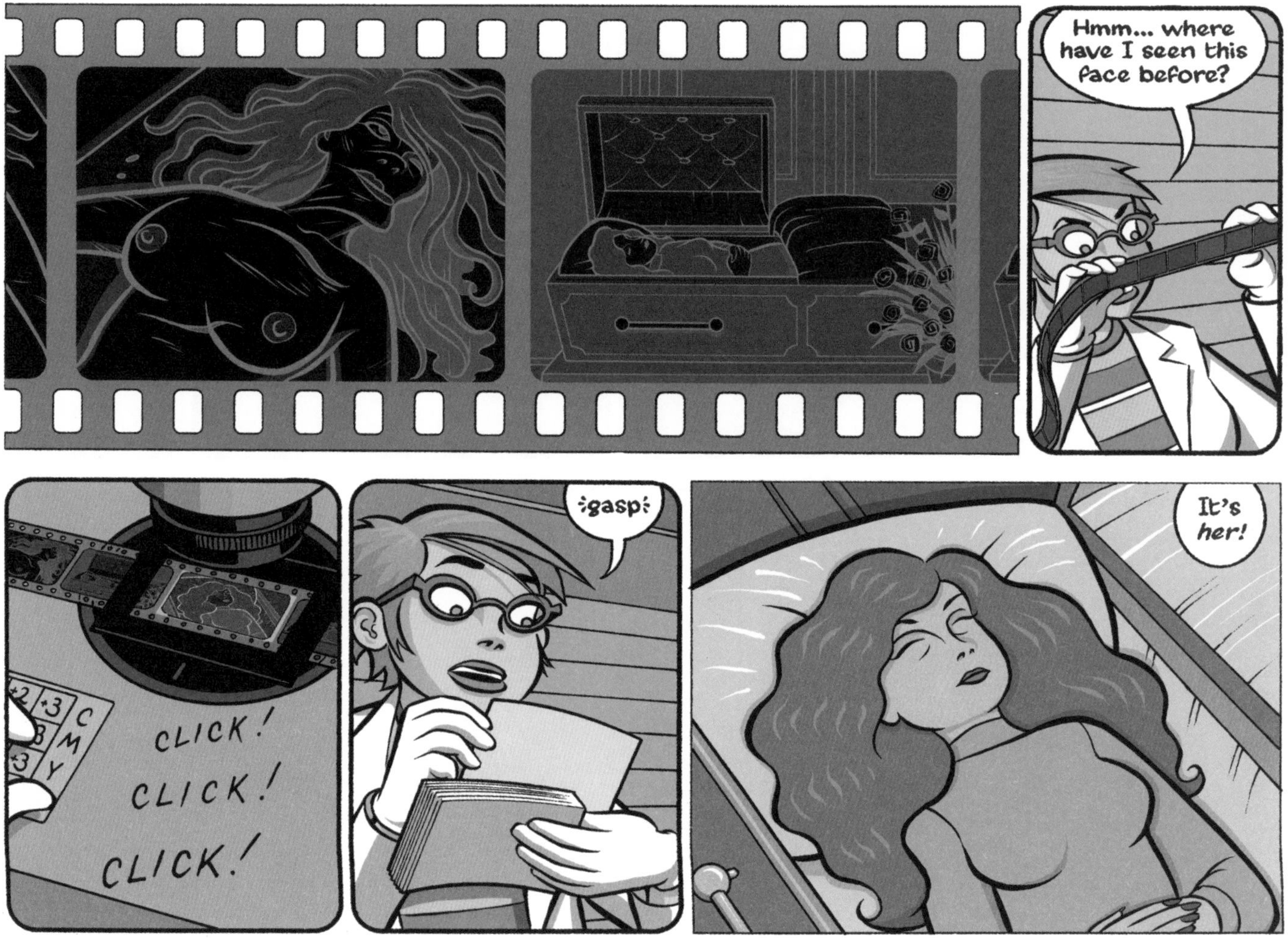
Hmm... where have I seen this face before?
CLICK!
CLICK!
CLICK!
:gasp:
It's her!

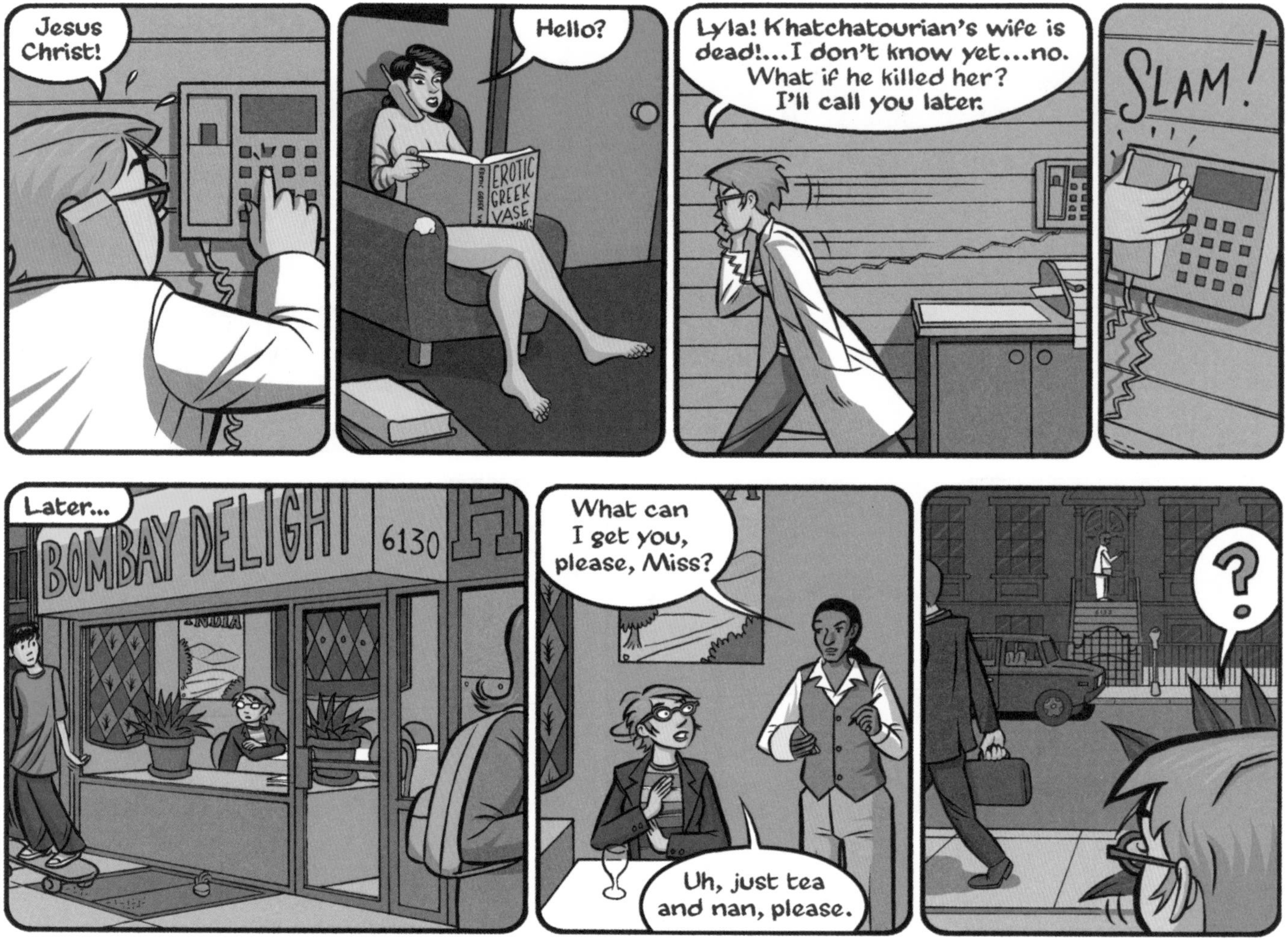
Jesus Christ!
Hello?
EROTIC GREEK VASE
Lyla! Khatchatourian's wife is dead!...I don't know yet...no. What if he killed her? I'll call you later.
SLAM!
Later...
BOMBAY DELIGHT
6130
INDIA
What can I get you, please, Miss?
Uh, just tea and nan, please.
?

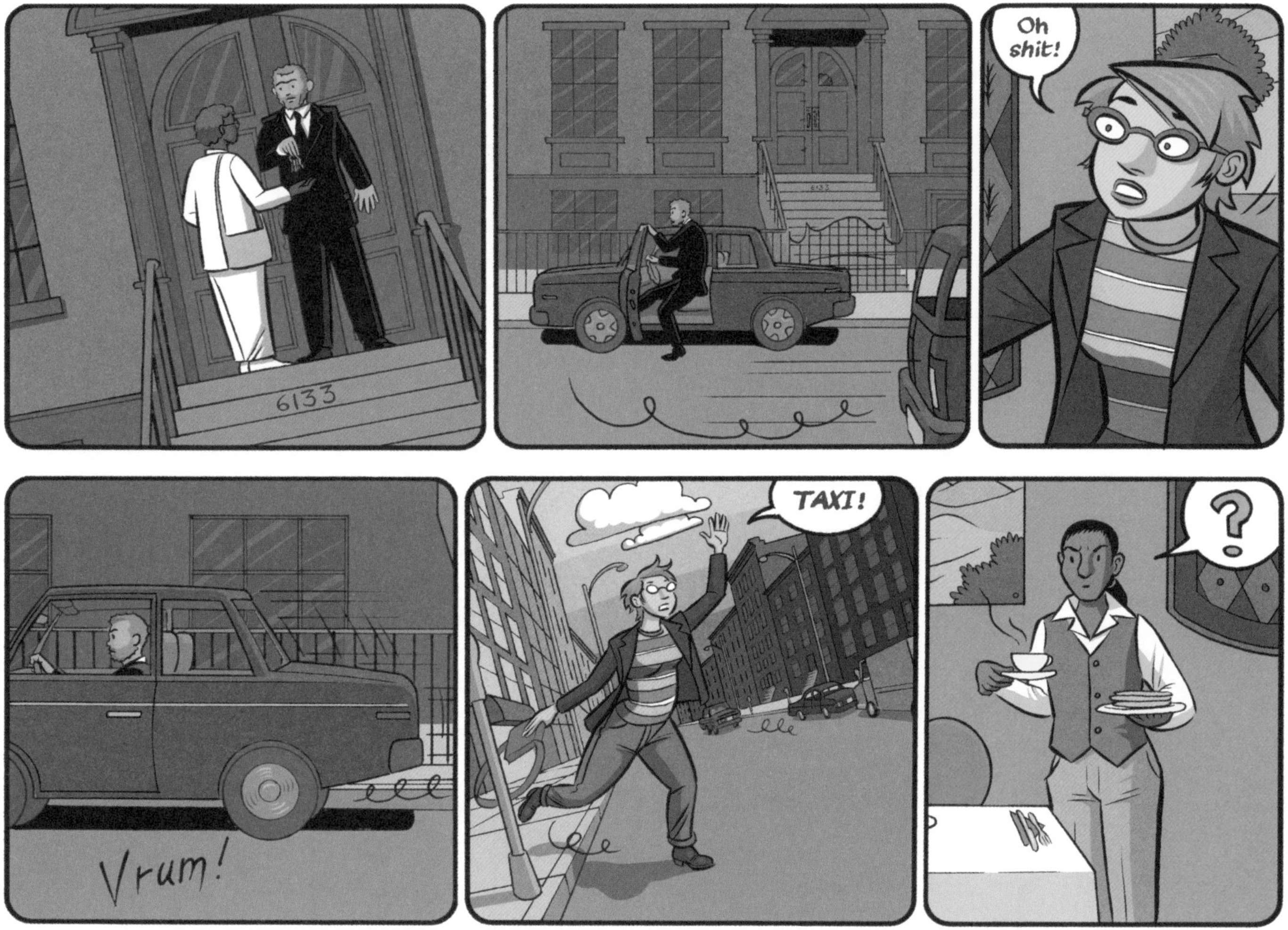
6133
Oh shit!
Vrum!
TAXI!
?

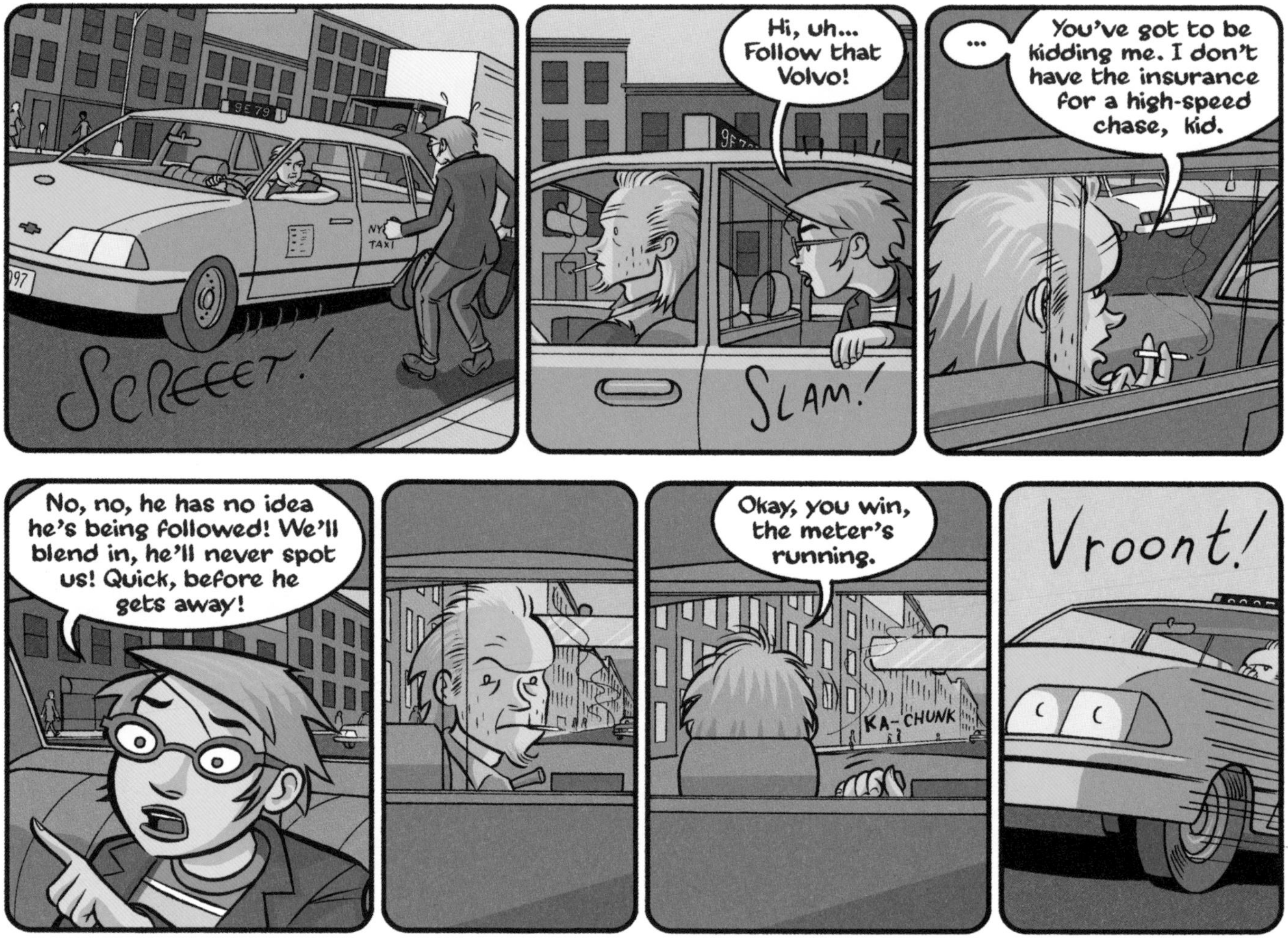
SCREEEET!
NY TAXI
Hi, uh... Follow that Volvo!
SLAM!
...
You've got to be kidding me. I don't have the insurance for a high-speed chase, kid.
No, no, he has no idea he's being followed! We'll blend in, he'll never spot us! Quick, before he gets away!
Okay, you win, the meter's running.
KA-CHUNK
Vroont!

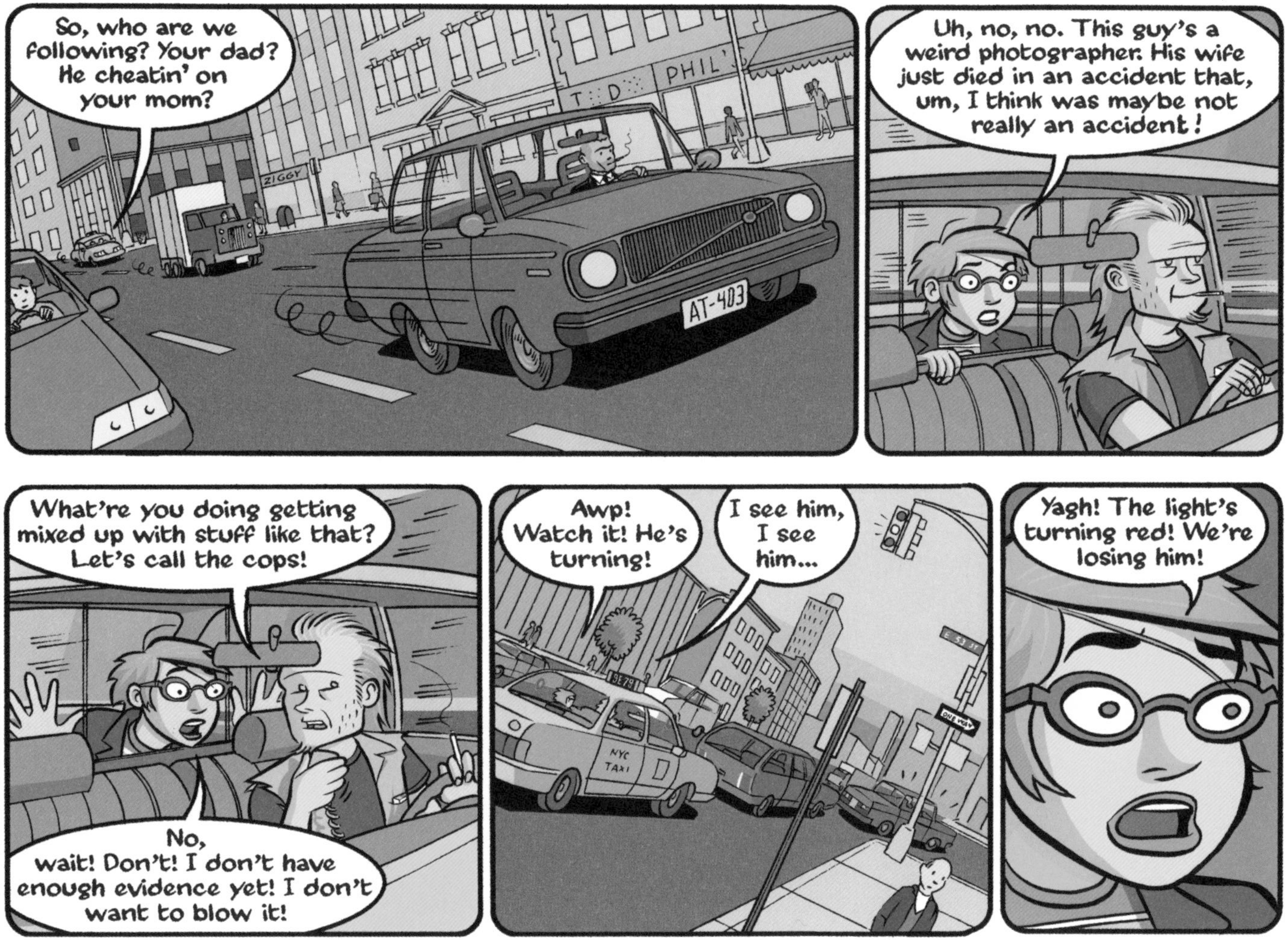
So, who are we following? Your dad? He cheatin' on your mom?
ZIGGY
AT-403
Uh, no, no. This guy's a weird photographer. His wife just died in an accident that, um, I think was maybe not really an accident!
What're you doing getting mixed up with stuff like that? Let's call the cops!
No, wait! Don't! I don't have enough evidence yet! I don't want to blow it!
Awp! Watch it! He's turning!
I see him, I see him...
NYC TAXI
Yagh! The light's turning red! We're losing him!

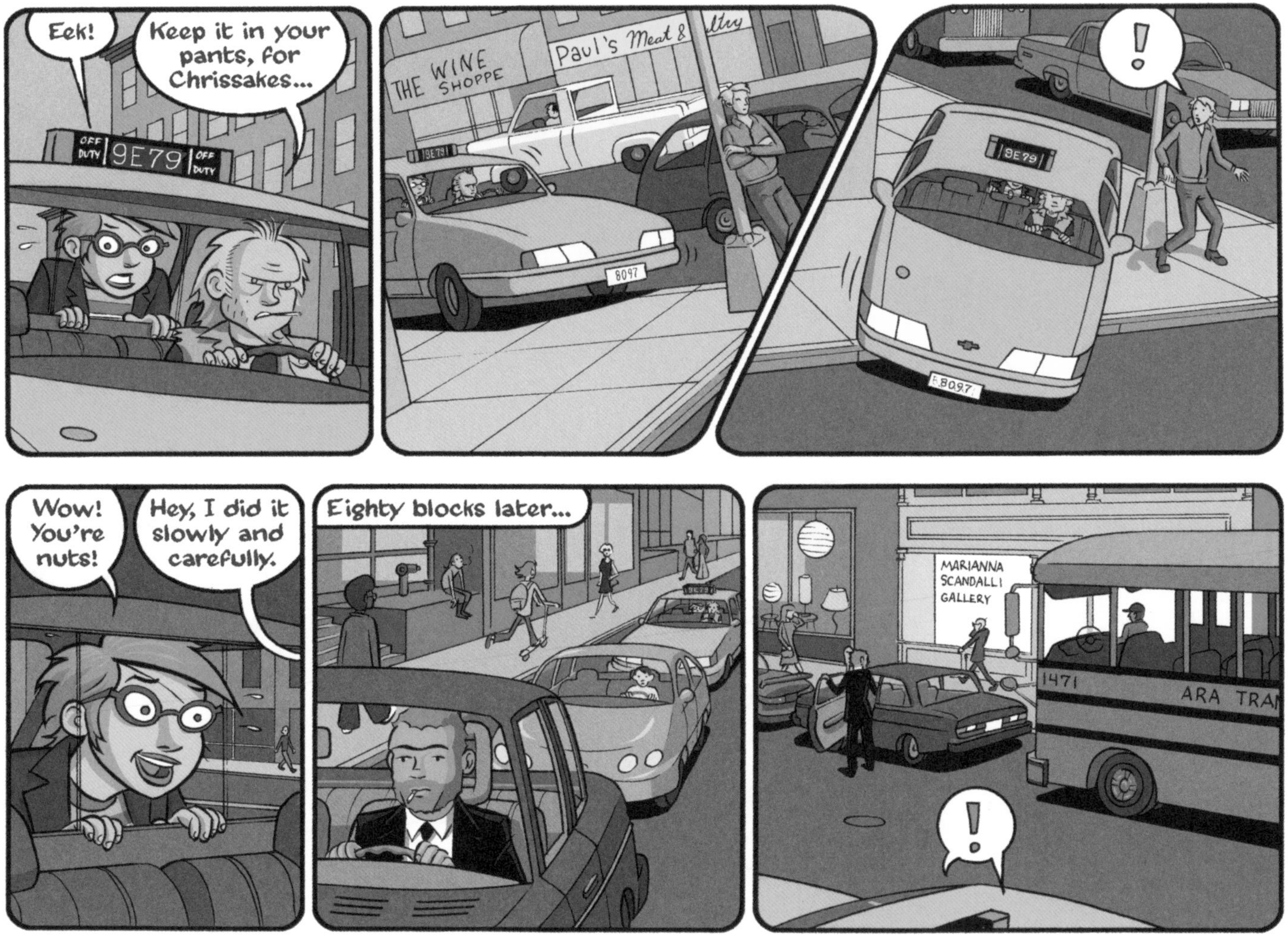
Eek!
Keep it in your pants, for Chrissakes...
OFF DUTY 9E79 OFF DUTY
THE WINE SHOPPE
Paul's Meat &
8097
!
9E79
8097
Wow! You're nuts!
Hey, I did it slowly and carefully.
Eighty blocks later...
MARIANNA SCANDALLI GALLERY
1471
!

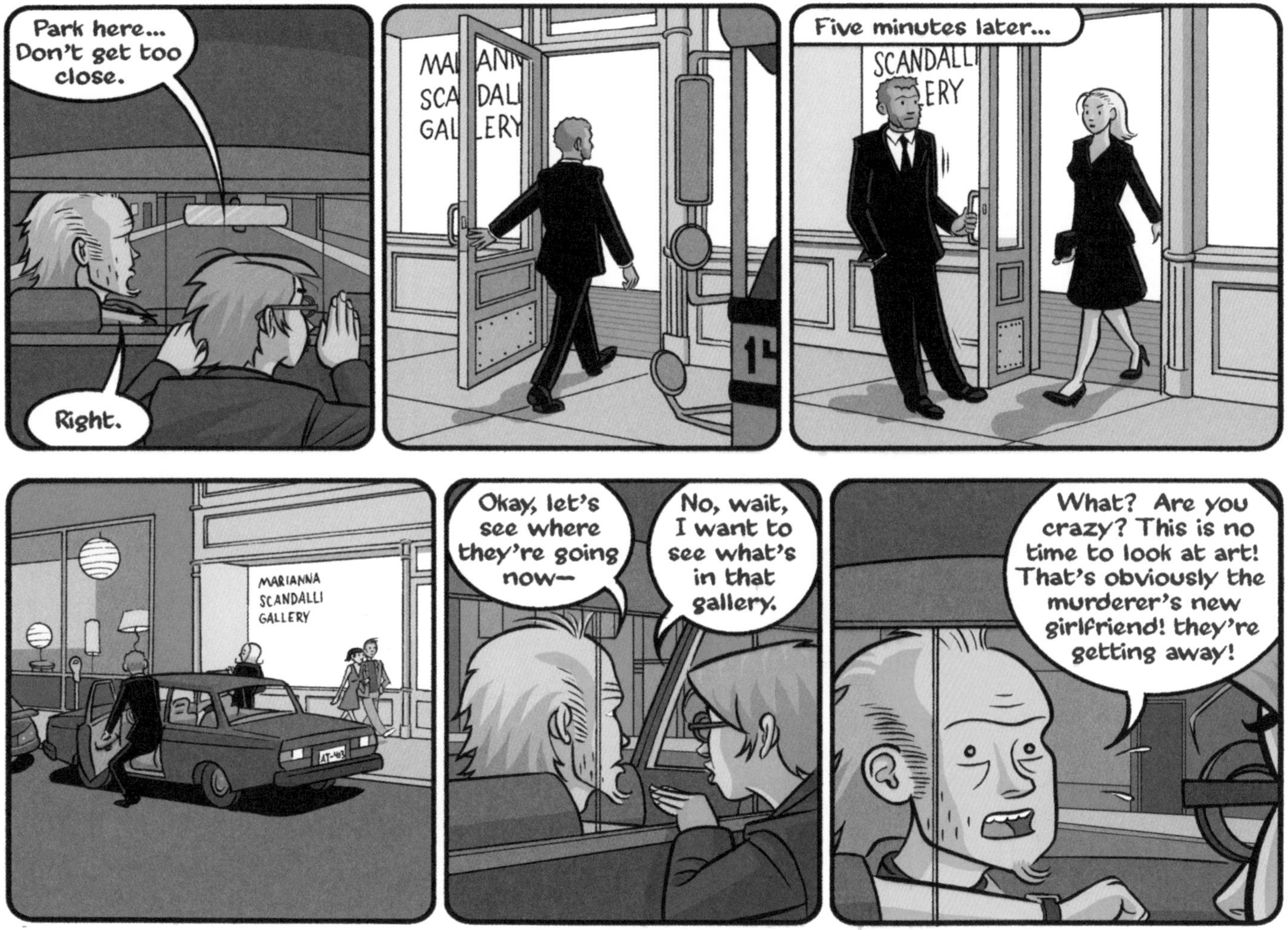
Park here... Don't get too close.
Right.
MARIANNA SCANDALLI GALLERY
Five minutes later...
SCANDALLI GALLERY
MARIANNA SCANDALLI GALLERY
Okay, let's see where they're going now—
No, wait, I want to see what's in that gallery.
What? Are you crazy? This is no time to look at art! That's obviously the murderer's new girlfriend! they're getting away!

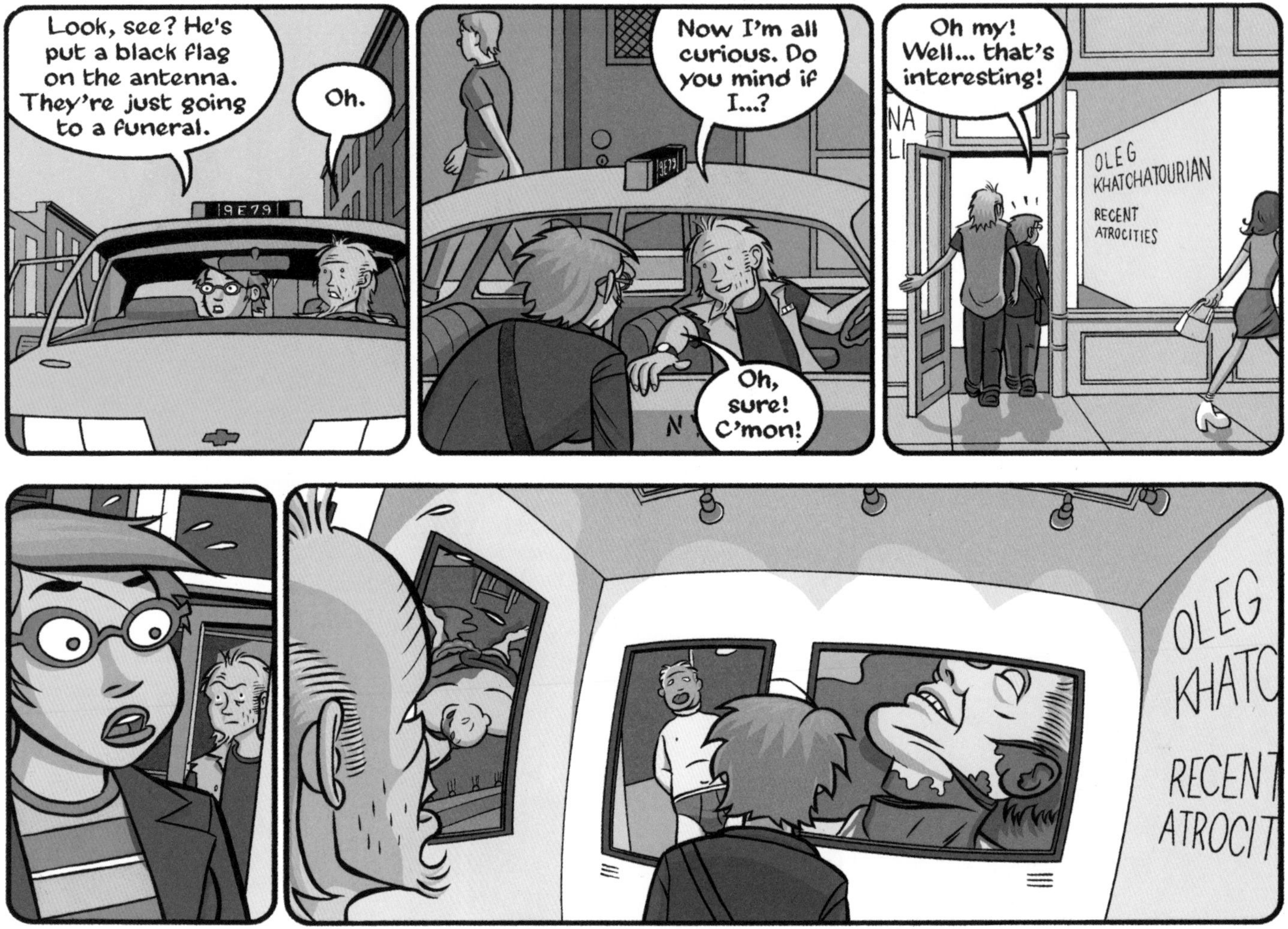
Look, see? He's put a black flag on the antenna. They're just going to a funeral.
Oh.
9E79
Now I'm all curious. Do you mind if I...?
Oh, sure! C'mon!
Oh my! Well... that's interesting!
OLEG KHATCHATOURIAN
RECENT ATROCITIES
OLEG KHATC
RECENT ATROCIT

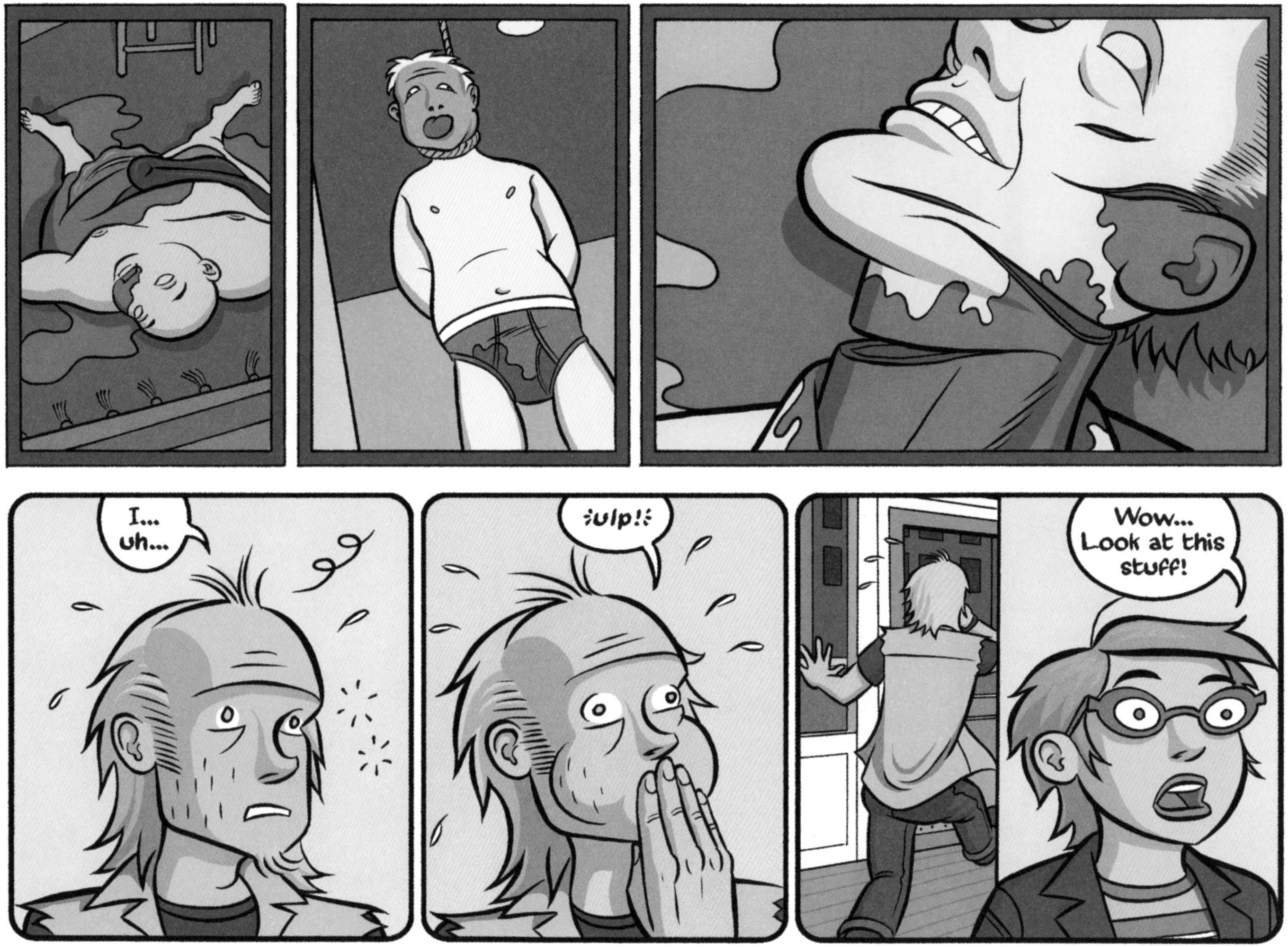
I... uh...
¦ulp!¦
Wow... Look at this stuff!

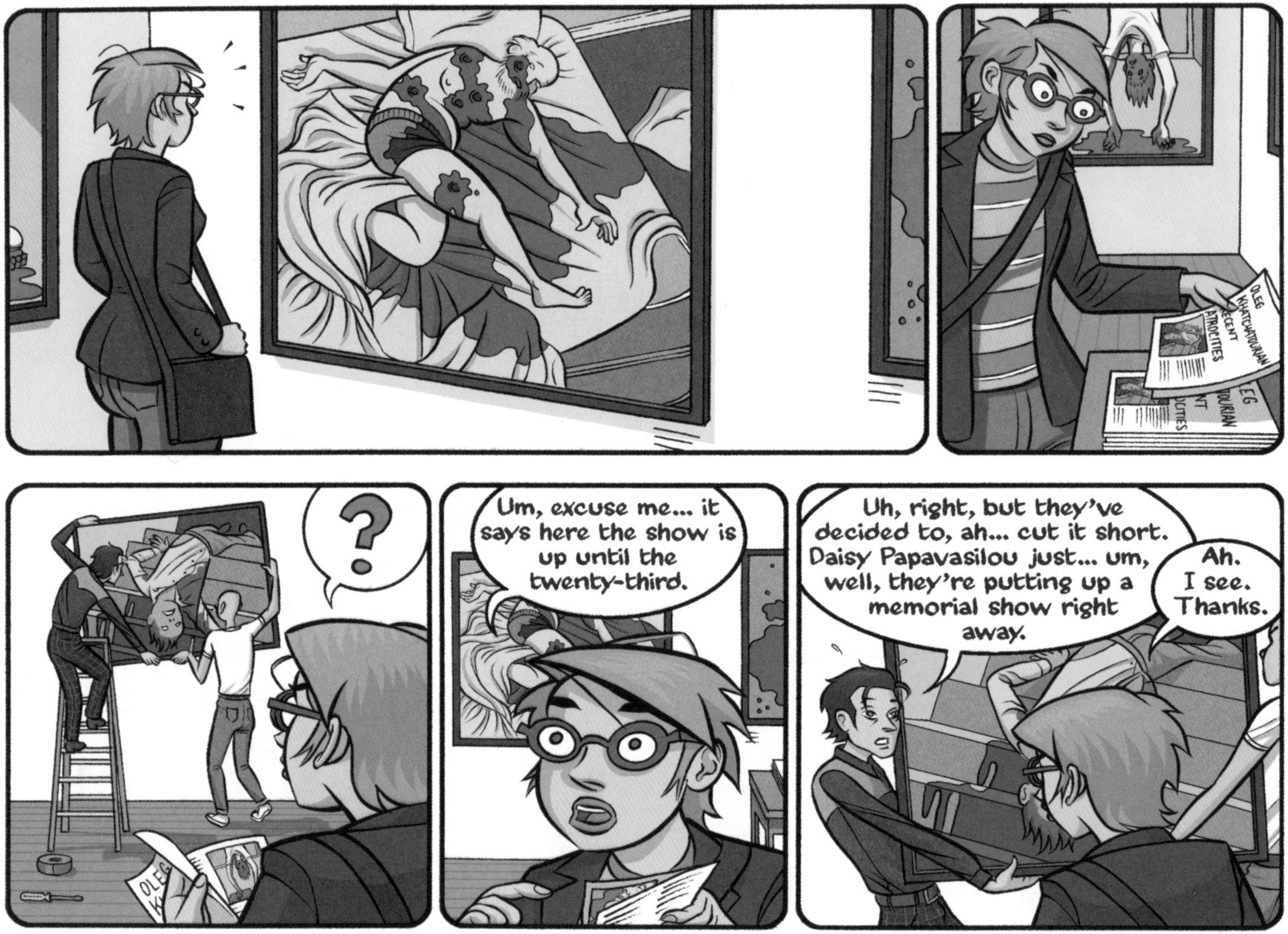
OLEG KHATCHATOURIAN RECENT ATROCITIES
?
Um, excuse me... it says here the show is up until the twenty-third.
Uh, right, but they've decided to, ah... cut it short. Daisy Papavasilou just... um, well, they're putting up a memorial show right away.
Ah. I see. Thanks.

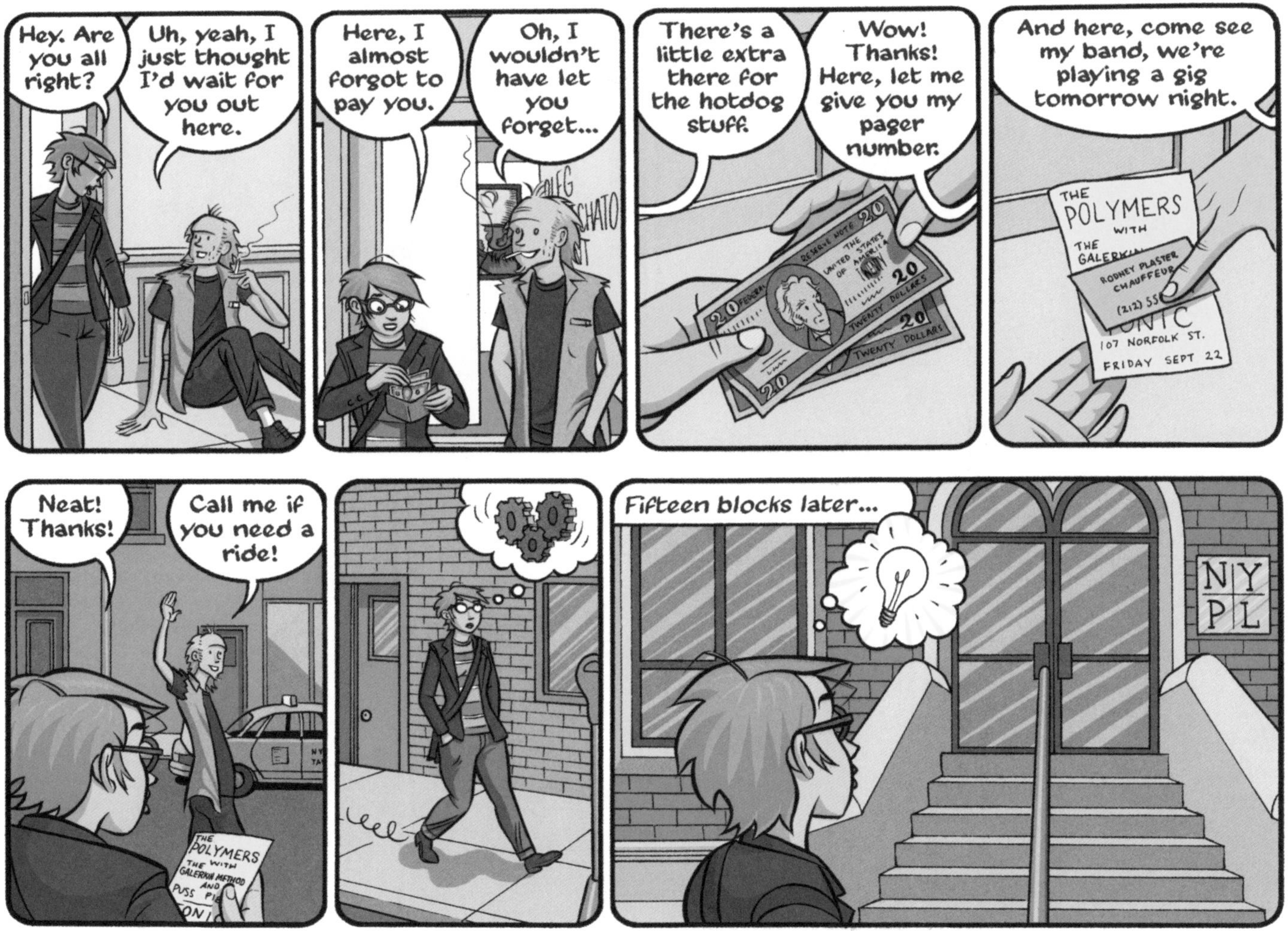

Hey. Are you all right?
Uh, yeah, I just thought I'd wait for you out here.
Here, I almost forgot to pay you.
Oh, I wouldn't have let you forget...
There's a little extra there for the hotdog stuff.
Wow! Thanks! Here, let me give you my pager number.
And here, come see my band, we're playing a gig tomorrow night.
THE POLYMERS
WITH
RODNEY PLASTER
CHAUFFEUR
107 NORFOLK ST.
FRIDAY SEPT 22
Neat! Thanks!
Call me if you need a ride!
Fifteen blocks later...
NY
PL

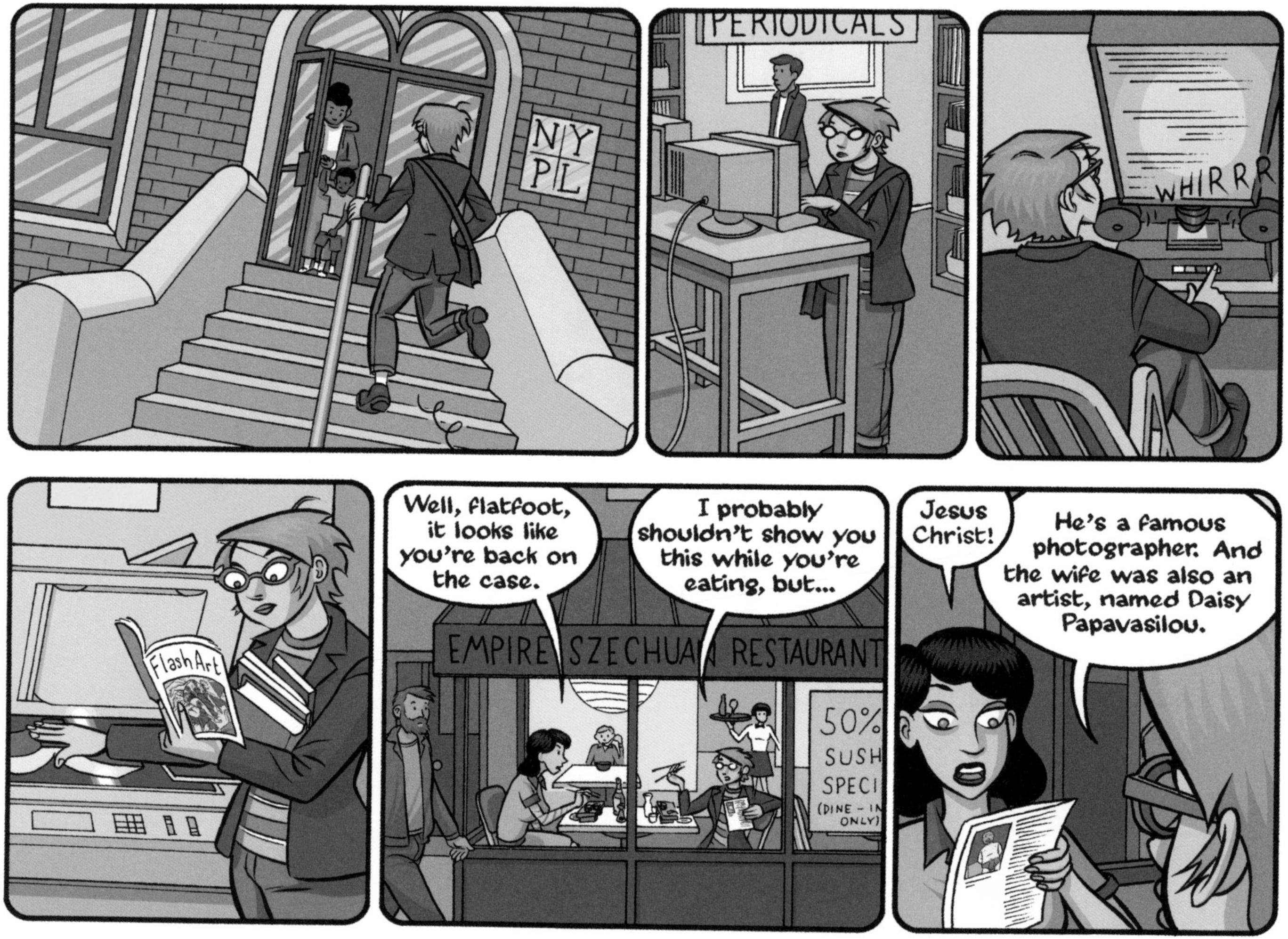
NY PL
PERIODICALS
WHIRRR
FlashArt
Well, flatfoot, it looks like you're back on the case.
I probably shouldn't show you this while you're eating, but...
EMPIRE SZECHUAN RESTAURANT
50% SUSH SPECI (DINE-IN ONLY)
Jesus Christ!
He's a famous photographer. And the wife was also an artist, named Daisy Papavasilou.

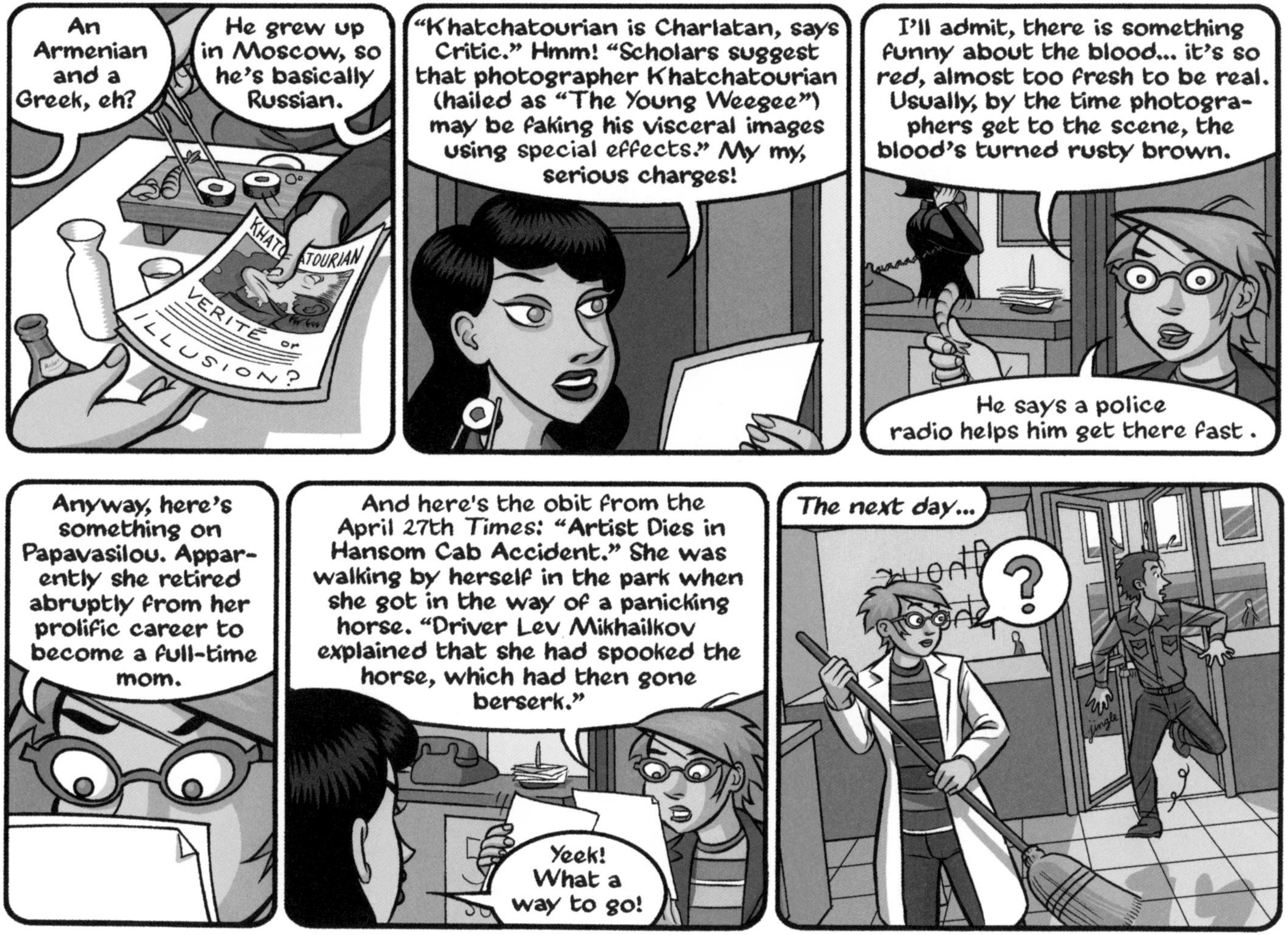
An Armenian and a Greek, eh?
He grew up in Moscow, so he's basically Russian.
KHATCHATOURIAN
VERITÉ or ILLUSION?
"Khatchatourian is Charlatan, says Critic." Hmm! "Scholars suggest that photographer Khatchatourian (hailed as "The Young Weegee") may be faking his visceral images using special *effects*." My my, serious charges!
I'll admit, there is something funny about the blood... it's so *red*, almost too fresh to be real. Usually, by the time photographers get to the scene, the blood's turned rusty brown.
He says a police radio helps him get there fast .
Anyway, here's something on Papavasilou. Apparently she retired abruptly from her prolific career to become a full-time mom.
And here's the obit from the April 27th *Times*: "Artist Dies in Hansom Cab Accident." She was walking by herself in the park when she got in the way of a panicking horse. "Driver Lev Mikhailkov explained that she had spooked the horse, which had then gone berserk."
Yeek! What a way to go!
The next day...
?
jingle

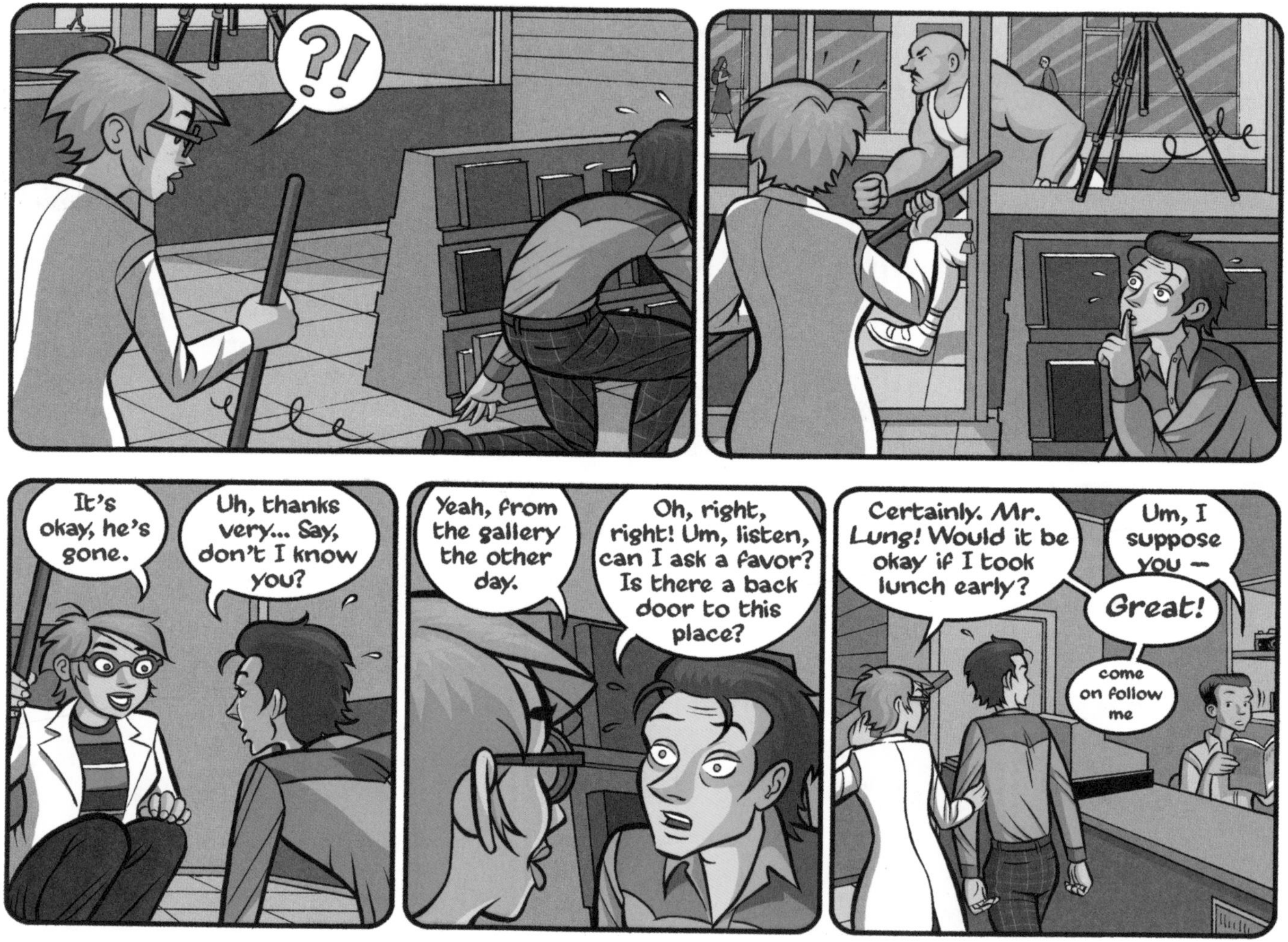
?!
It's okay, he's gone.
Uh, thanks very... Say, don't I know you?
Yeah, from the gallery the other day.
Oh, right, right! Um, listen, can I ask a favor? Is there a back door to this place?
Certainly. *Mr. Lung!* Would it be okay if I took lunch early?
Um, I suppose you —
Great!
come on follow me

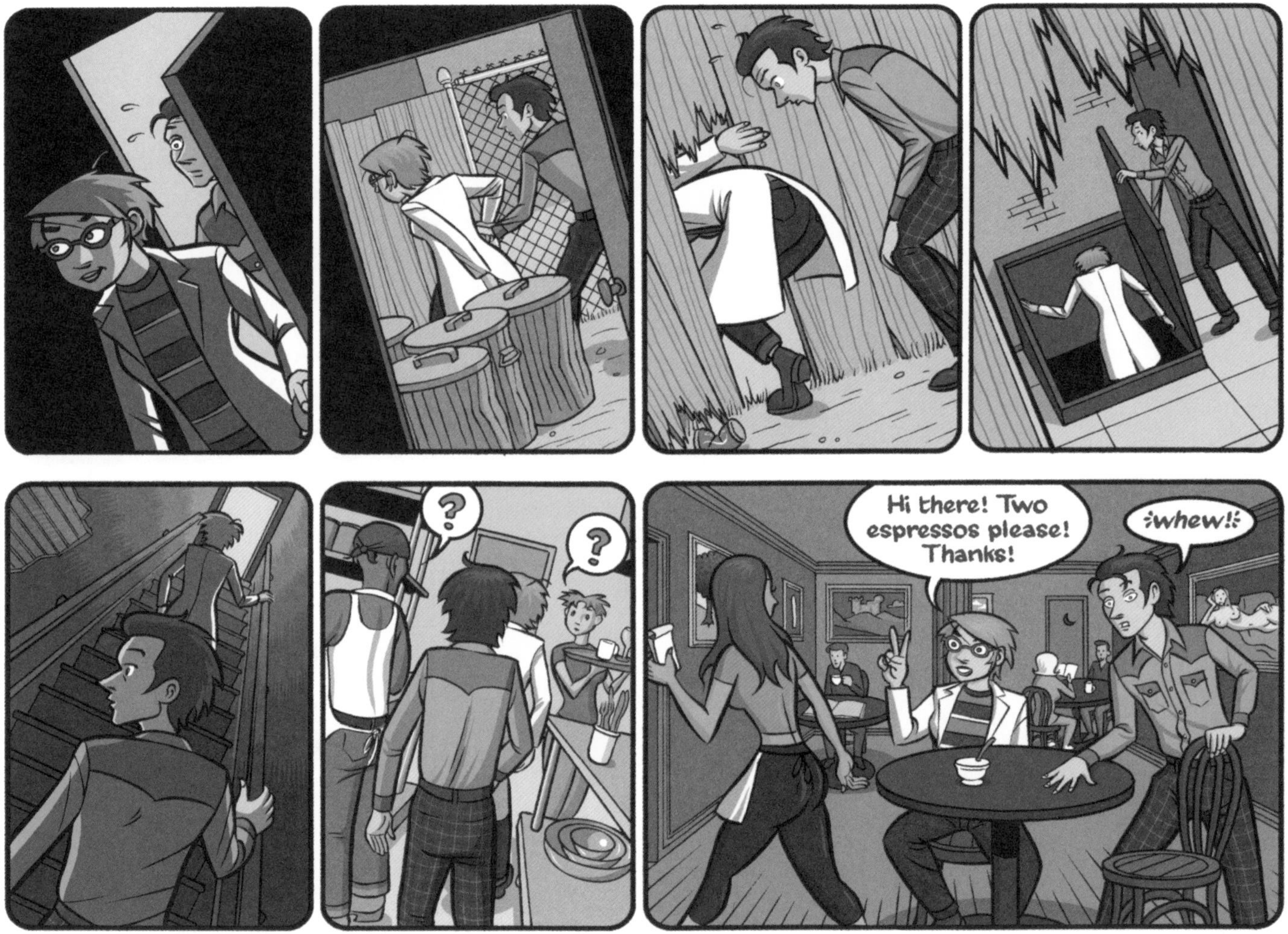
?
?
Hi there! Two espressos please! Thanks!
whew!

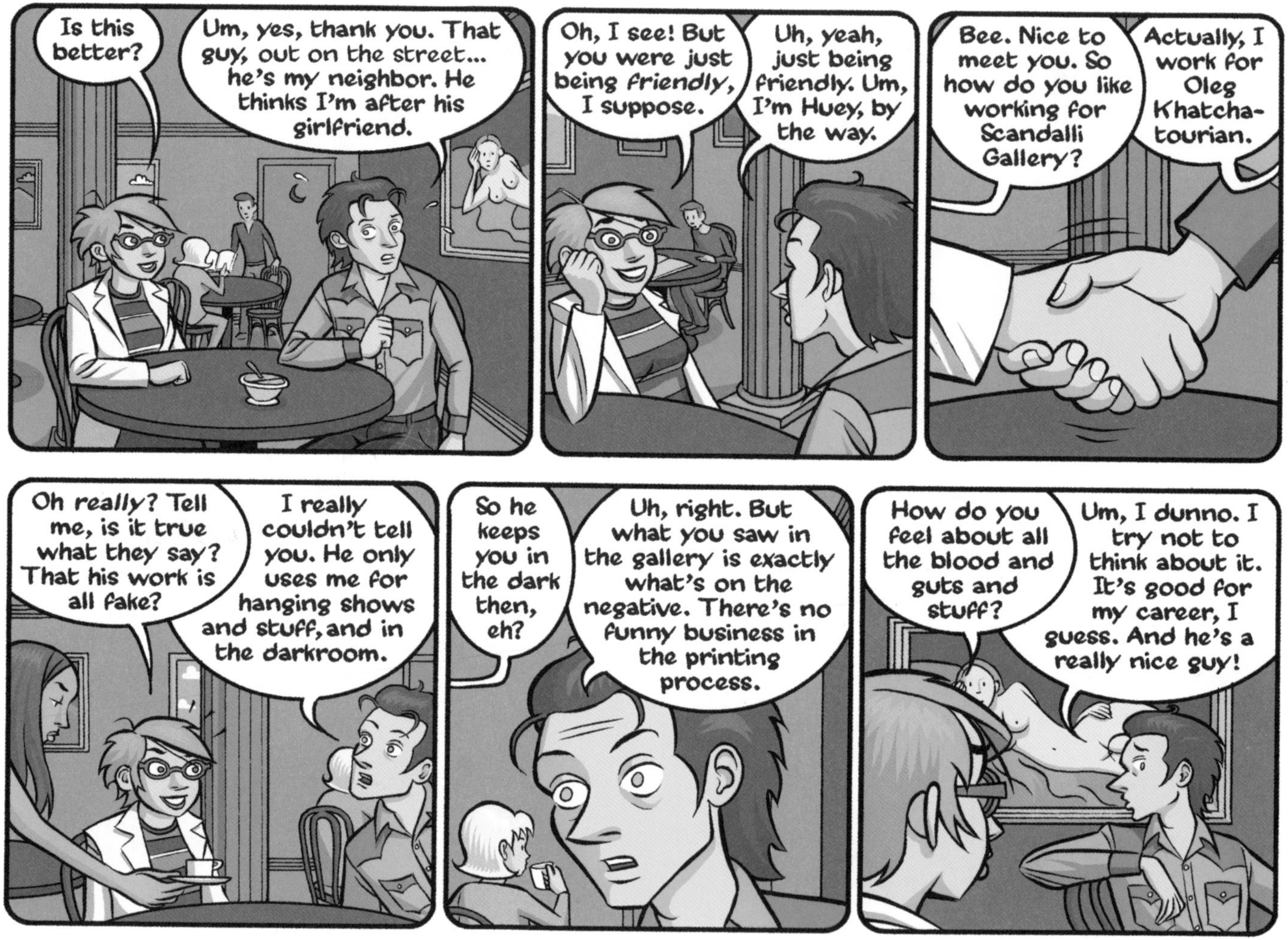
Is this better?
Um, yes, thank you. That guy, out on the street... he's my neighbor. He thinks I'm after his girlfriend.
Oh, I see! But you were just being *friendly*, I suppose.
Uh, yeah, just being friendly. Um, I'm Huey, by the way.
Bee. Nice to meet you. So how do you like working for Scandalli Gallery?
Actually, I work for Oleg Khatcha-tourian.
Oh *really*? Tell me, is it true what they say? That his work is all fake?
I really couldn't tell you. He only uses me for hanging shows and stuff, and in the darkroom.
So he keeps you in the dark then, eh?
Uh, right. But what you saw in the gallery is exactly what's on the negative. There's no funny business in the printing process.
How do you feel about all the blood and guts and stuff?
Um, I dunno. I try not to think about it. It's good for my career, I guess. And he's a really nice guy!

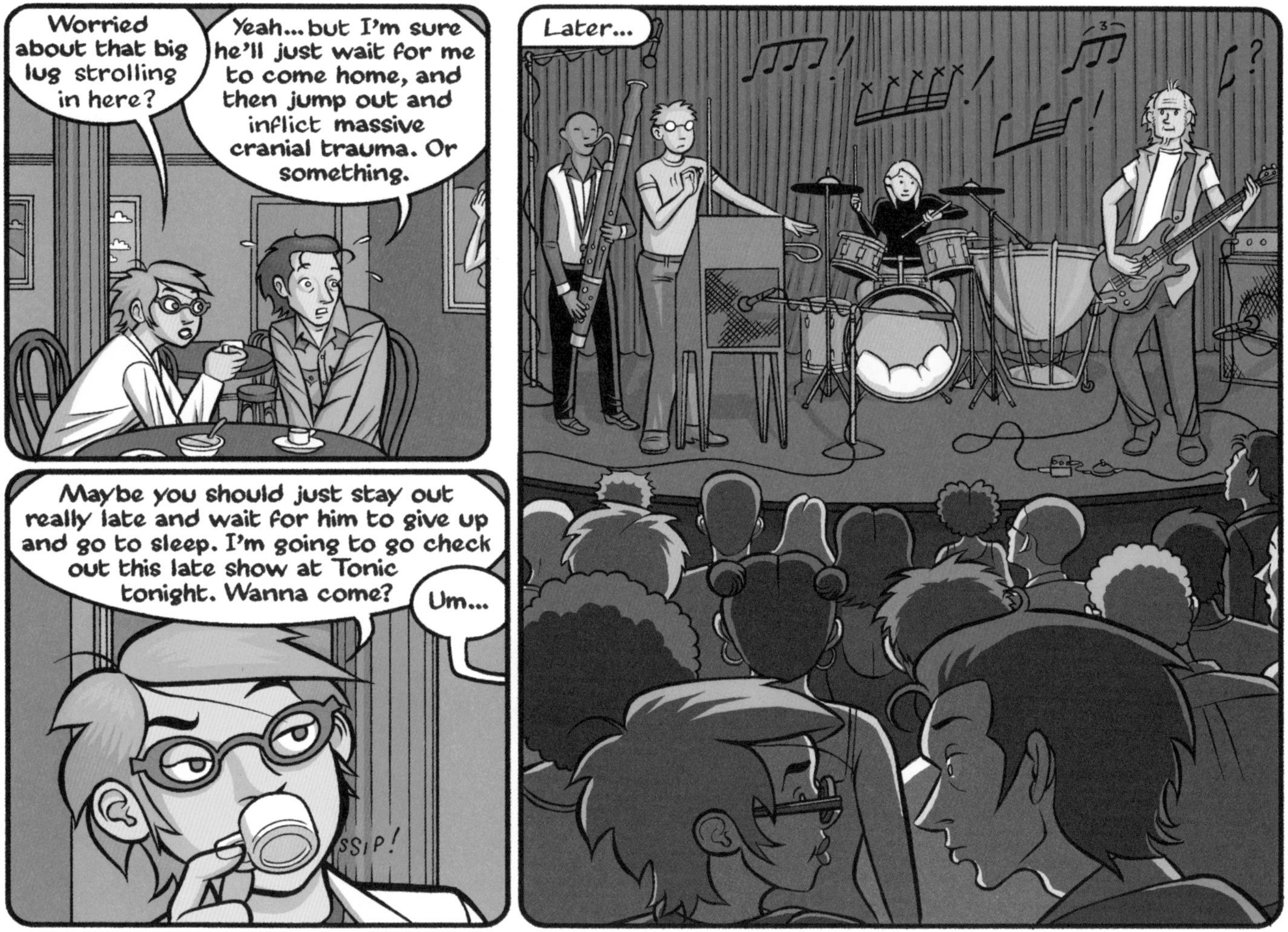
Worried about that big lug strolling in here?
Yeah... but I'm sure he'll just wait for me to come home, and then jump out and inflict massive cranial trauma. Or something.
Maybe you should just stay out really late and wait for him to give up and go to sleep. I'm going to go check out this late show at Tonic tonight. Wanna come?
Um...
SSIP!
Later...

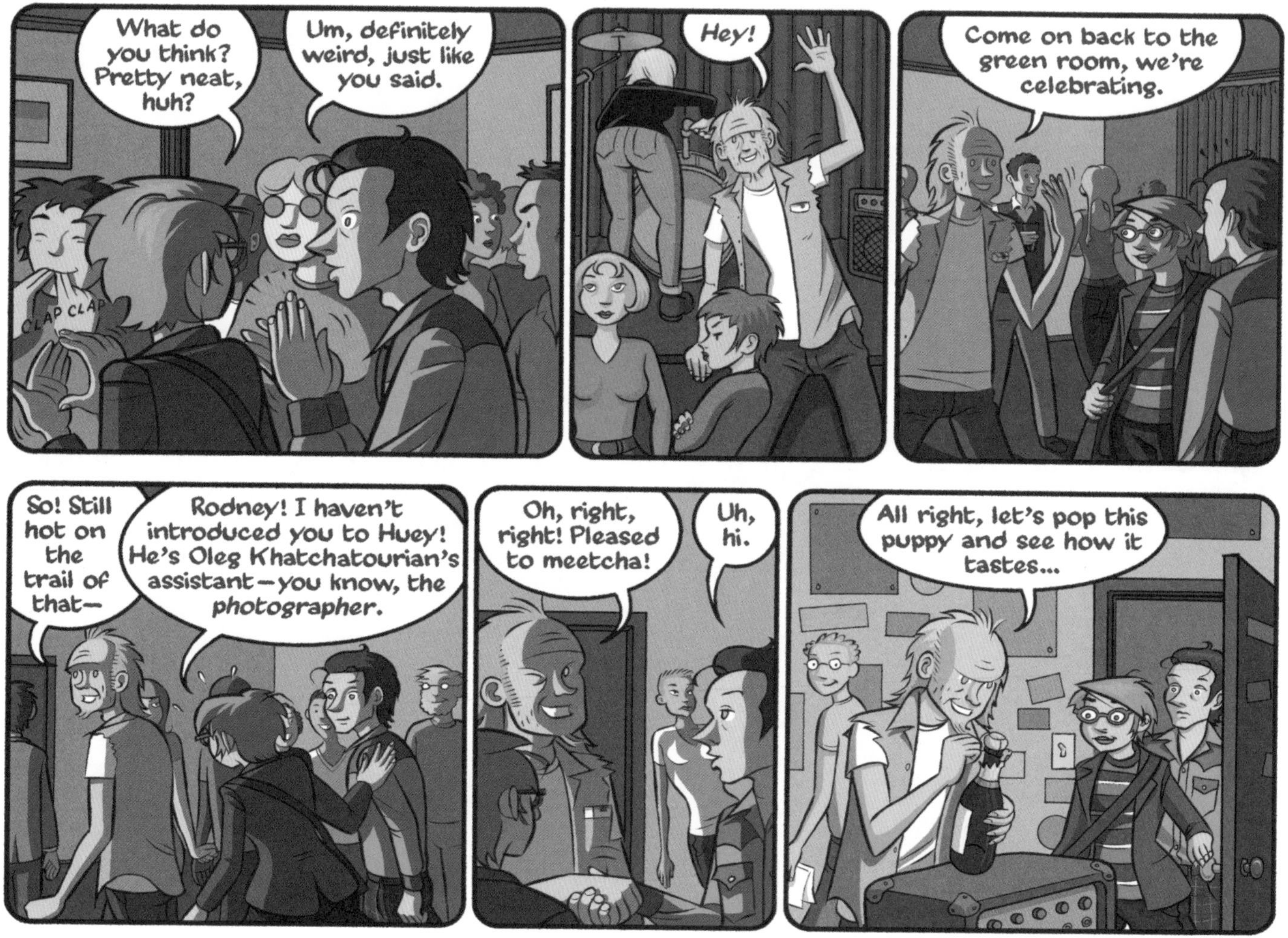
What do you think? Pretty neat, huh?
Um, definitely weird, just like you said.
CLAP CLAP
Hey!
Come on back to the green room, we're celebrating.
So! Still hot on the trail of that—
Rodney! I haven't introduced you to Huey! He's Oleg Khatchatourian's assistant—you know, the *photographer.*
Oh, right, right! Pleased to meetcha!
Uh, hi.
All right, let's pop this puppy and see how it tastes...

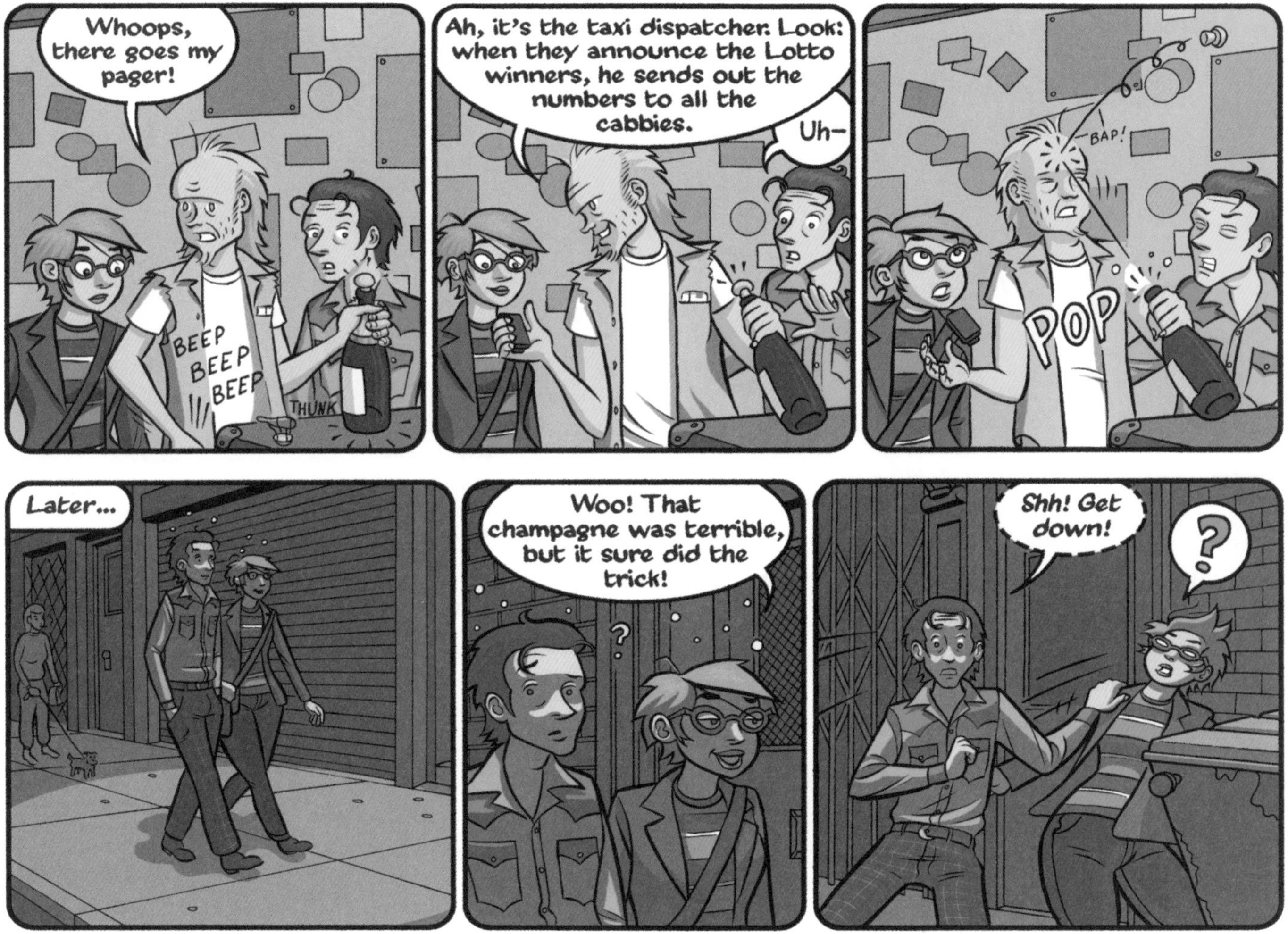
Whoops, there goes my pager!
BEEP BEEP BEEP
THUNK
Ah, it's the taxi dispatcher. Look: when they announce the Lotto winners, he sends out the numbers to all the cabbies.
Uh–
BAP!
POP
Later...
Woo! That champagne was terrible, but it sure did the trick!
?
Shh! Get down!
?

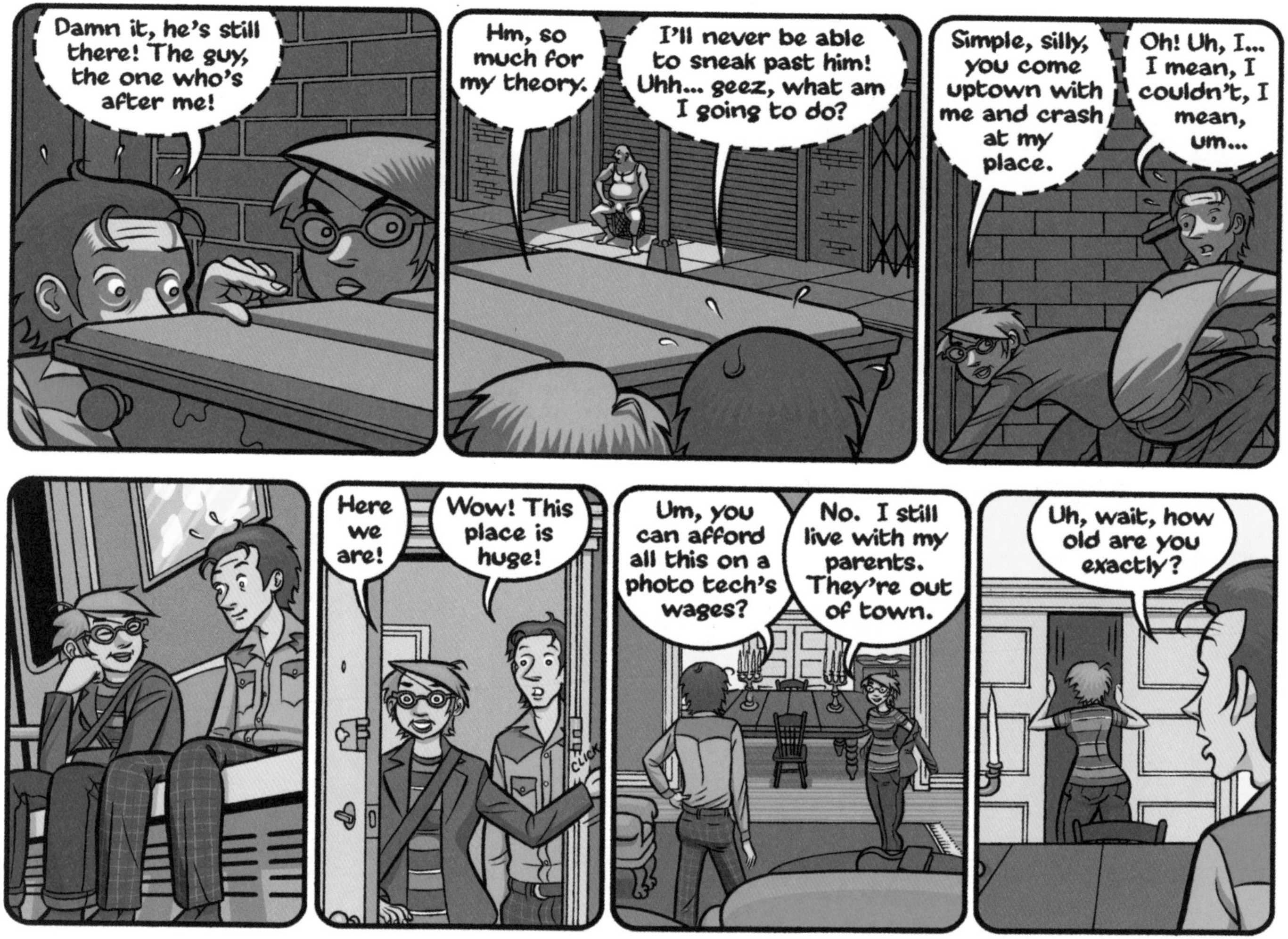
Damn it, he's still there! The guy, the one who's after me!
Hm, so much for my theory.
I'll never be able to sneak past him! Uhh... geez, what am I going to do?
Simple, silly, you come uptown with me and crash at my place.
Oh! Uh, I... I mean, I couldn't, I mean, um...
Here we are!
Wow! This place is huge!
CLICK
Um, you can afford all this on a photo tech's wages?
No. I still live with my parents. They're out of town.
Uh, wait, how old are you exactly?

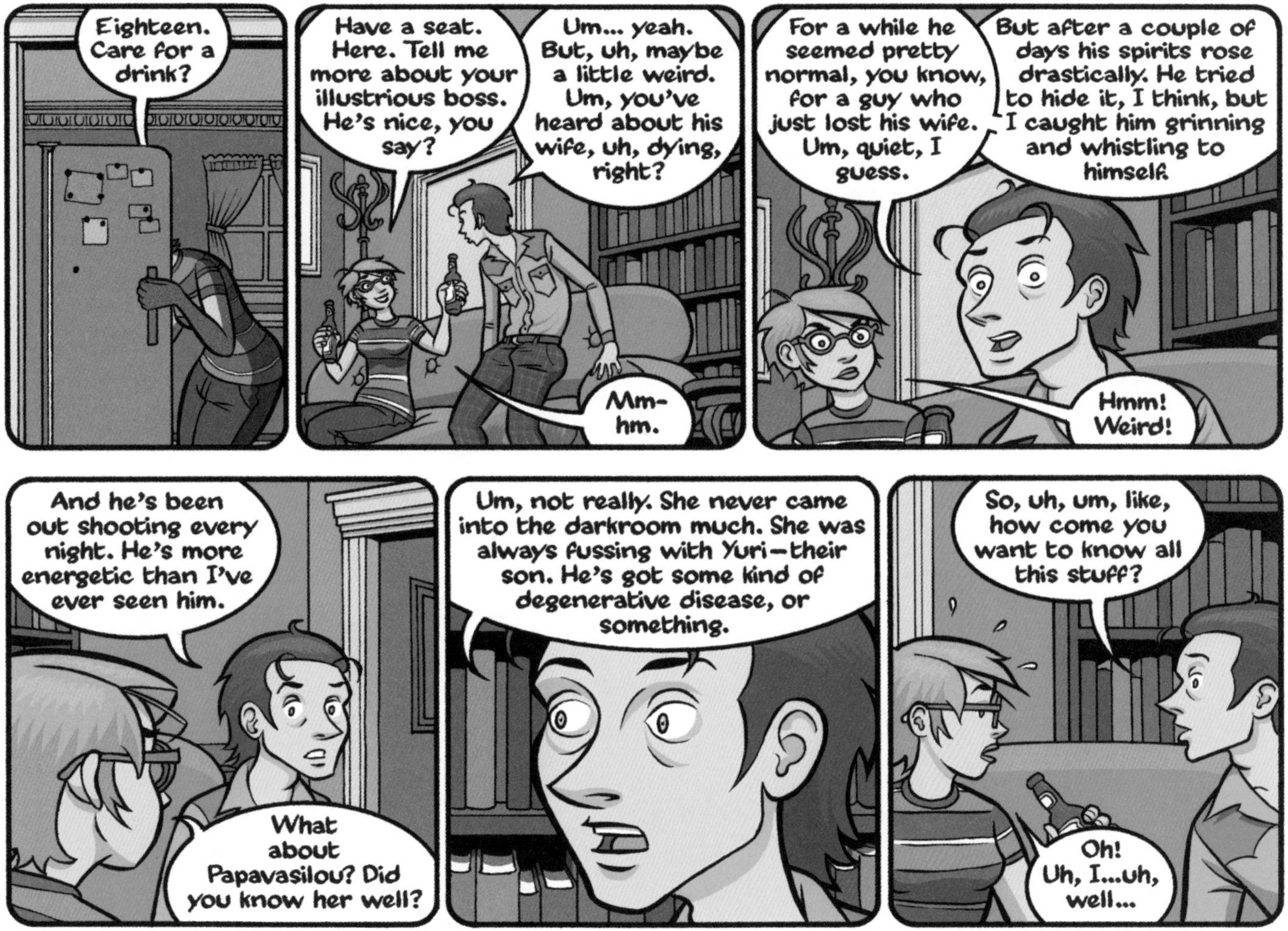
Eighteen. Care for a drink?
Have a seat. Here. Tell me more about your illustrious boss. He's nice, you say?
Um... yeah. But, uh, maybe a little weird. Um, you've heard about his wife, uh, dying, right?
Mm-hm.
For a while he seemed pretty normal, you know, for a guy who just lost his wife. Um, quiet, I guess.
But after a couple of days his spirits rose drastically. He tried to hide it, I think, but I caught him grinning and whistling to himself.
Hmm! Weird!
And he's been out shooting every night. He's more energetic than I've ever seen him.
What about Papavasilou? Did you know her well?
Um, not really. She never came into the darkroom much. She was always fussing with Yuri—their son. He's got some kind of degenerative disease, or something.
So, uh, um, like, how come you want to know all this stuff?
Oh! Uh, I...uh, well...

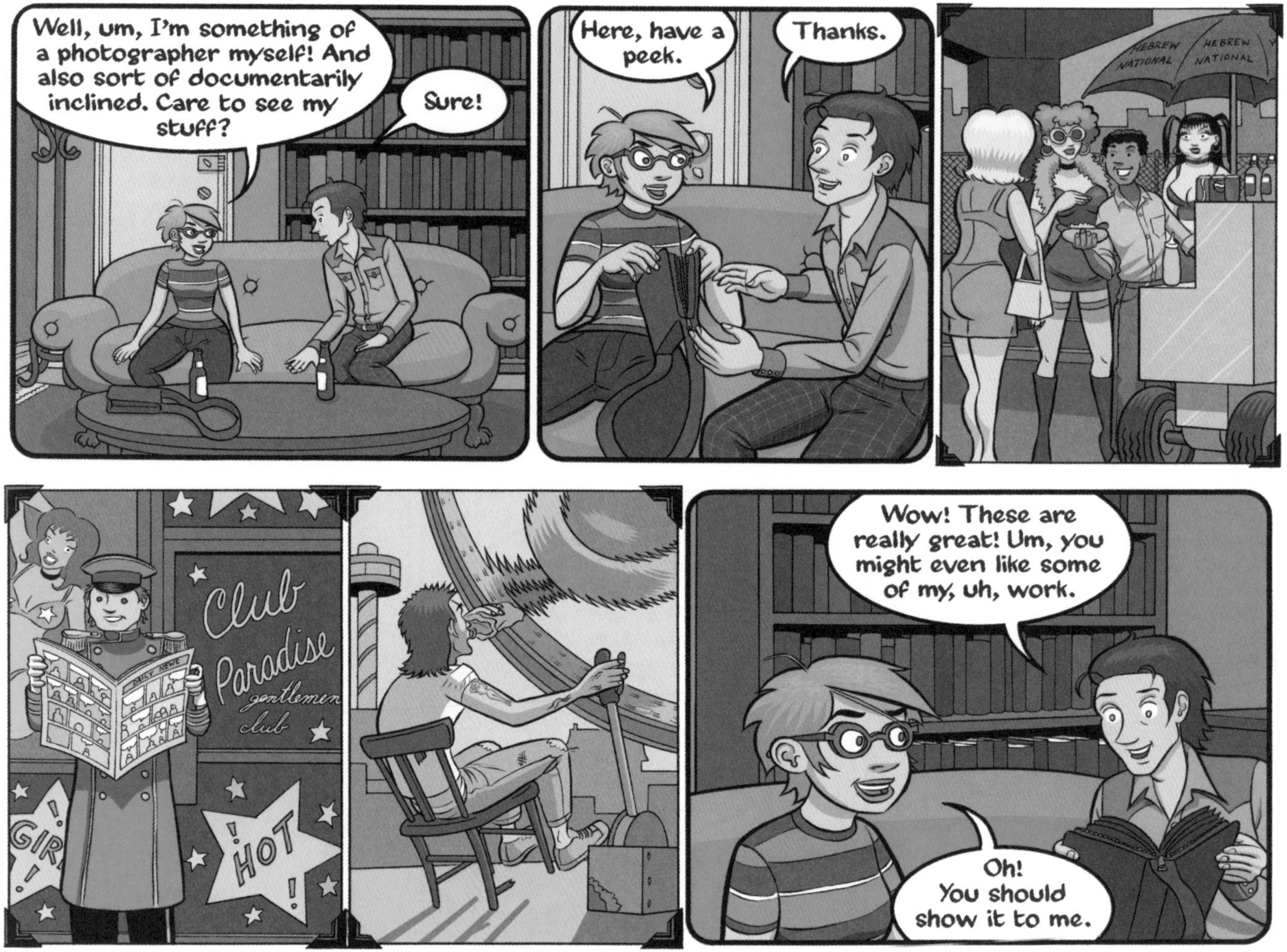
Well, um, I'm something of a photographer myself! And also sort of documentarily inclined. Care to see my stuff?
Sure!
Here, have a peek.
Thanks.
HEBREW NATIONAL
HEBREW NATIONAL
Club Paradise gentlemen club
DAILY NEWS
HOT
Wow! These are really great! Um, you might even like some of my, uh, work.
Oh! You should show it to me.

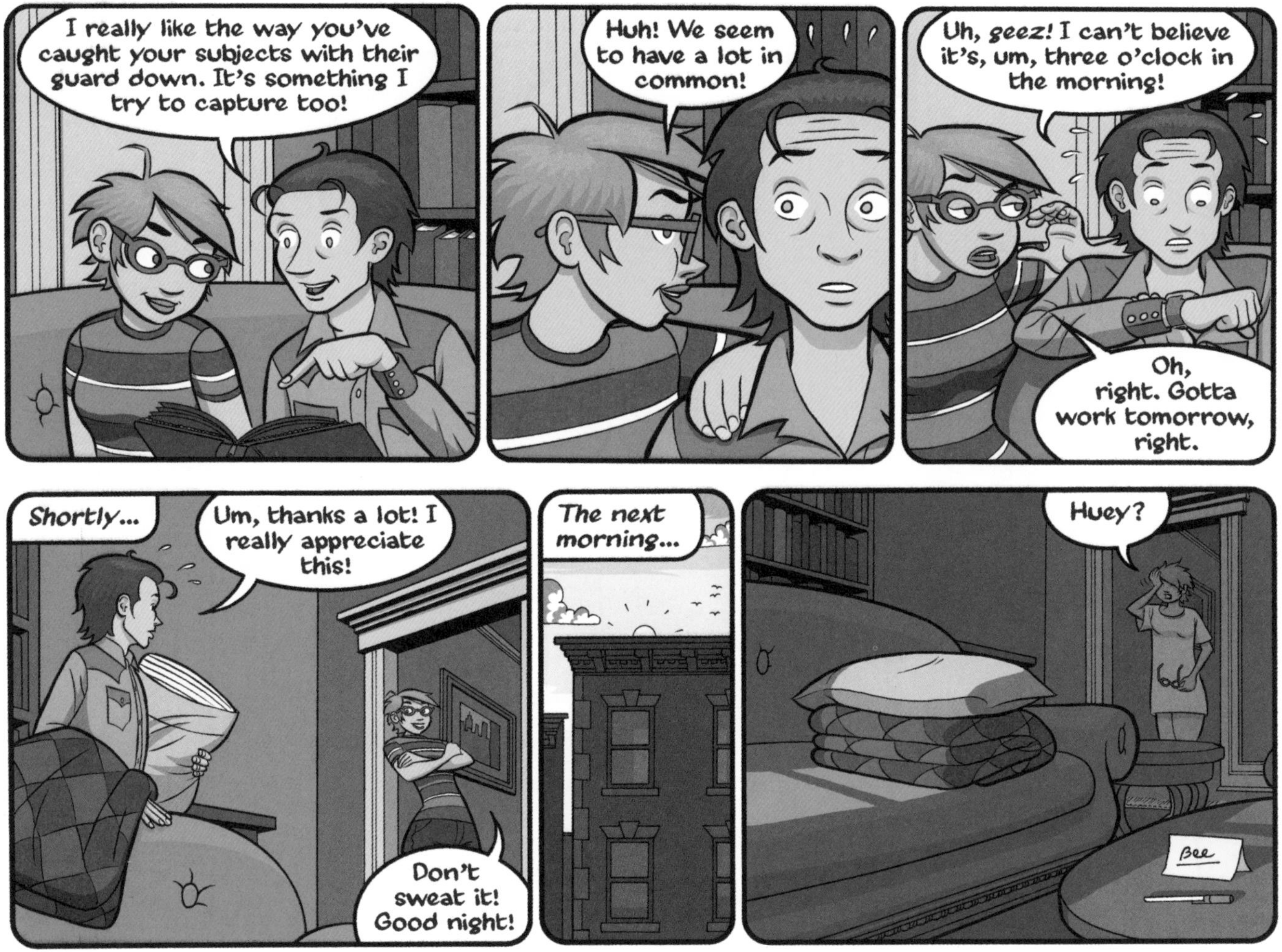
I really like the way you've caught your subjects with their guard down. It's something I try to capture too!
Huh! We seem to have a lot in common!
Uh, geez! I can't believe it's, um, three o'clock in the morning!
Oh, right. Gotta work tomorrow, right.
Shortly...
Um, thanks a lot! I really appreciate this!
Don't sweat it! Good night!
The next morning...
Huey?
Bee

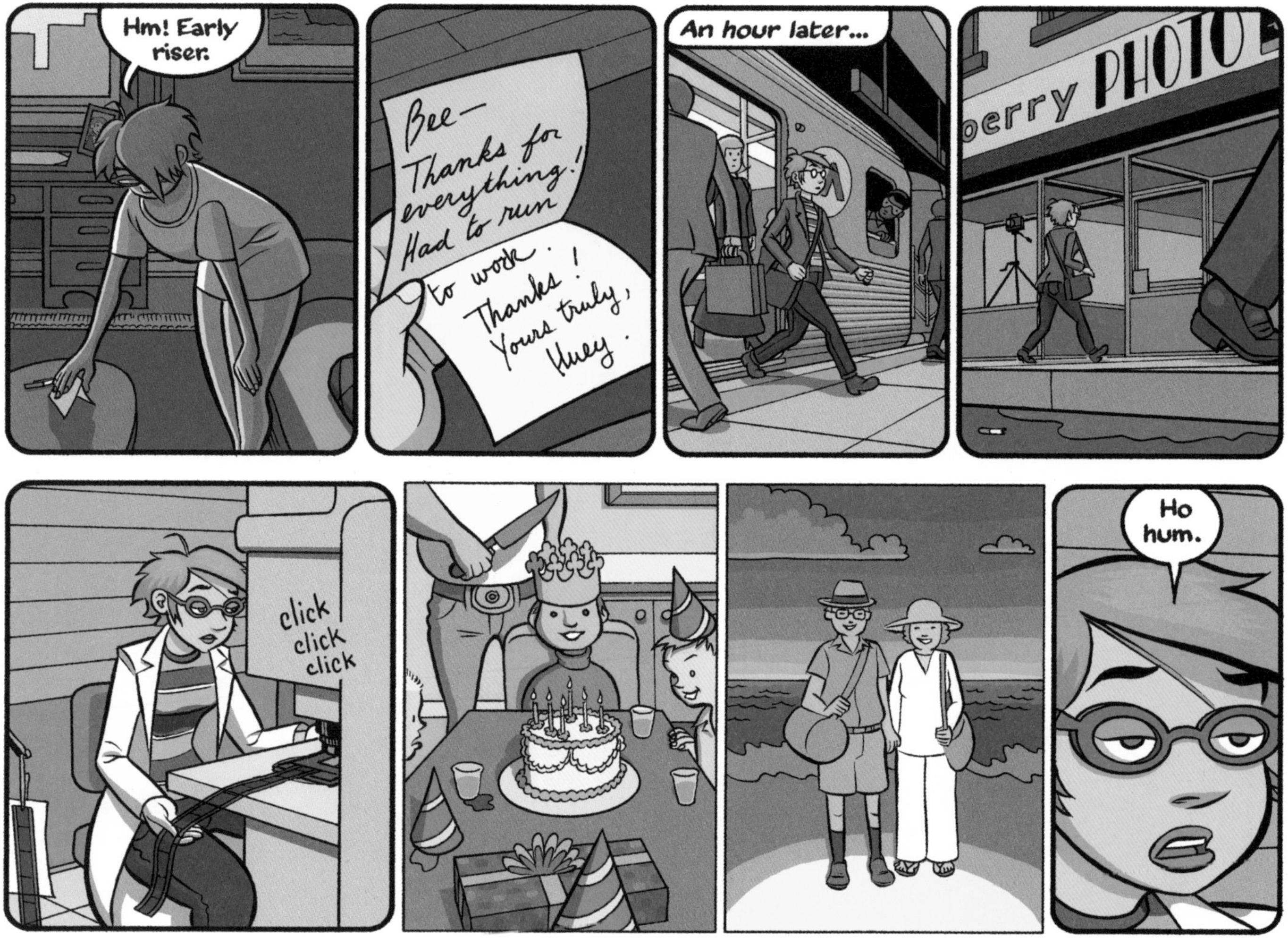
Hm! Early riser.
Bee—
Thanks for everything!
Had to run to work.
Thanks!
Yours truly,
Huey.
An hour later...
berry PHOTO
click
click
click
Ho hum.

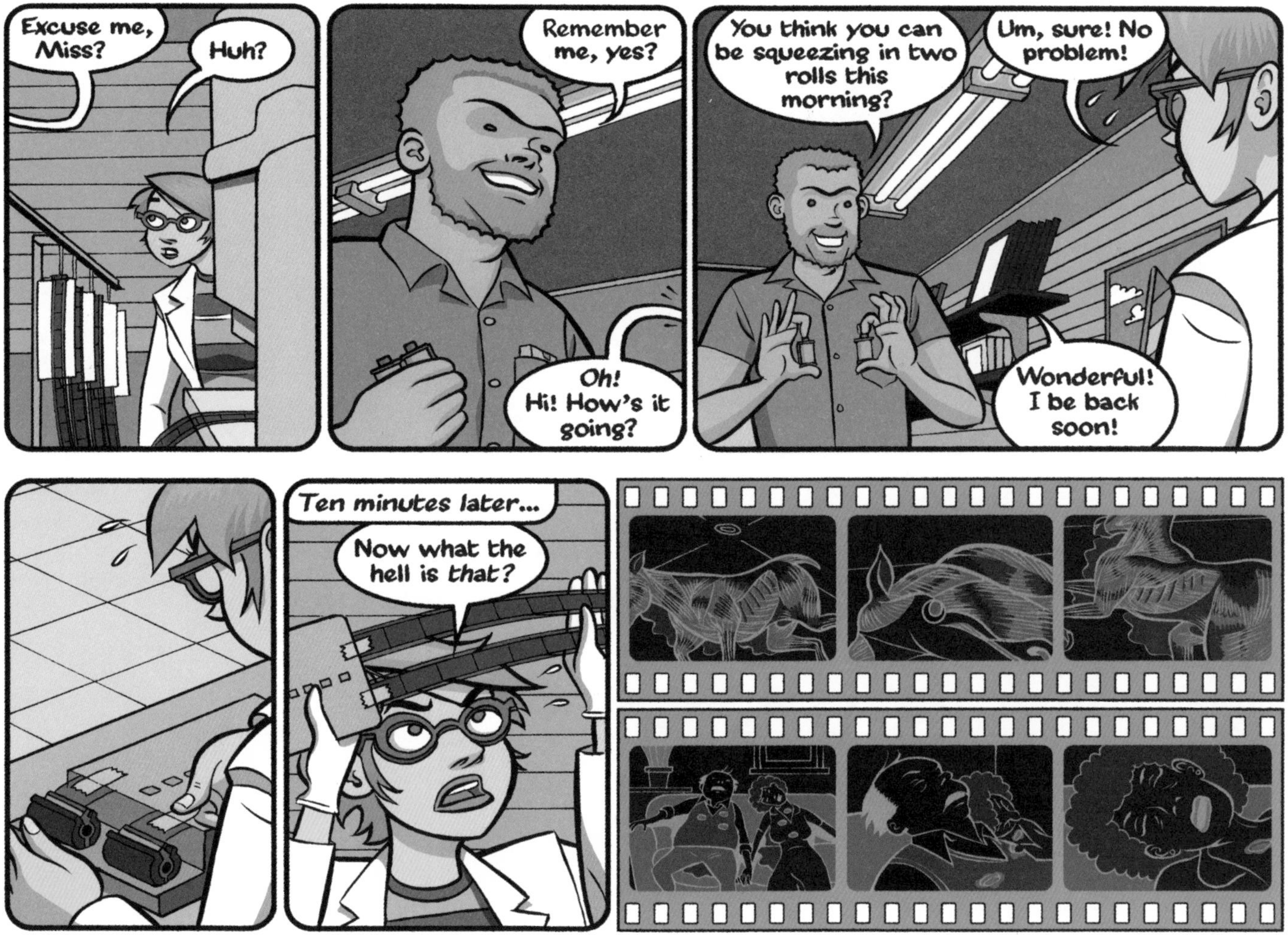
Excuse me, Miss?
Huh?
Remember me, yes?
Oh! Hi! How's it going?
You think you can be squeezing in two rolls this morning?
Um, sure! No problem!
Wonderful! I be back soon!
Ten minutes later...
Now what the hell is *that*?

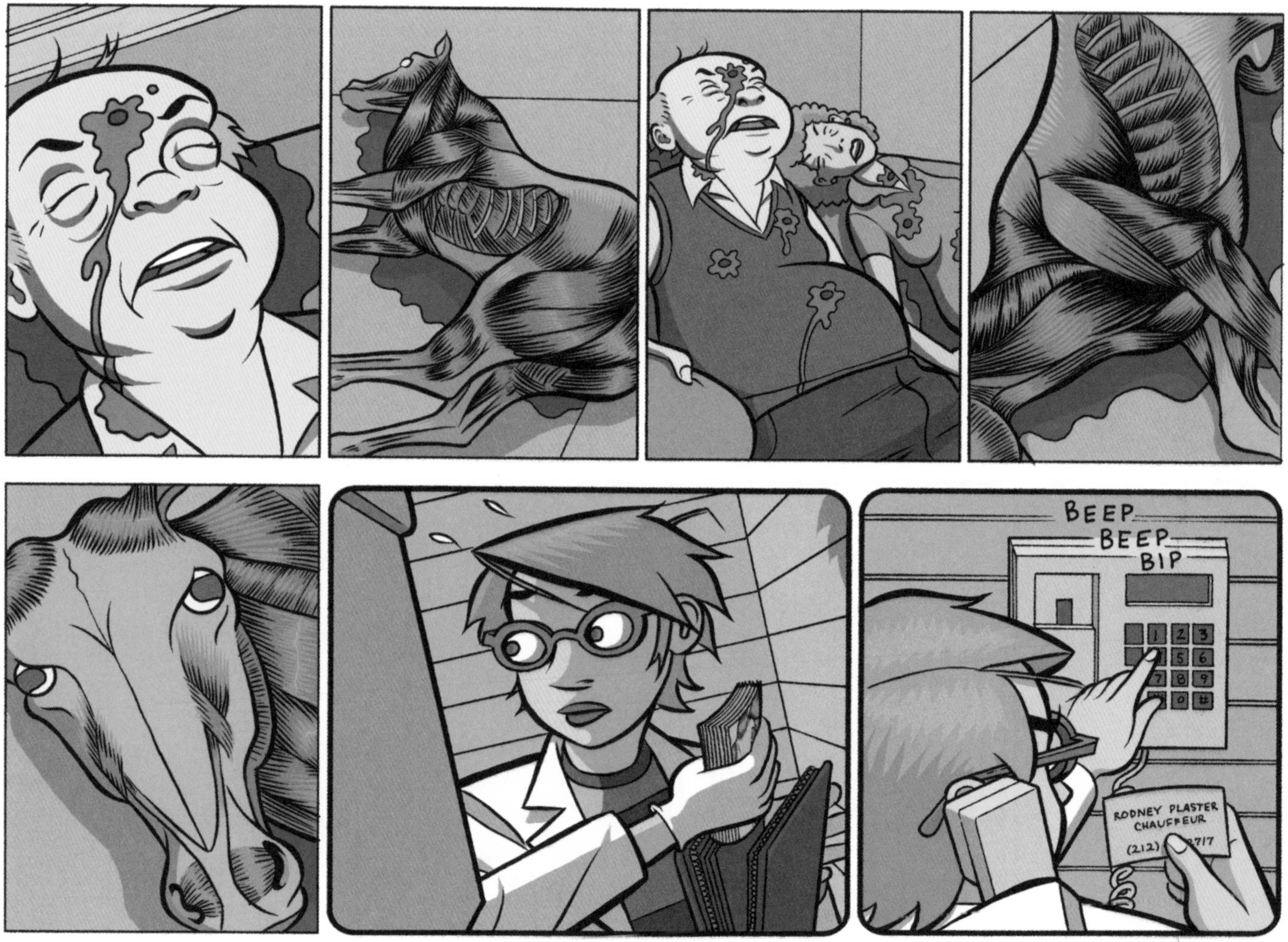
BEEP
BEEP
BIP
RODNEY PLASTER
CHAUFFEUR
(212)

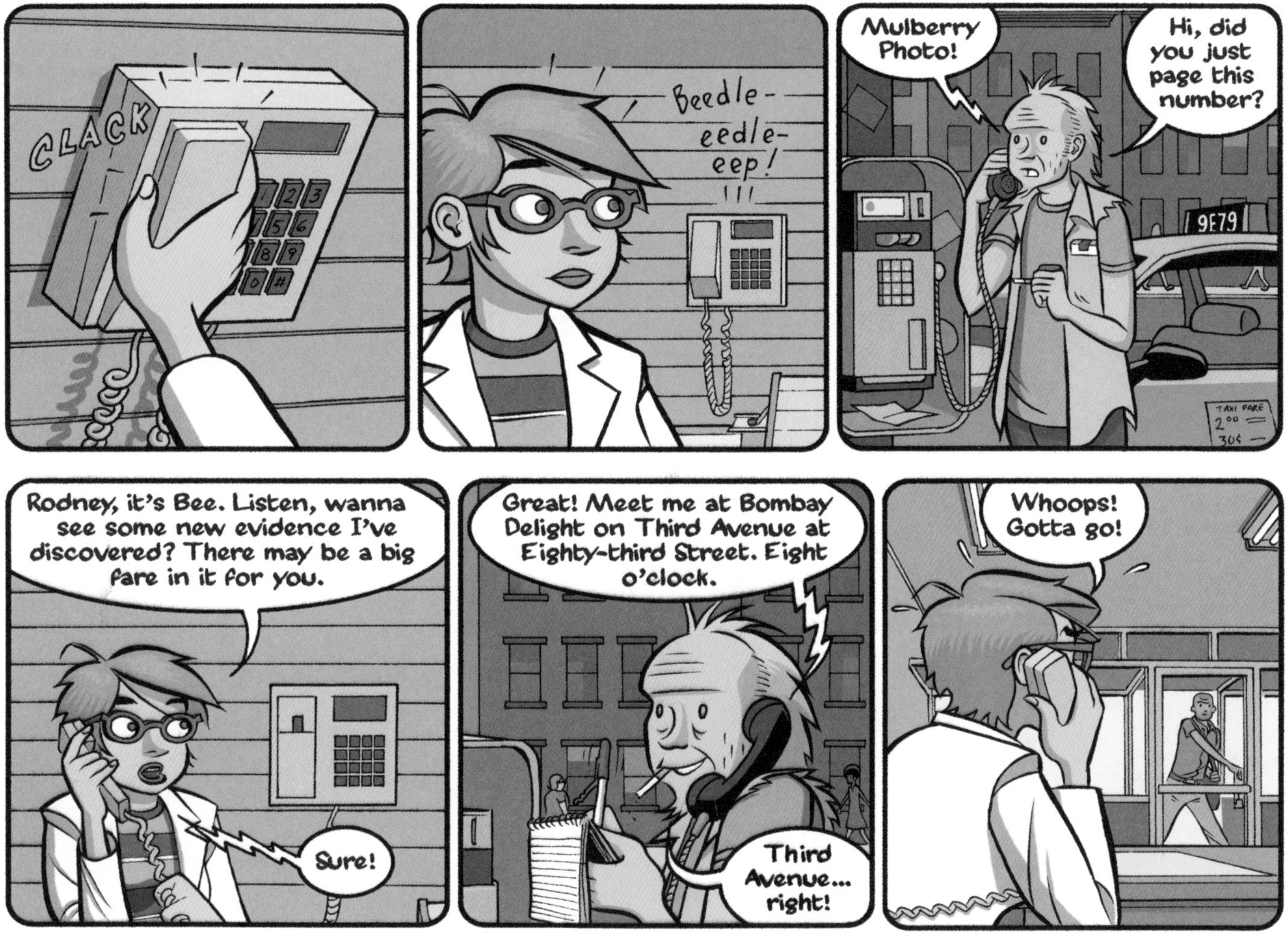
CLACK
Beedle-eedle-eep!
Mulberry Photo!
Hi, did you just page this number?
9E79
TAXI FARE
Rodney, it's Bee. Listen, wanna see some new evidence I've discovered? There may be a big fare in it for you.
Sure!
Great! Meet me at Bombay Delight on Third Avenue at Eighty-third Street. Eight o'clock.
Third Avenue... right!
Whoops! Gotta go!

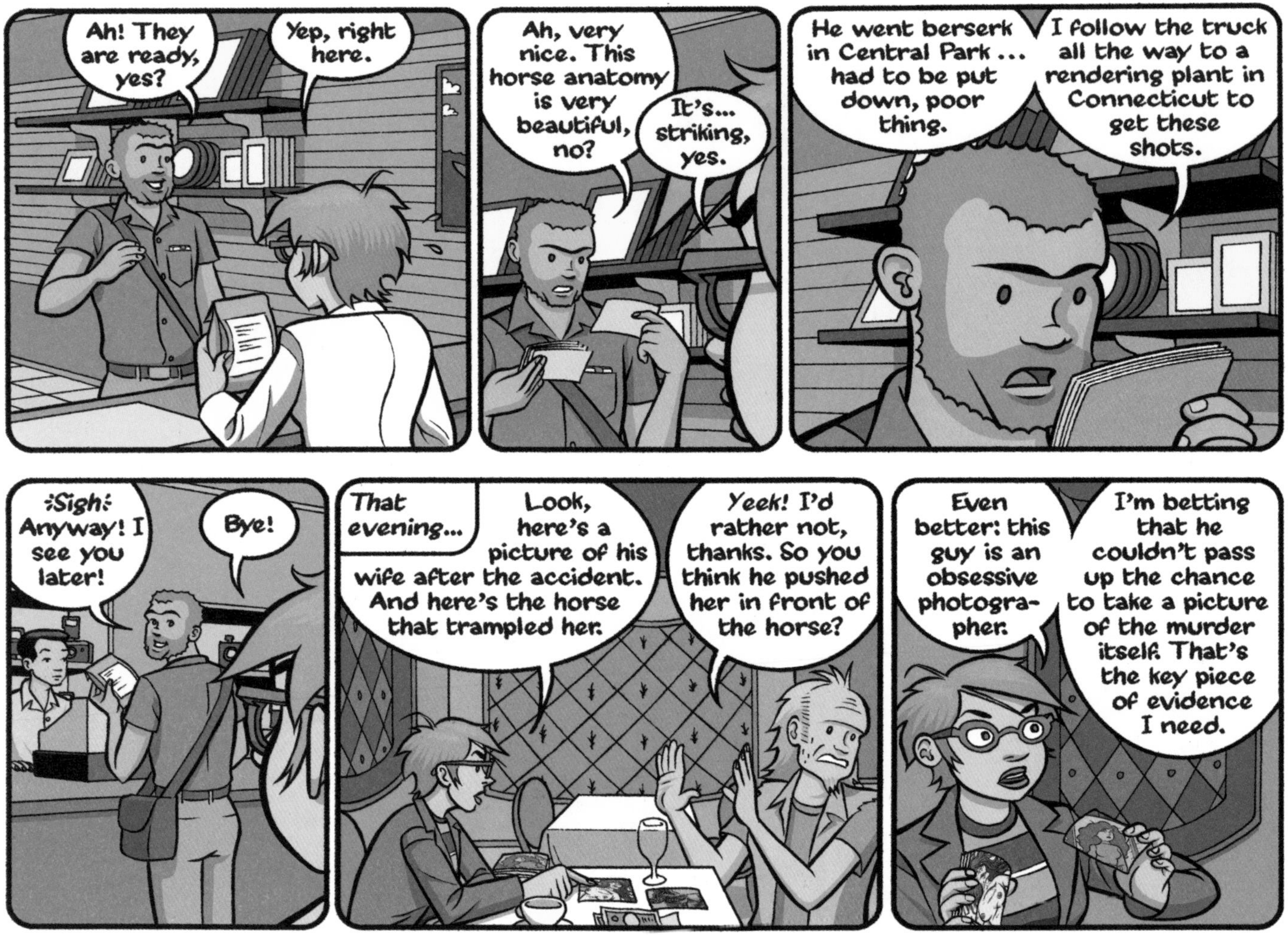

Ah! They are ready, yes?
Yep, right here.
Ah, very nice. This horse anatomy is very beautiful, no?
It's... striking, yes.
He went berserk in Central Park . . . had to be put down, poor thing.
I follow the truck all the way to a rendering plant in Connecticut to get these shots.
:Sigh: Anyway! I see you later!
Bye!
That evening...
Look, here's a picture of his wife after the accident. And here's the horse that trampled her.
Yeek! I'd rather not, thanks. So you think he pushed her in front of the horse?
Even better: this guy is an obsessive photographer.
I'm betting that he couldn't pass up the chance to take a picture of the murder itself. That's the key piece of evidence I need.

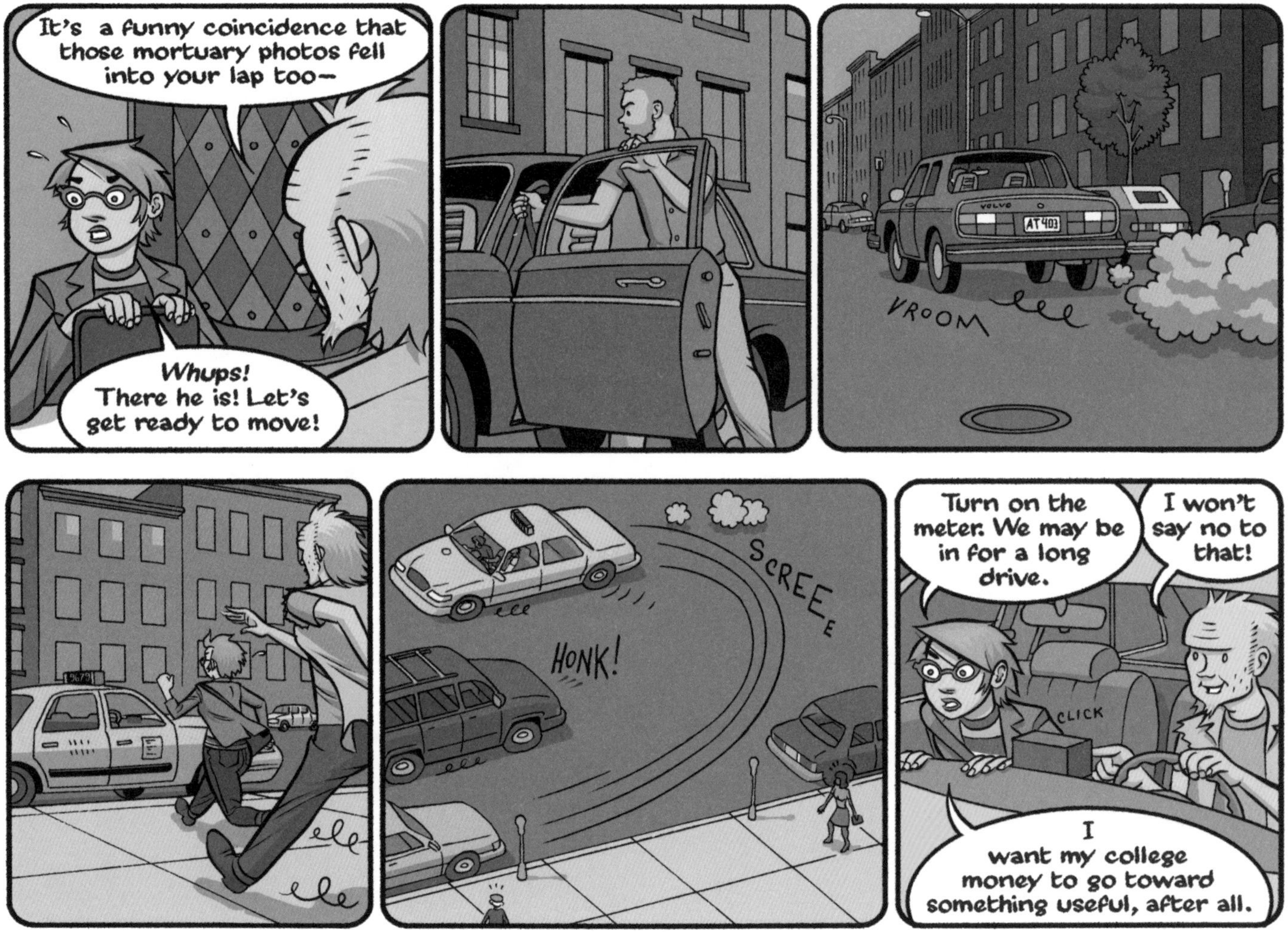

It's a funny coincidence that those mortuary photos fell into your lap too—
Whups! There he is! Let's get ready to move!
VOLVO
AT 403
VROOM
HONK!
SCREEEE
Turn on the meter. We may be in for a long drive.
I won't say no to that!
CLICK
I want my college money to go toward something useful, after all.

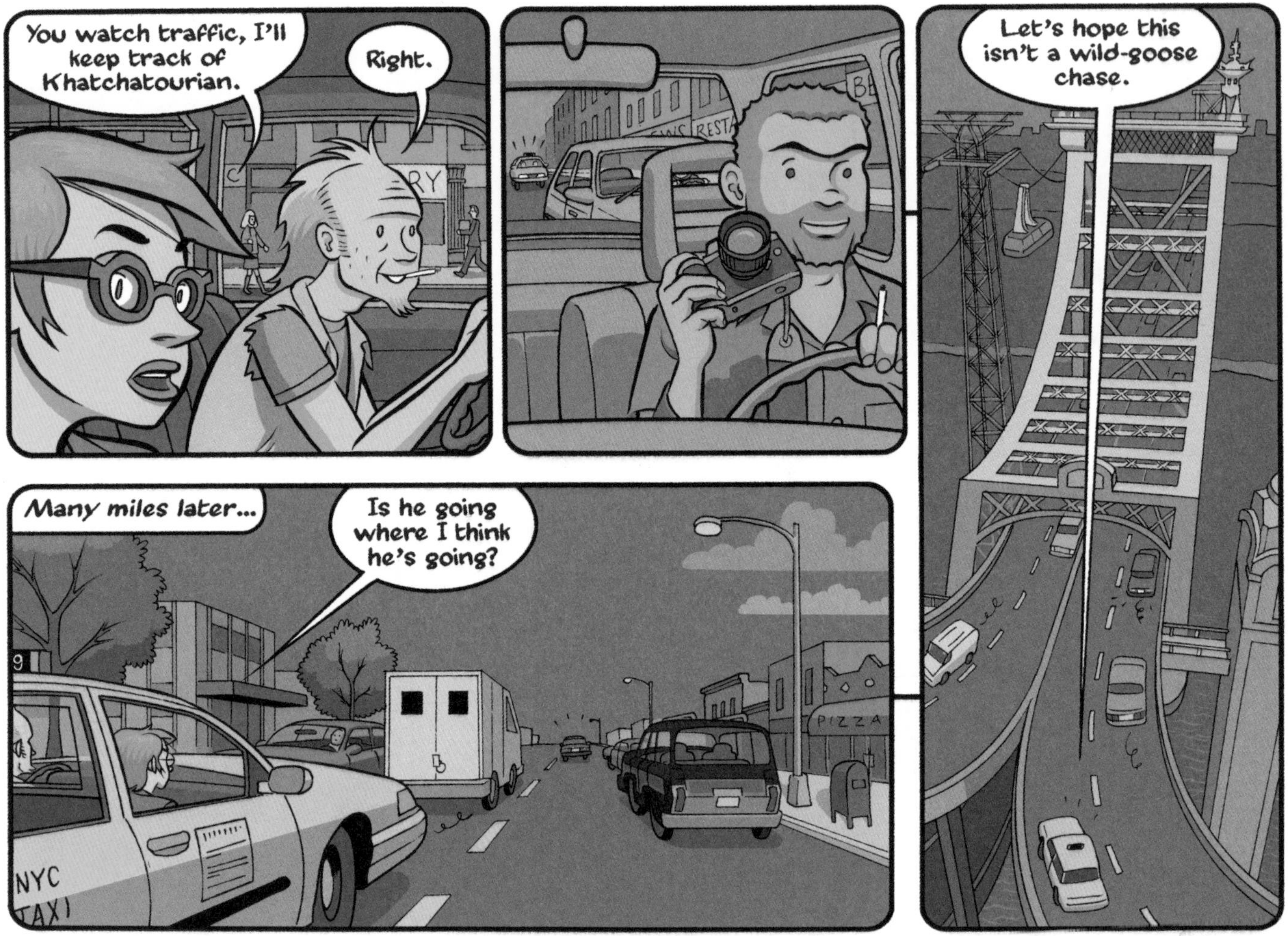
You watch traffic, I'll keep track of Khatchatourian.
Right.
BE
RESTA
RY
Many miles later...
Is he going where I think he's going?
PIZZA
NYC TAXI
Let's hope this isn't a wild-goose chase.

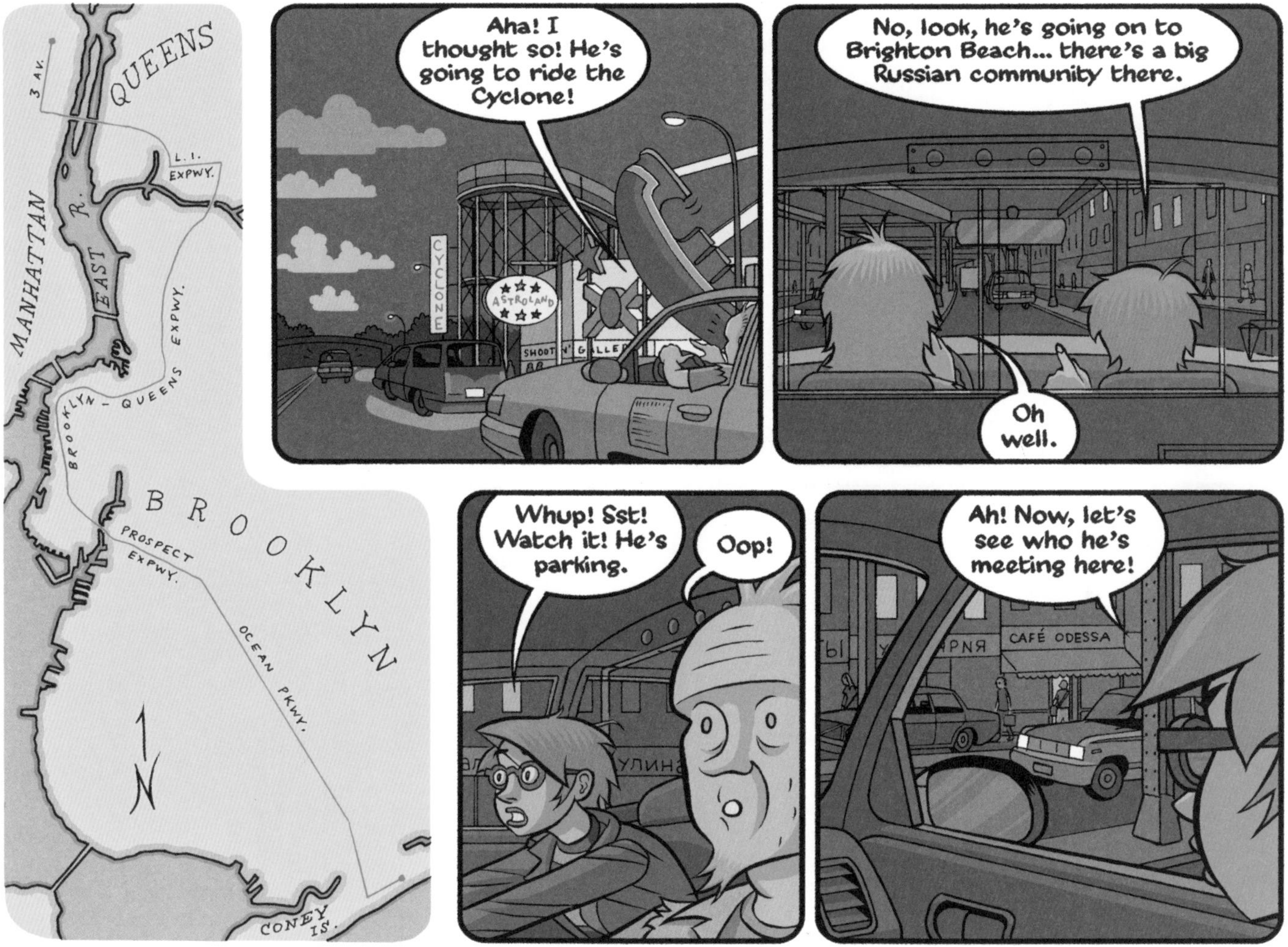
QUEENS
3 AV.
MANHATTAN
EAST R.
L. I. EXPWY.
BROOKLYN - QUEENS EXPWY.
BROOKLYN
PROSPECT EXPWY.
OCEAN PKWY.
CONEY IS.
N
Aha! I thought so! He's going to ride the Cyclone!
CYCLONE
ASTROLAND
No, look, he's going on to Brighton Beach... there's a big Russian community there.
Oh well.
Whup! Sst! Watch it! He's parking.
Oop!
Ah! Now, let's see who he's meeting here!
CAFÉ ODESSA

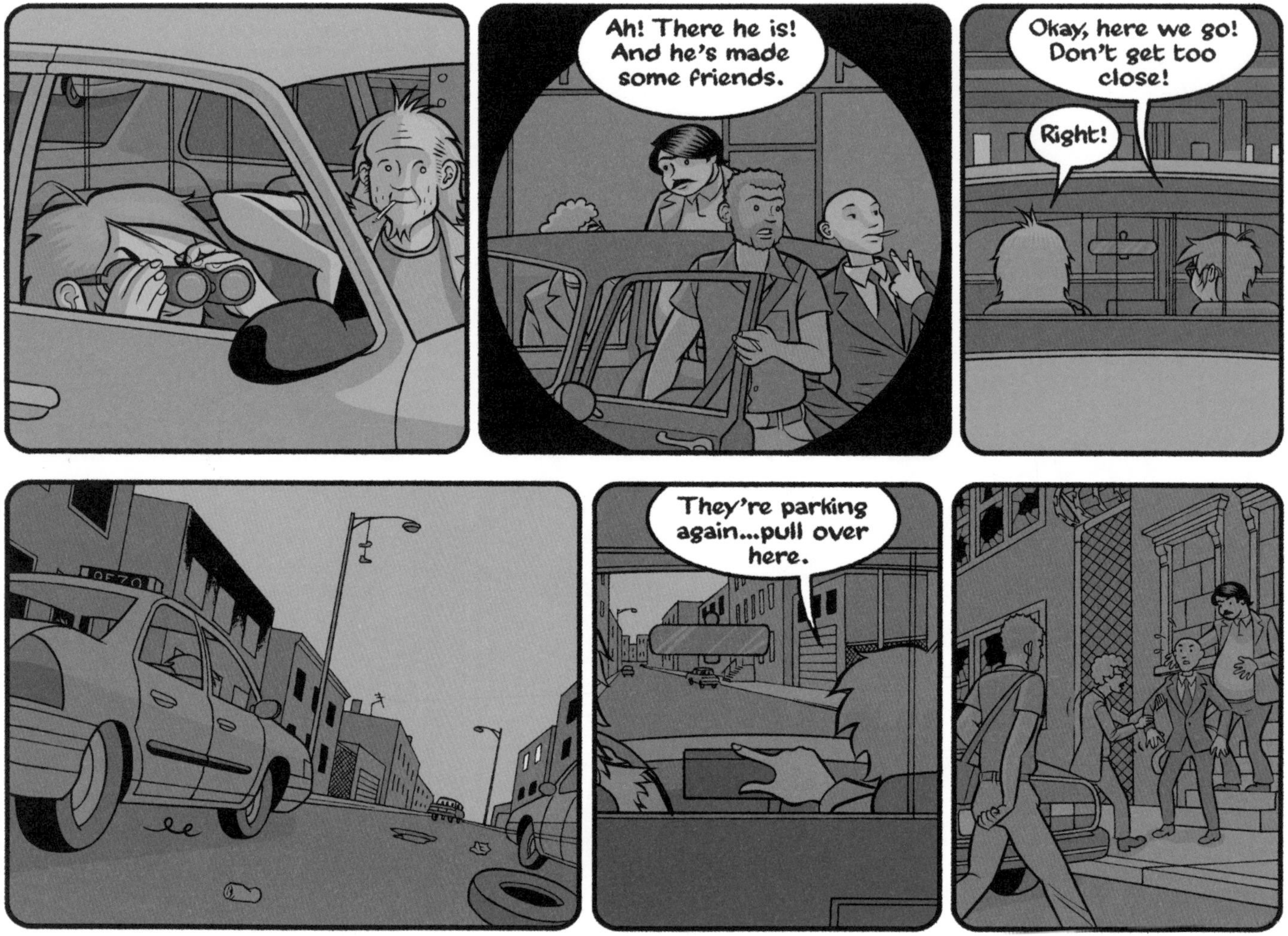
Ah! There he is! And he's made some friends.
Okay, here we go! Don't get too close!
Right!
They're parking again...pull over here.

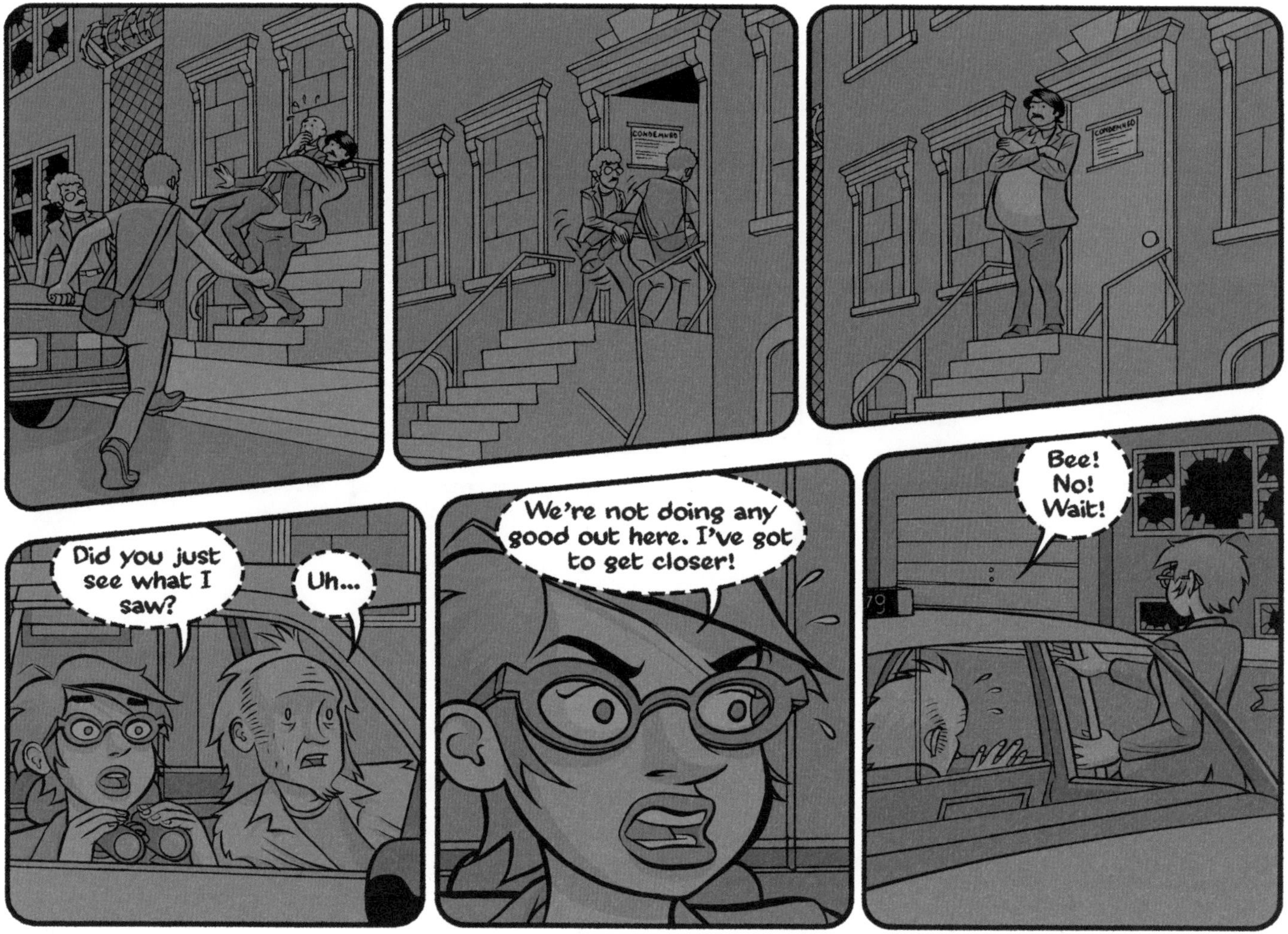
Did you just see what I saw?
Uh...
We're not doing any good out here. I've got to get closer!
Bee! No! Wait!

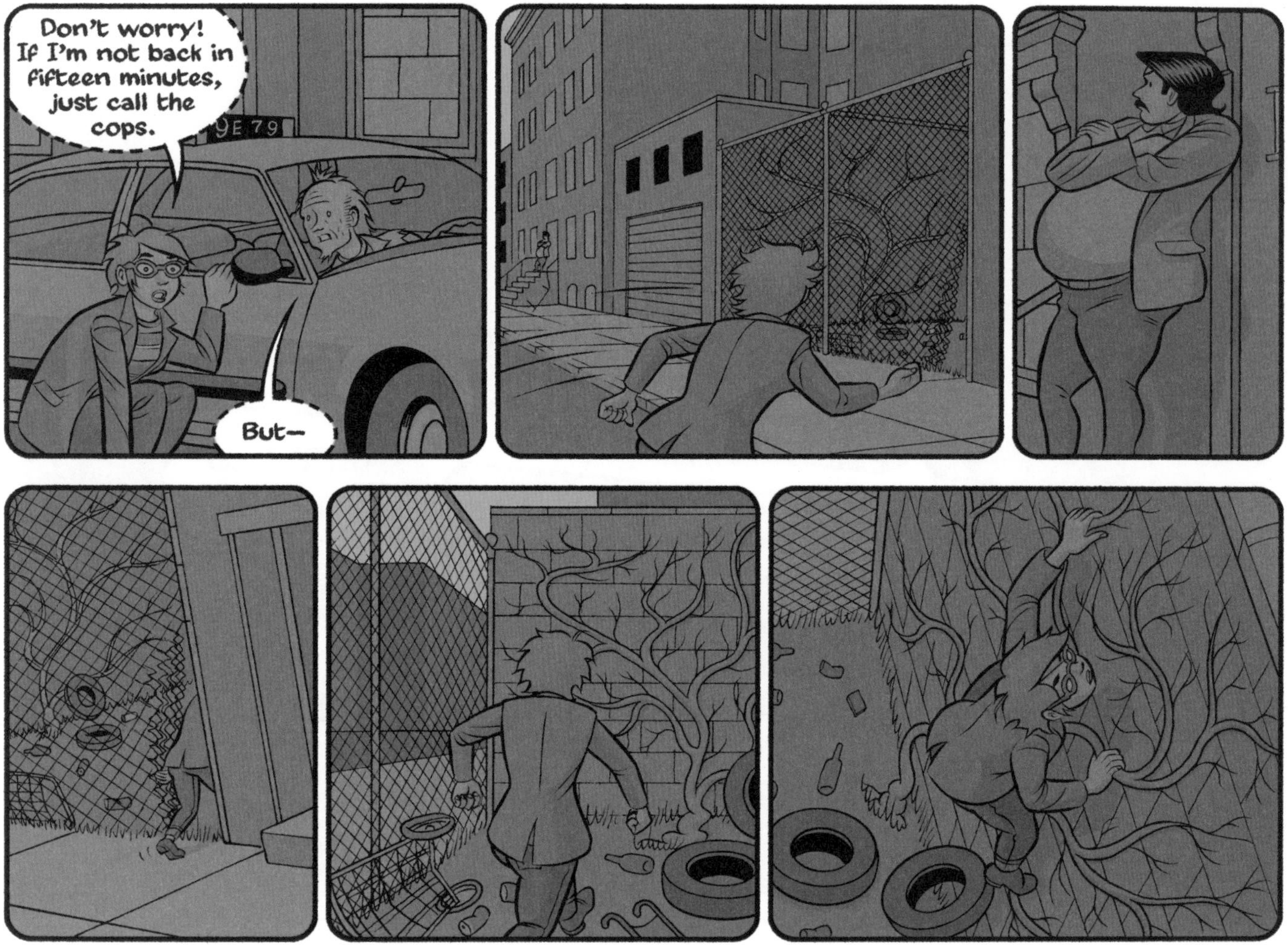
Don't worry! If I'm not back in fifteen minutes, just call the cops.
9E 79
But—

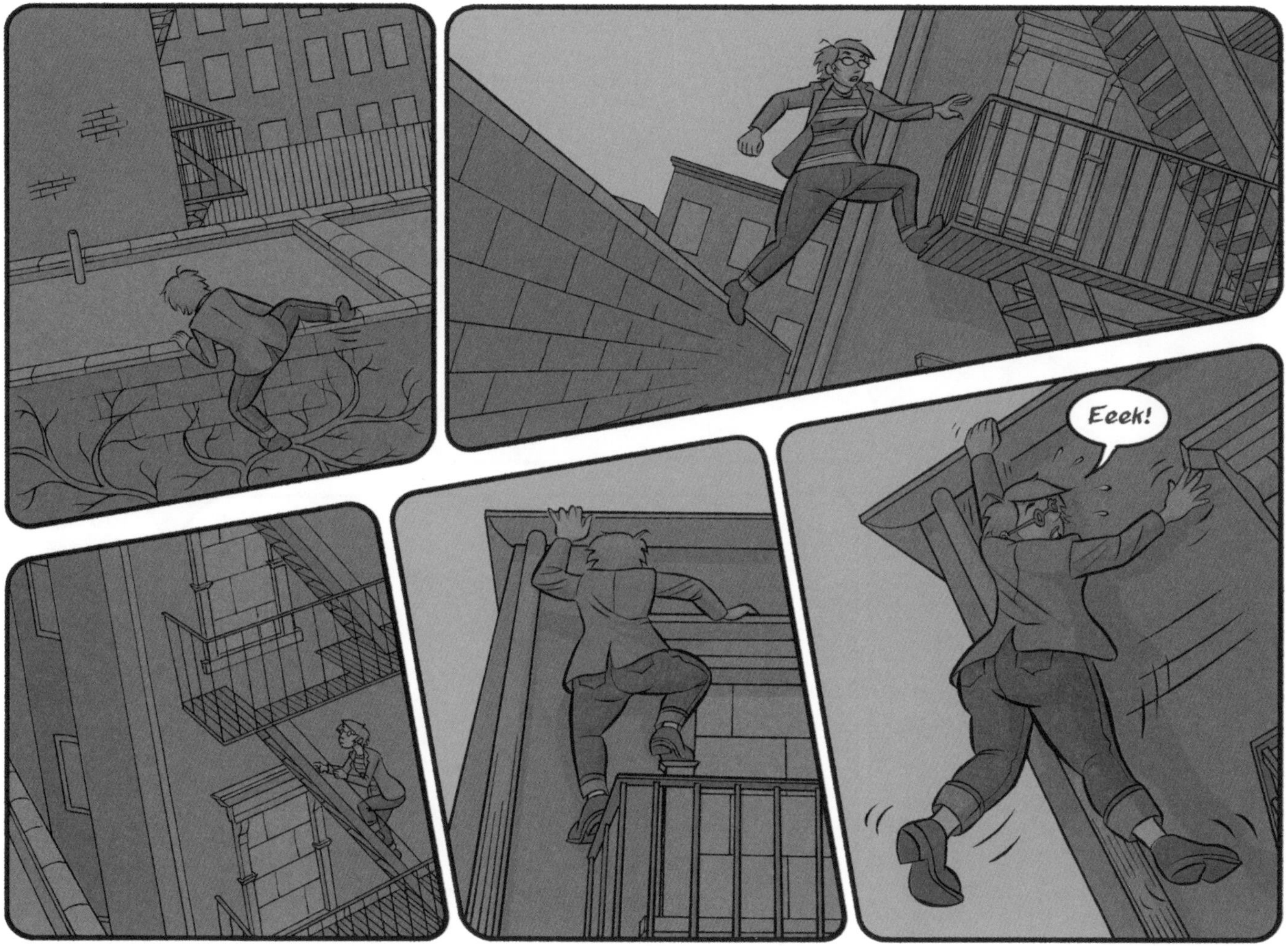
Eeek!

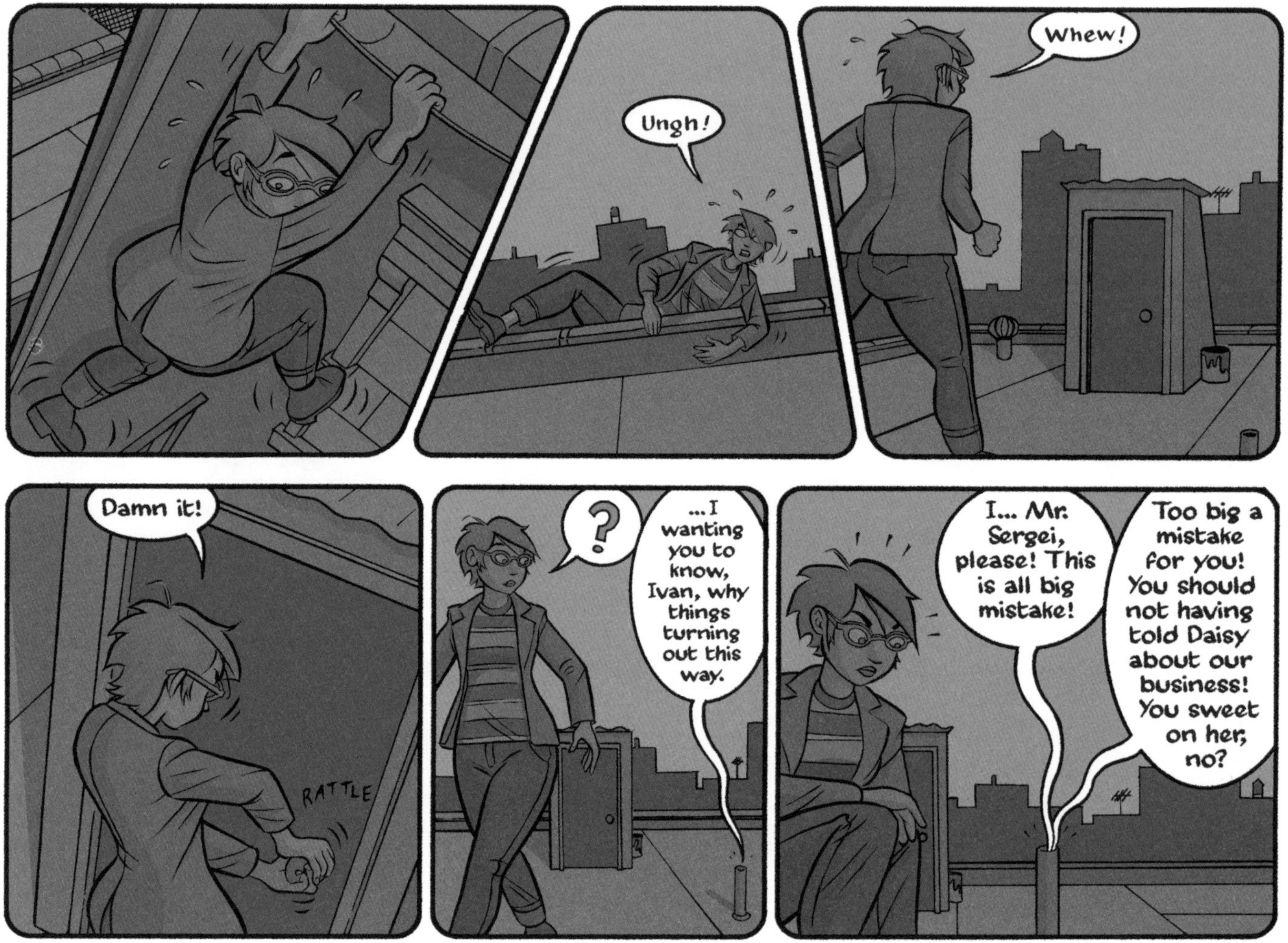
Ungh!
Whew!
Damn it!
RATTLE
?
...I wanting you to know, Ivan, why things turning out this way.
I... Mr. Sergei, please! This is all big mistake!
Too big a mistake for you! You should not having told Daisy about our business! You sweet on her, no?

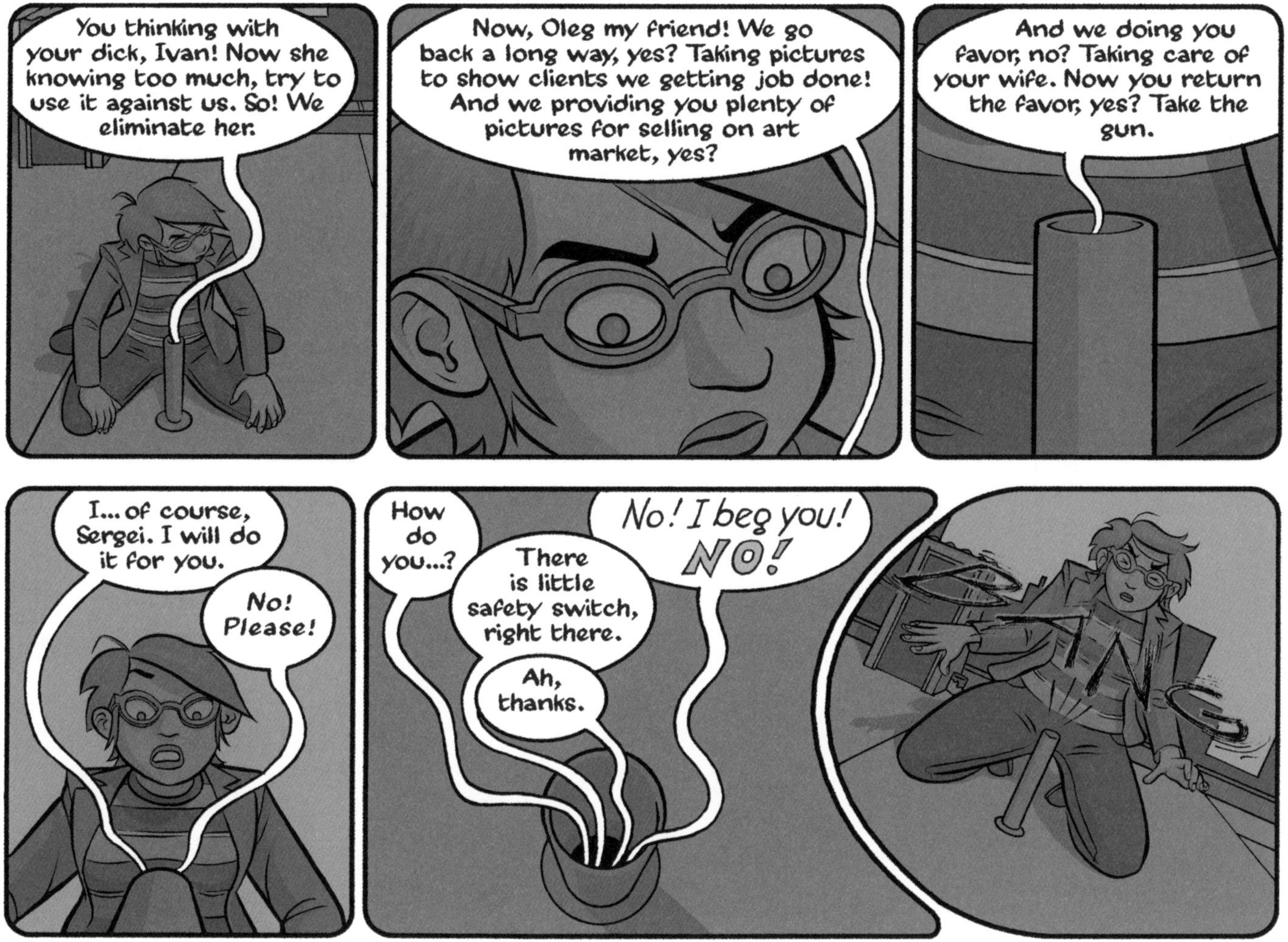
You thinking with your dick, Ivan! Now she knowing too much, try to use it against us. So! We eliminate her.
Now, Oleg my friend! We go back a long way, yes? Taking pictures to show clients we getting job done! And we providing you plenty of pictures for selling on art market, yes?
And we doing you favor, no? Taking care of your wife. Now you return the favor, yes? Take the gun.
I... of course, Sergei. I will do it for you.
No! Please!
How do you...?
There is little safety switch, right there.
Ah, thanks.
No! I beg you! NO!

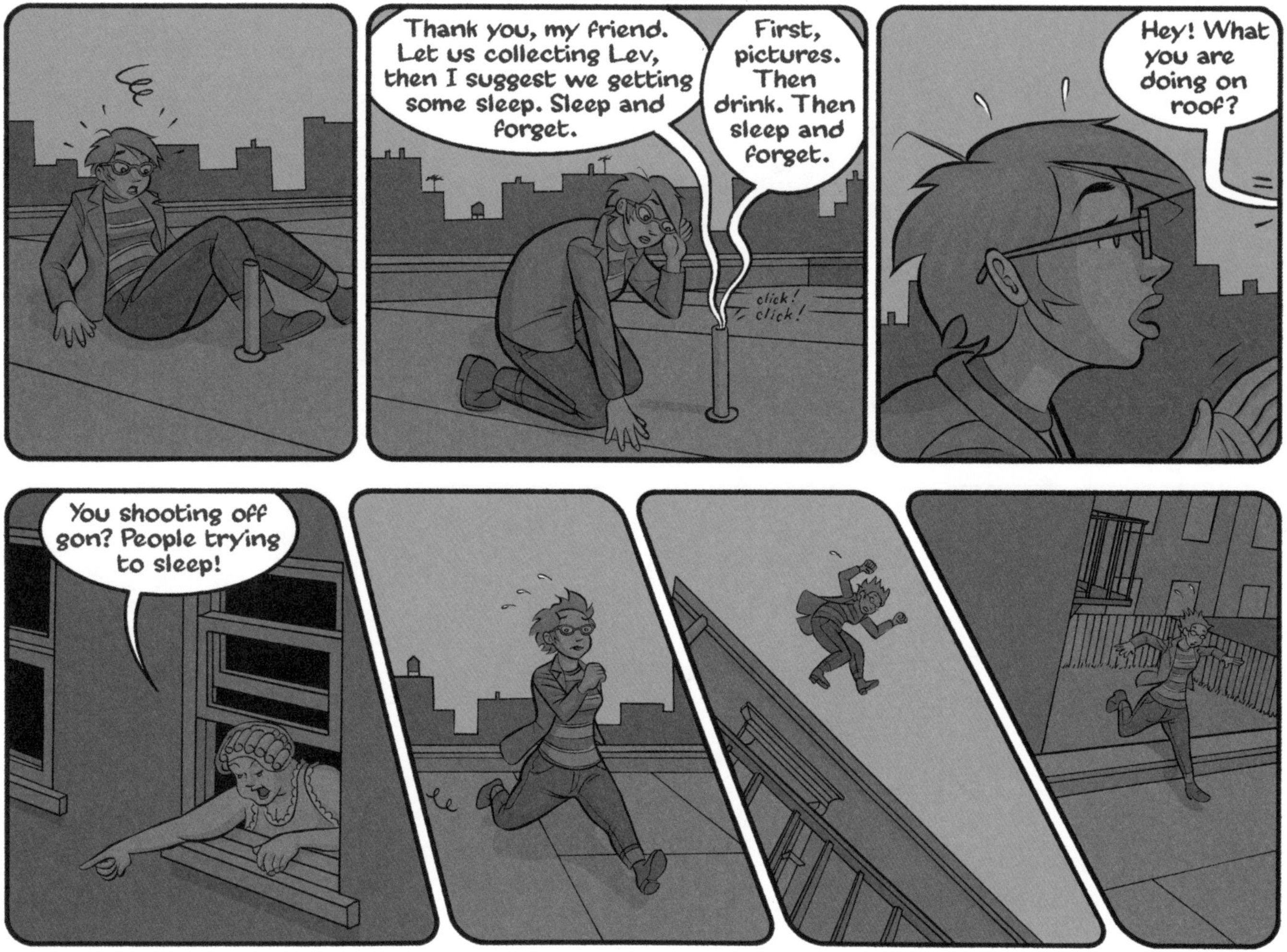
Thank you, my friend. Let us collecting Lev, then I suggest we getting some sleep. Sleep and forget.
First, pictures. Then drink. Then sleep and forget.
click! click!
Hey! What you are doing on roof?
You shooting off gon? People trying to sleep!

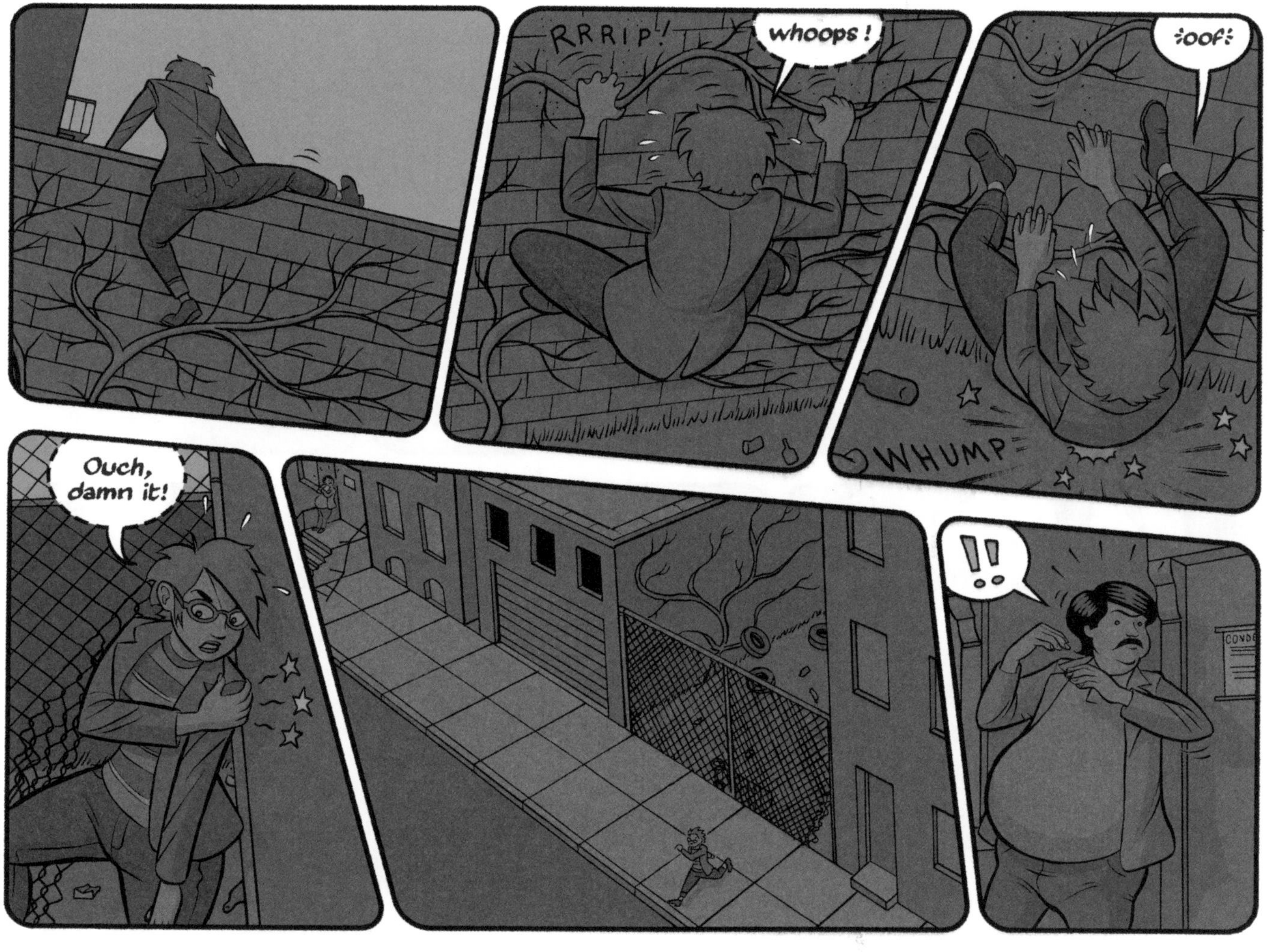
RRRIP!
whoops!
oof
WHUMP
Ouch, damn it!
!!

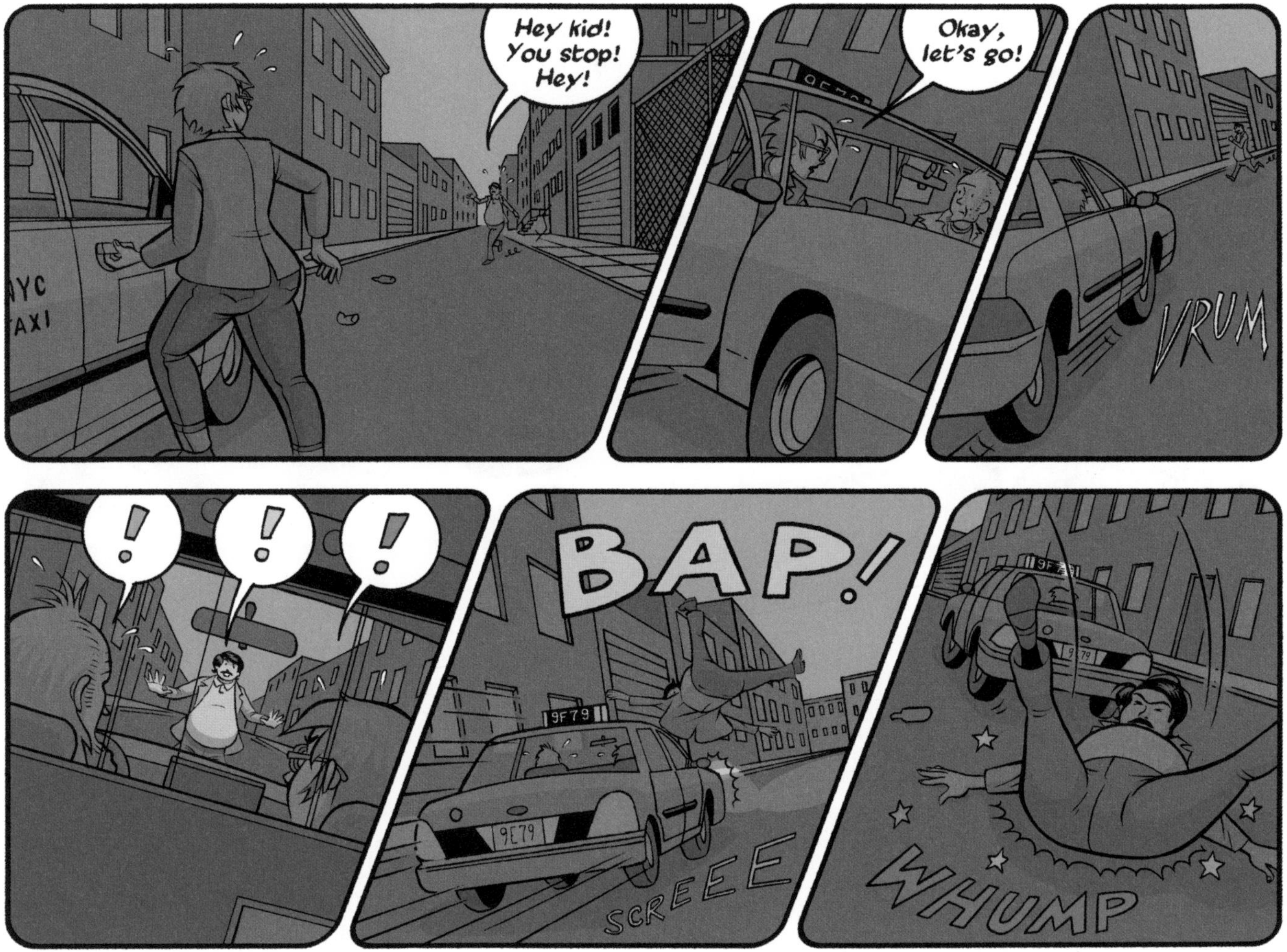
Hey kid! You stop! Hey!
Okay, let's go!
VRUM
!
!
!
BAP!
9F79
SCREEEE
WHUMP

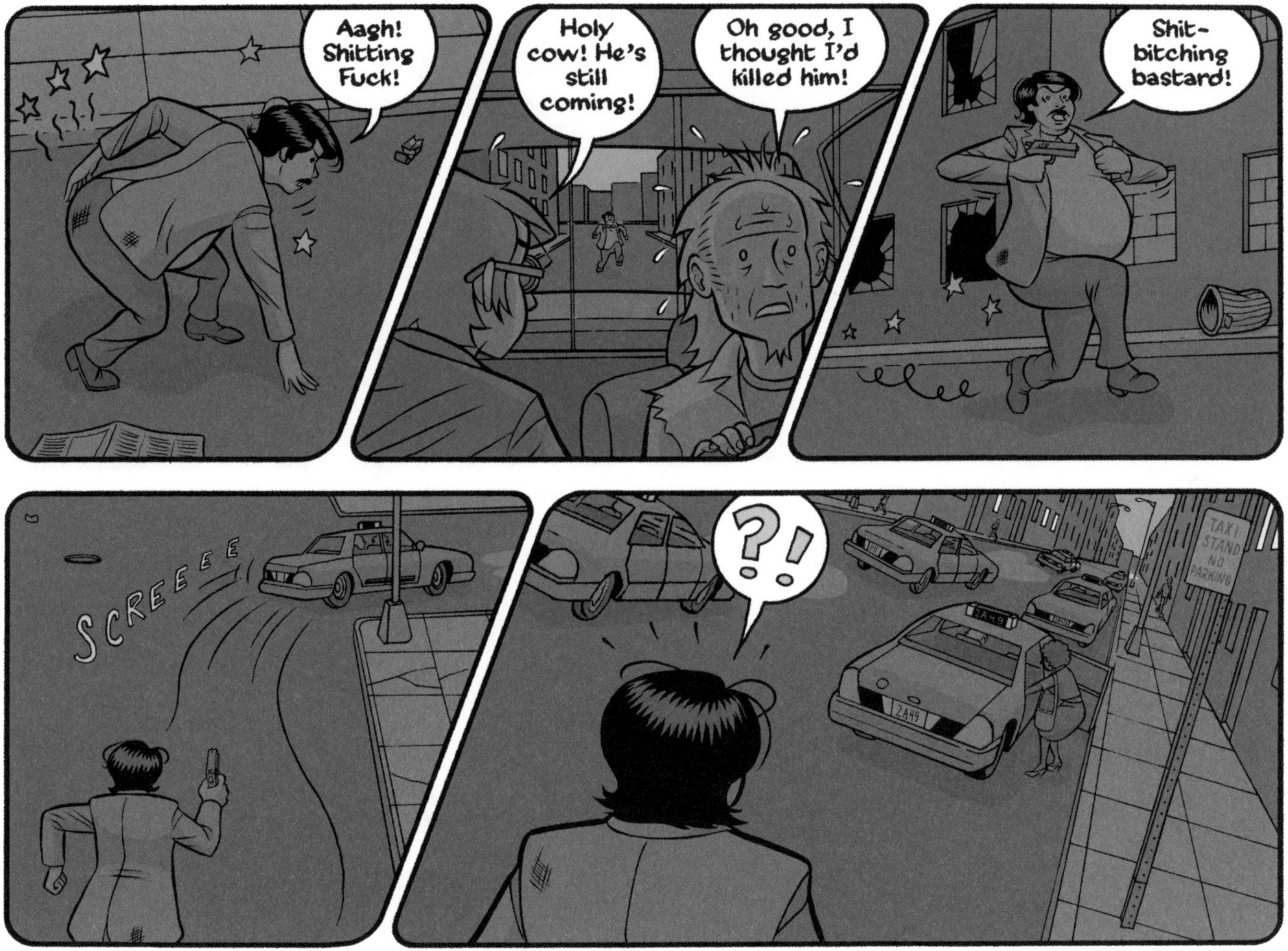
Aagh! Shitting Fuck!
Holy cow! He's still coming!
Oh good, I thought I'd killed him!
Shit-bitching bastard!
SCREEEEE
?!
TAXI STAND NO PARKING
2A49

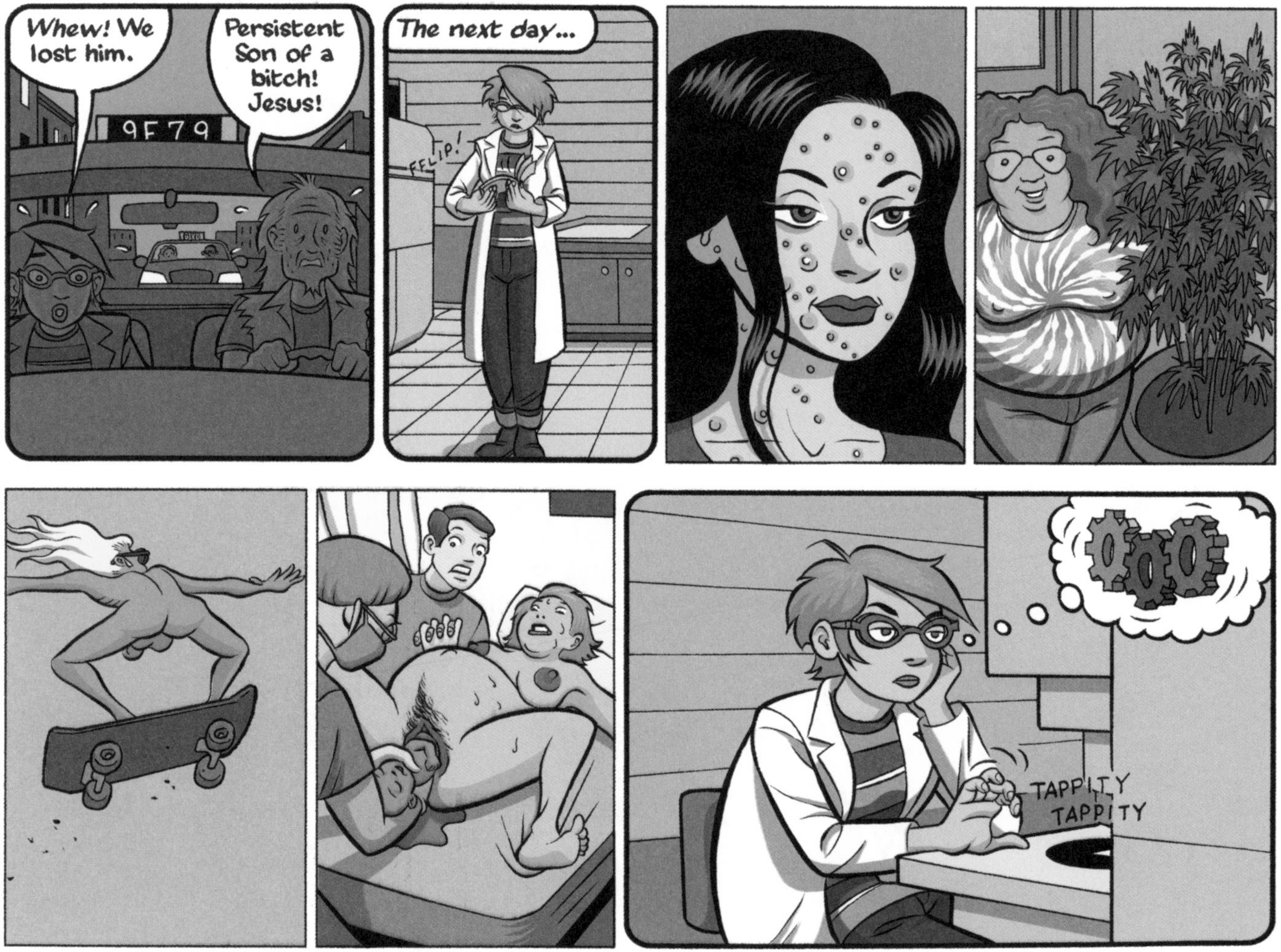
Whew! We lost him.
Persistent Son of a bitch! Jesus!
9F79
The next day...
FFLIP!
TAPPITY
TAPPITY

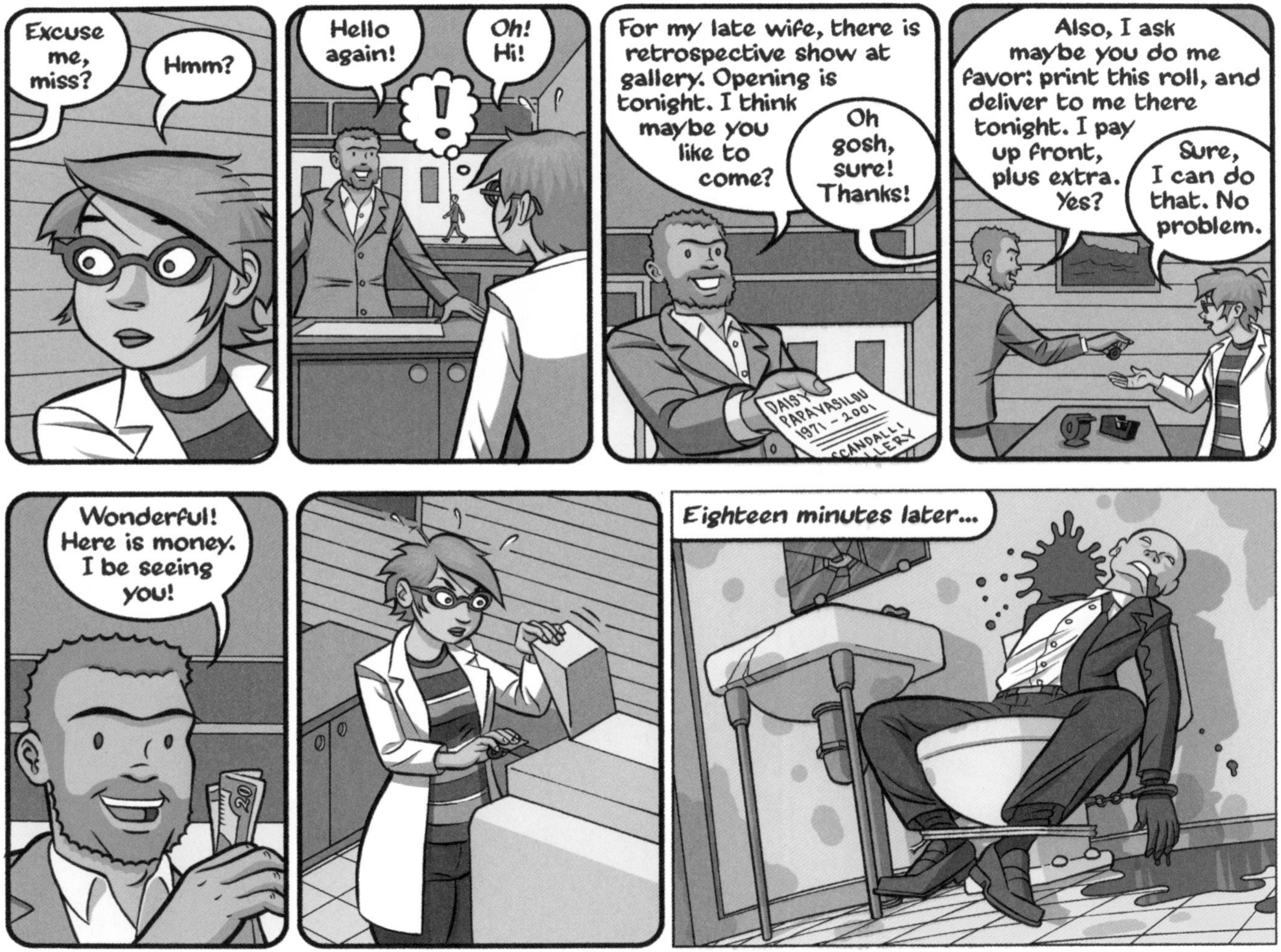

Excuse me, miss?
Hmm?
Hello again!
Oh! Hi!
!
For my late wife, there is retrospective show at gallery. Opening is tonight. I think maybe you like to come?
Oh gosh, sure! Thanks!
DAISY PAPAVASILOU 1971 - 2001
SCANDALLI GALLERY
Also, I ask maybe you do me favor: print this roll, and deliver to me there tonight. I pay up front, plus extra. Yes?
Sure, I can do that. No problem.
Wonderful! Here is money. I be seeing you!
20
Eighteen minutes later...

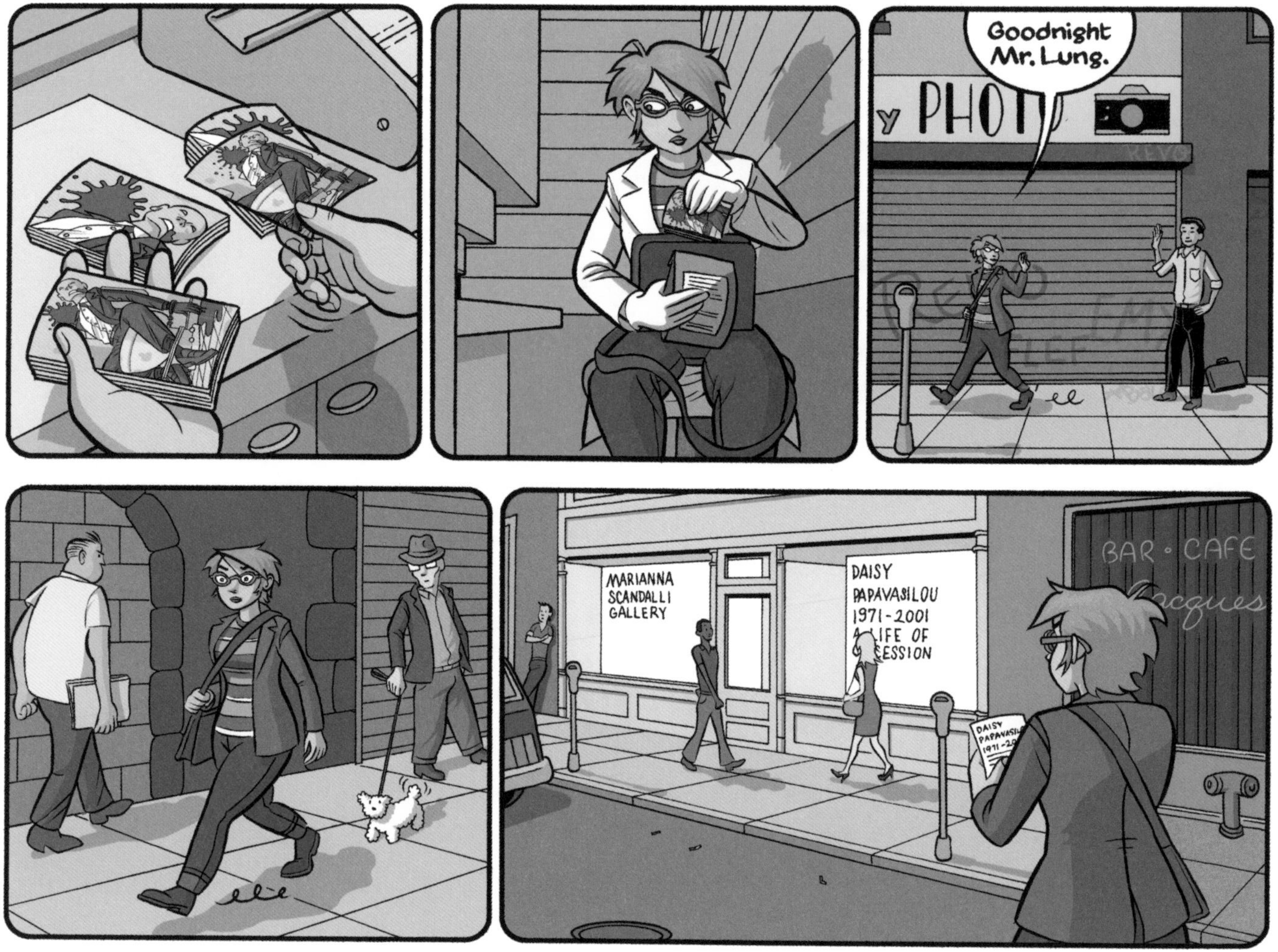
y PHOT
Goodnight Mr. Lung.
MARIANNA SCANDALLI GALLERY
DAISY PAPAVASILOU 1971-2001 A LIFE OF
ESSION
BAR • CAFE
acques
DAISY PAPAVASIL
1971-20

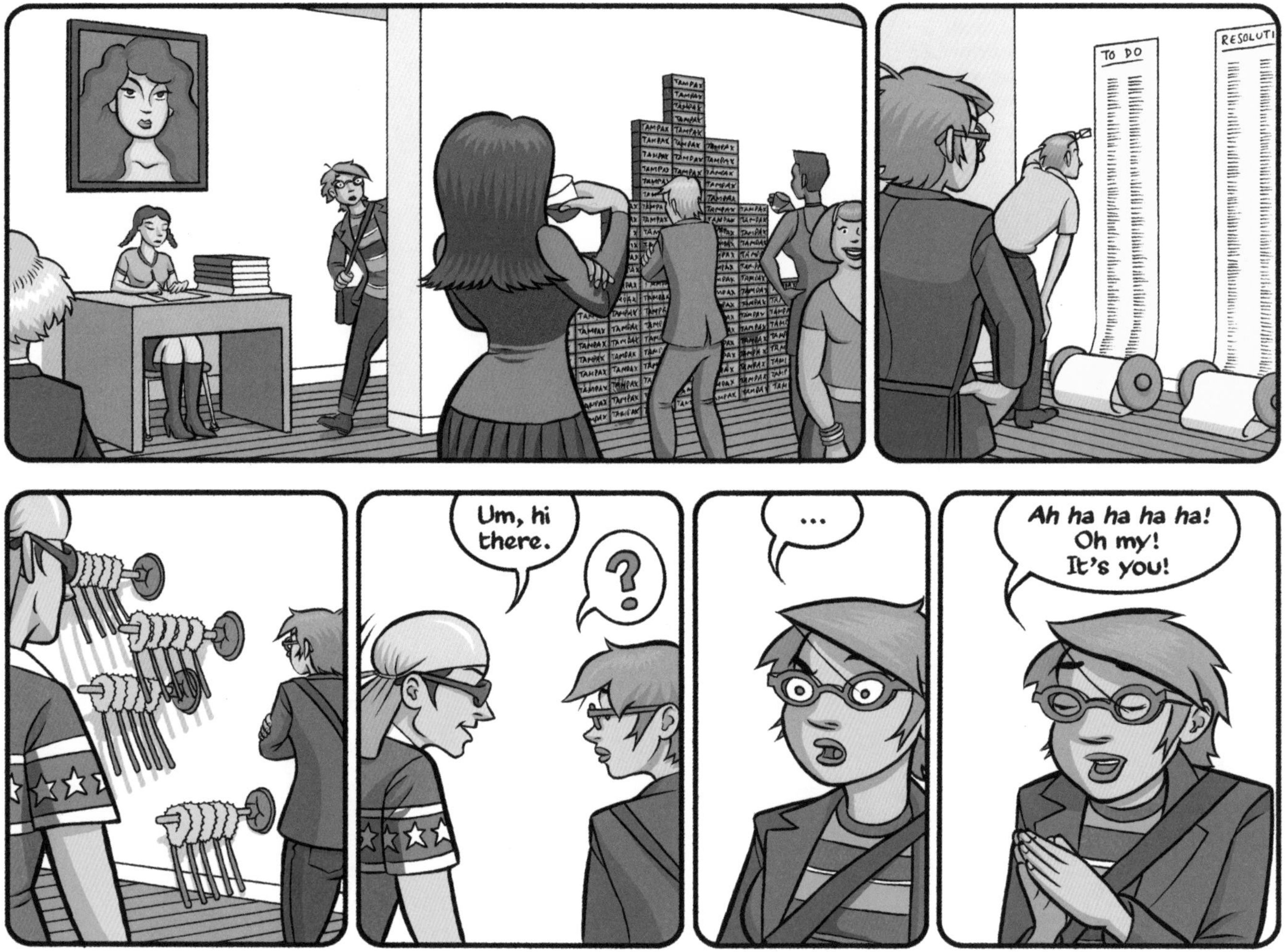
TAMPAX
TO DO
RESOLUTI
Um, hi there.
?
...
Ah ha ha ha ha! Oh my! It's you!

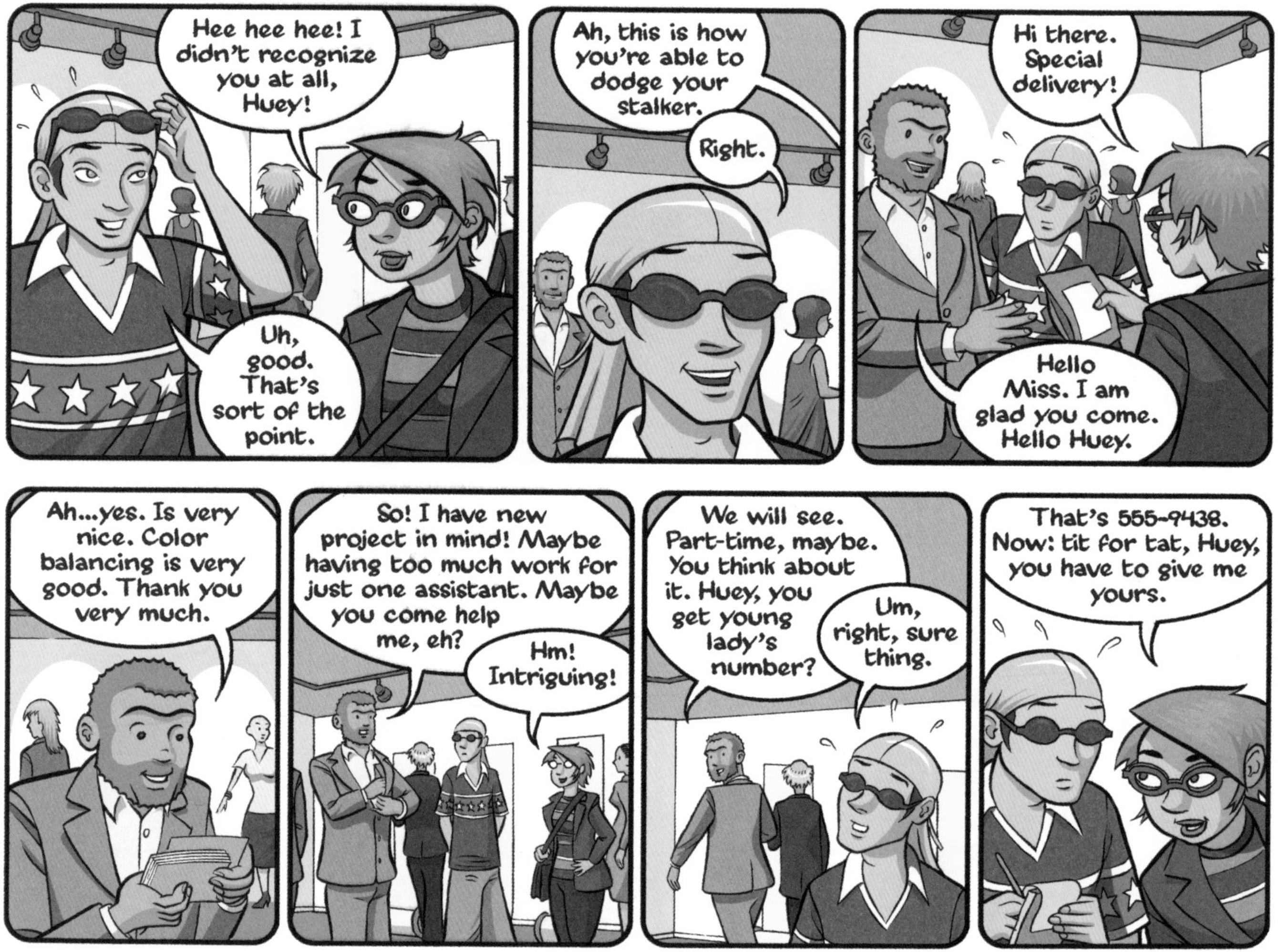
Hee hee hee! I didn't recognize you at all, Huey!
Uh, good. That's sort of the point.
Ah, this is how you're able to dodge your stalker.
Right.
Hi there. Special delivery!
Hello Miss. I am glad you come. Hello Huey.
Ah...yes. Is very nice. Color balancing is very good. Thank you very much.
So! I have new project in mind! Maybe having too much work for just one assistant. Maybe you come help me, eh?
Hm! Intriguing!
We will see. Part-time, maybe. You think about it. Huey, you get young lady's number?
Um, right, sure thing.
That's 555-9438. Now: tit for tat, Huey, you have to give me yours.

Later...

FlashArt

RIAN:
ERITÉ
ILLUSION

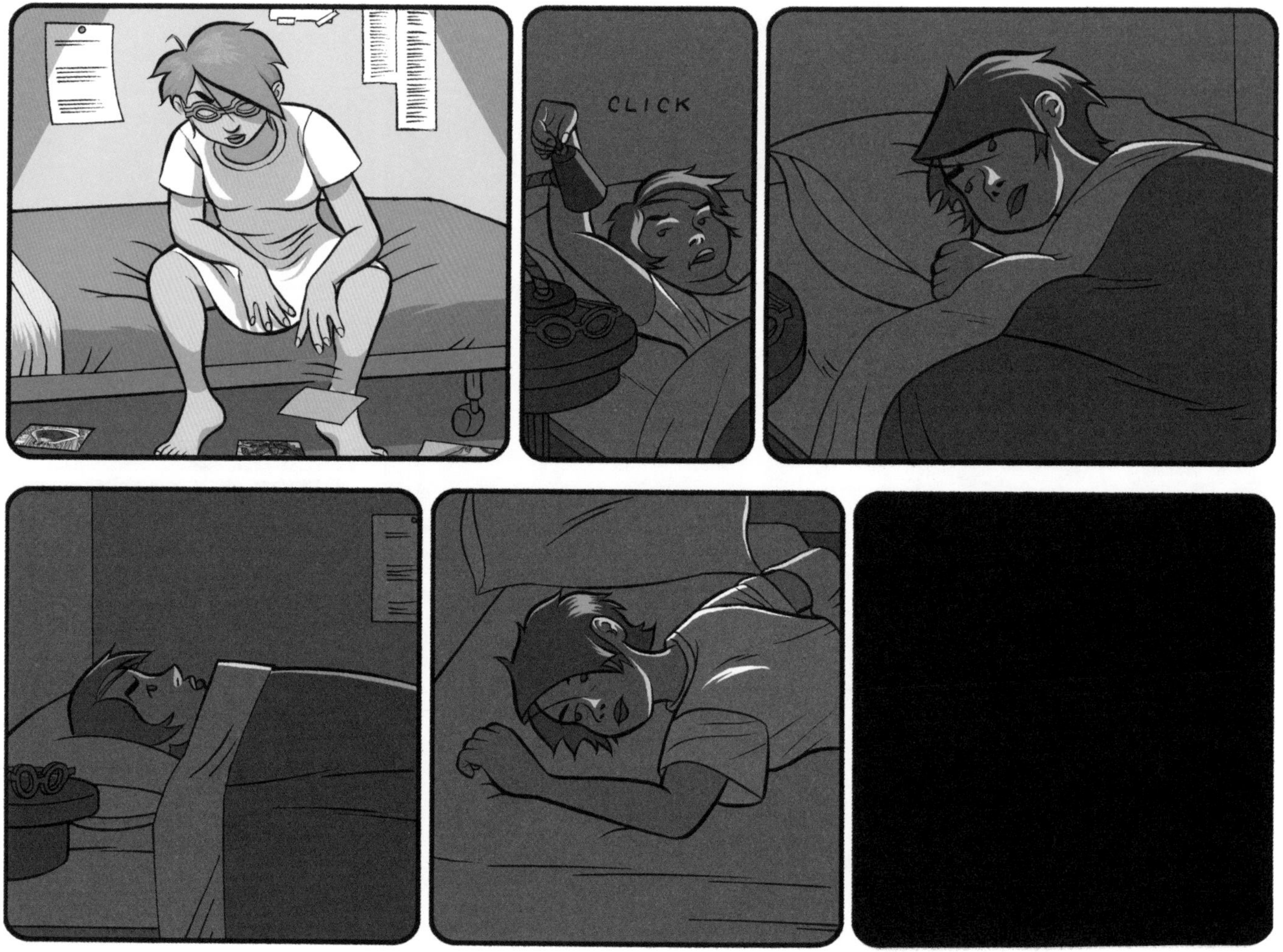
CLICK

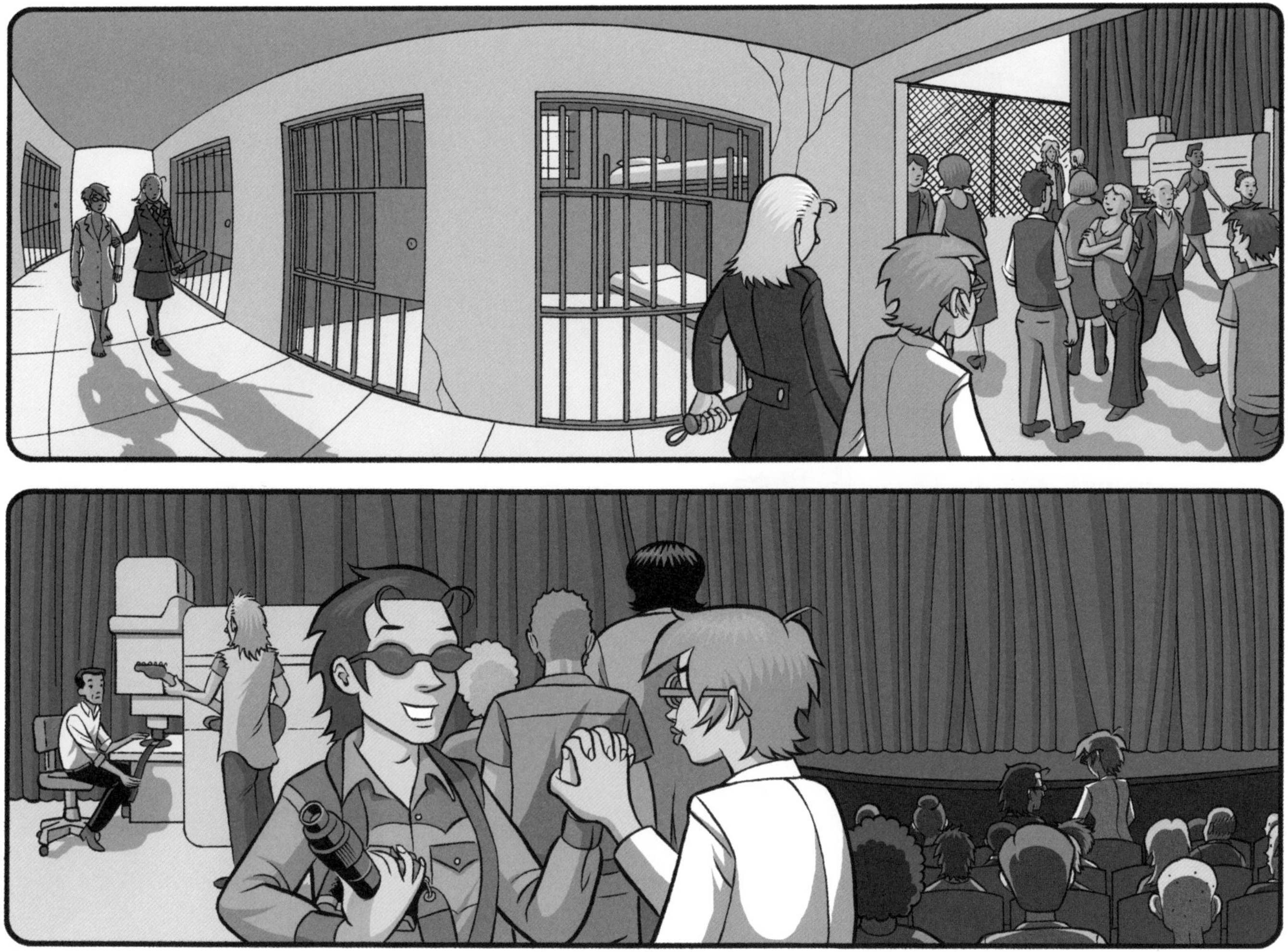

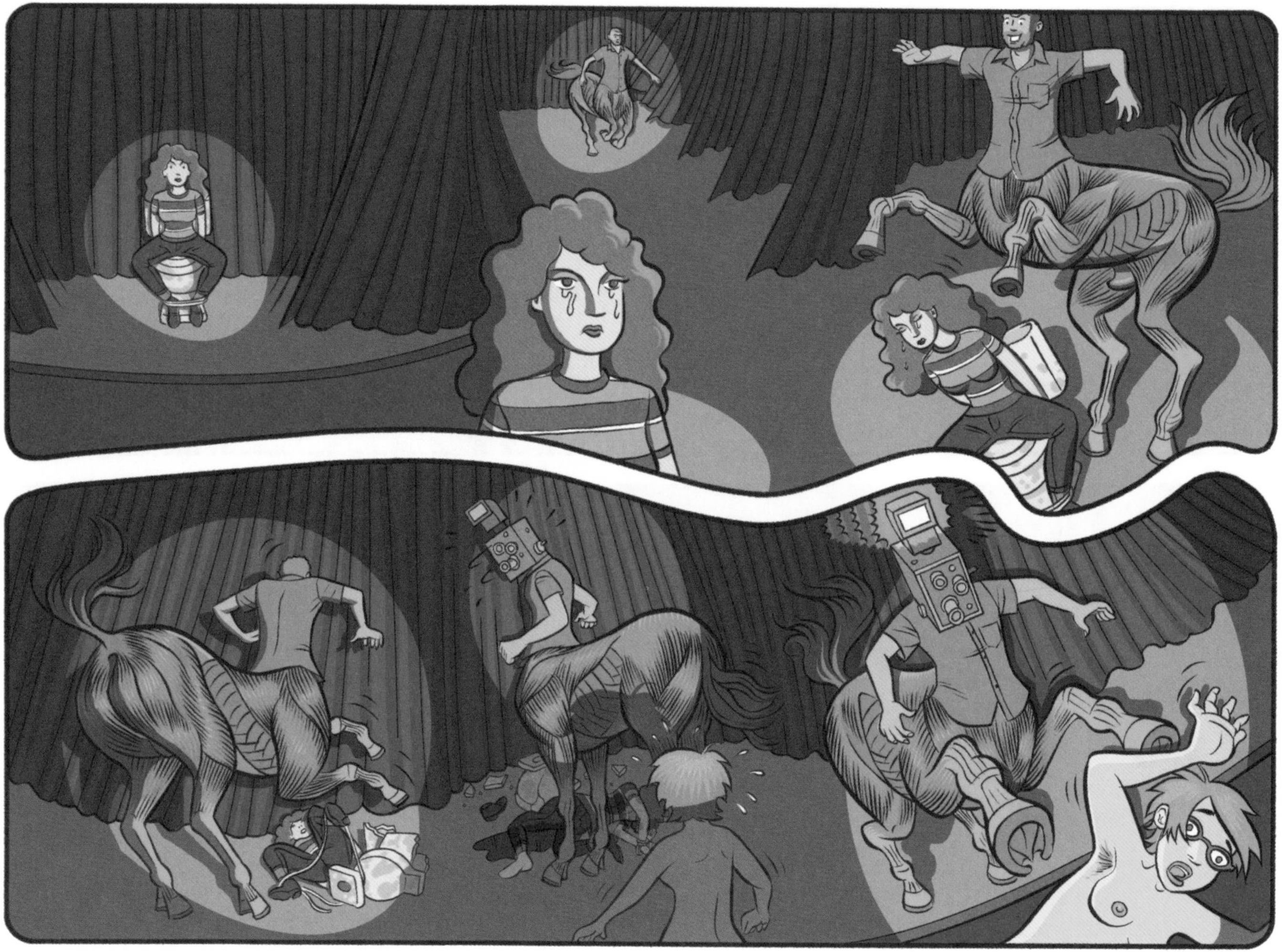

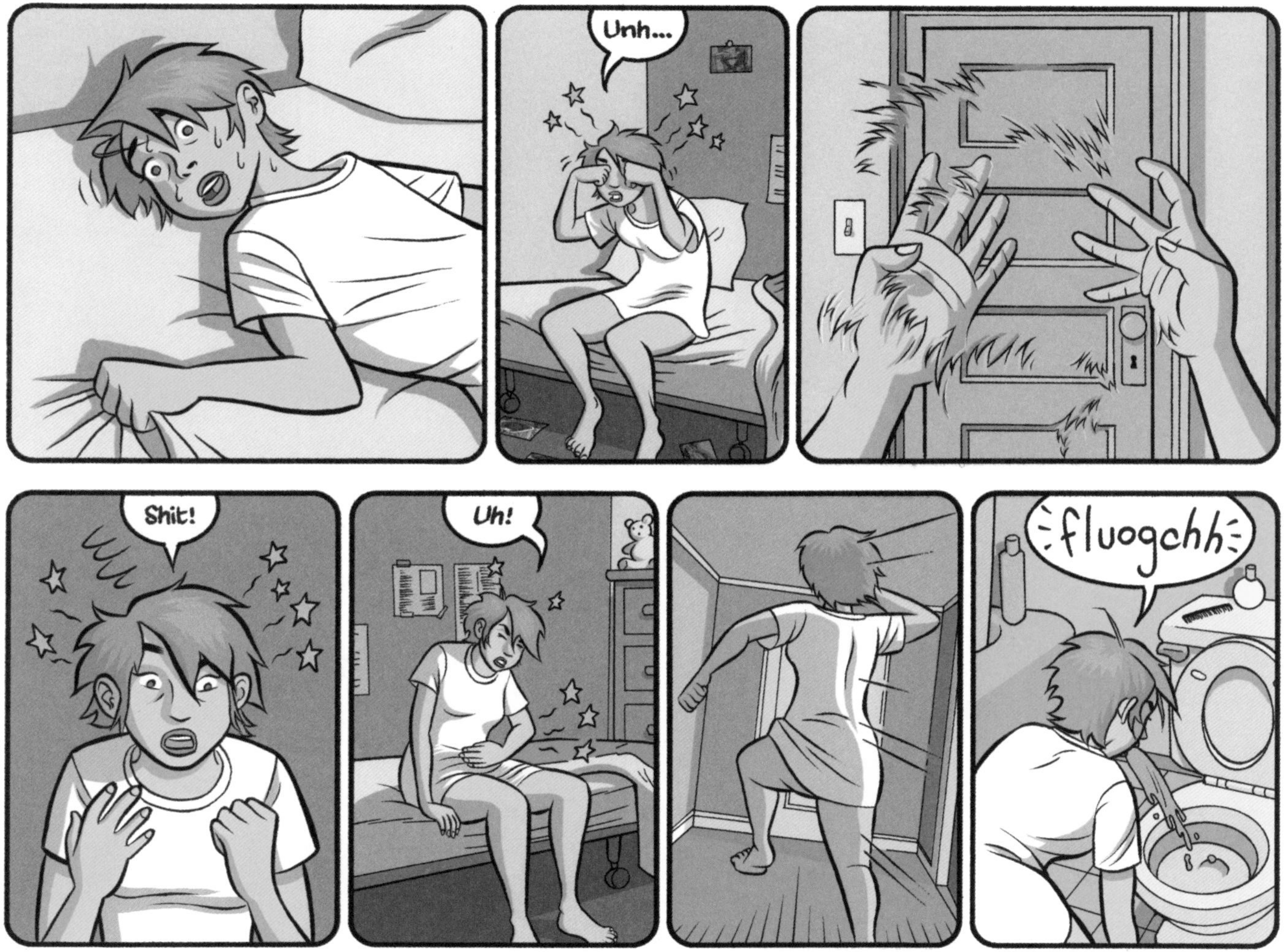
Unh...
Shit!
Uh!
fluogchh

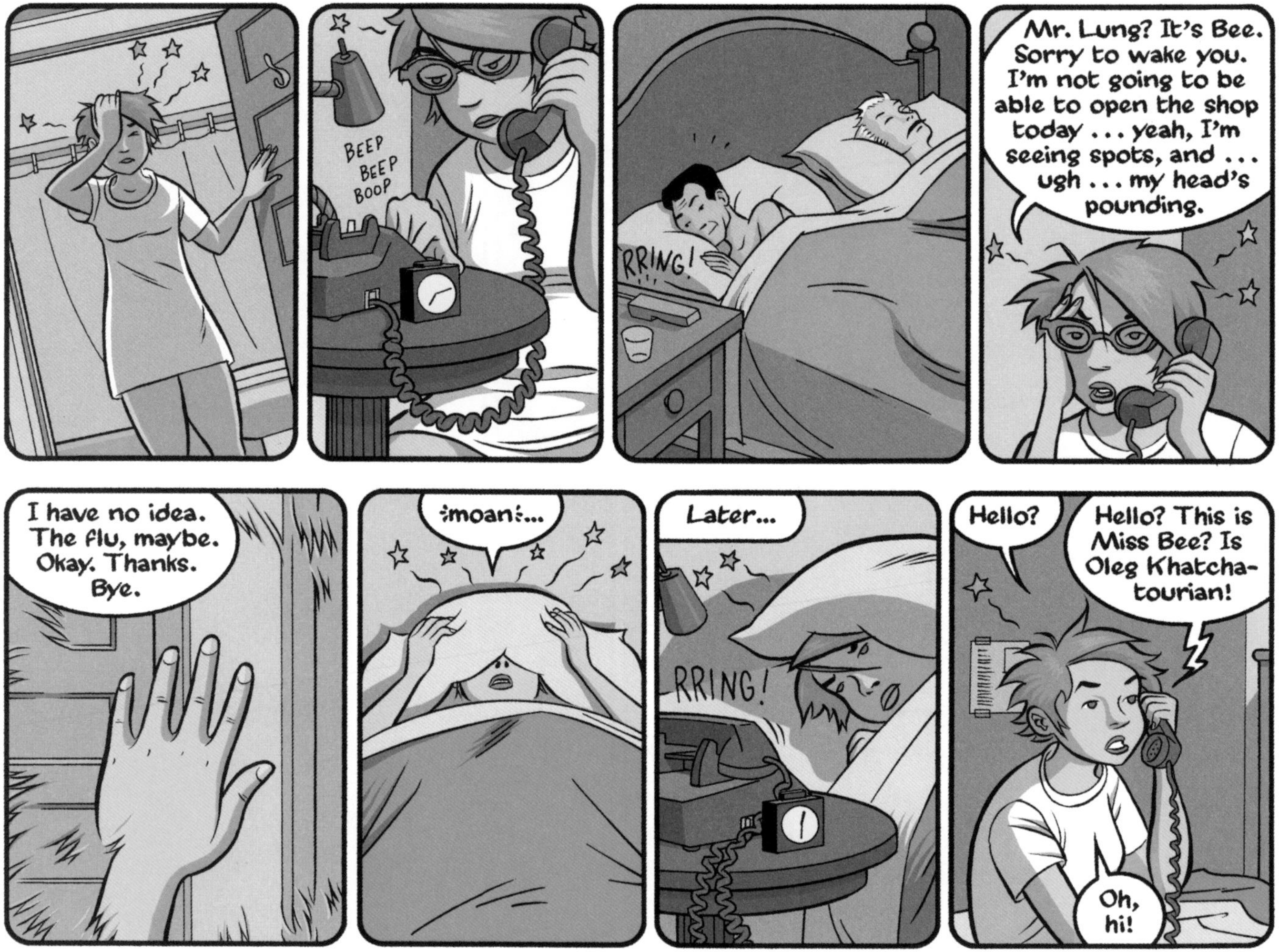
BEEP
BEEP
BOOP
RRING!
Mr. Lung? It's Bee. Sorry to wake you. I'm not going to be able to open the shop today . . . yeah, I'm seeing spots, and . . . ugh . . . my head's pounding.
I have no idea. The flu, maybe. Okay. Thanks. Bye.
:moan:...
Later...
RRING!
Hello?
Hello? This is Miss Bee? Is Oleg Khatchatourian!
Oh, hi!

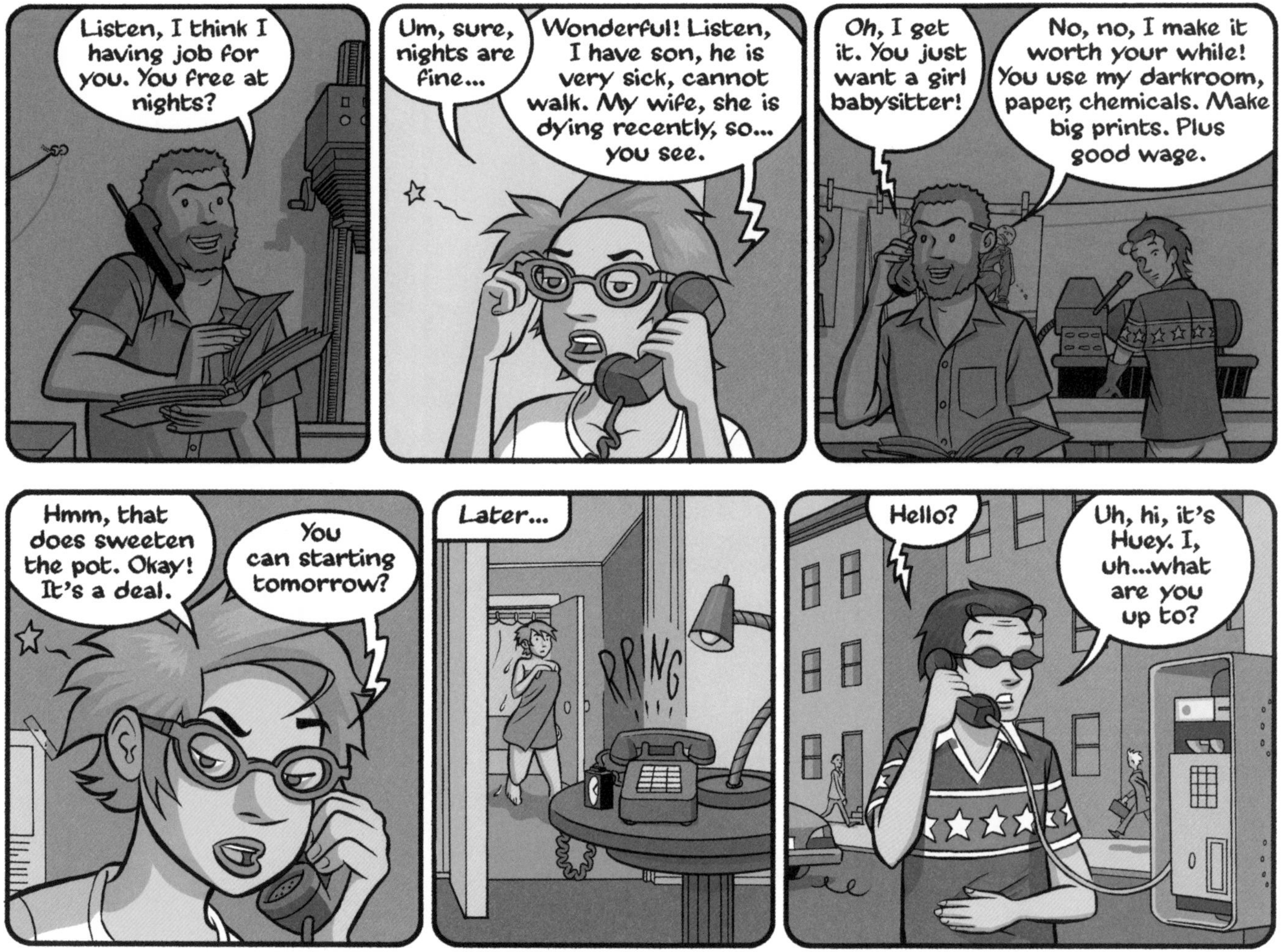
Listen, I think I having job for you. You free at nights?
Um, sure, nights are fine...
Wonderful! Listen, I have son, he is very sick, cannot walk. My wife, she is dying recently, so... you see.
Oh, I get it. You just want a girl babysitter!
No, no, I make it worth your while! You use my darkroom, paper, chemicals. Make big prints. Plus good wage.
Hmm, that does sweeten the pot. Okay! It's a deal.
You can starting tomorrow?
Later...
RRING
Hello?
Uh, hi, it's Huey. I, uh...what are you up to?

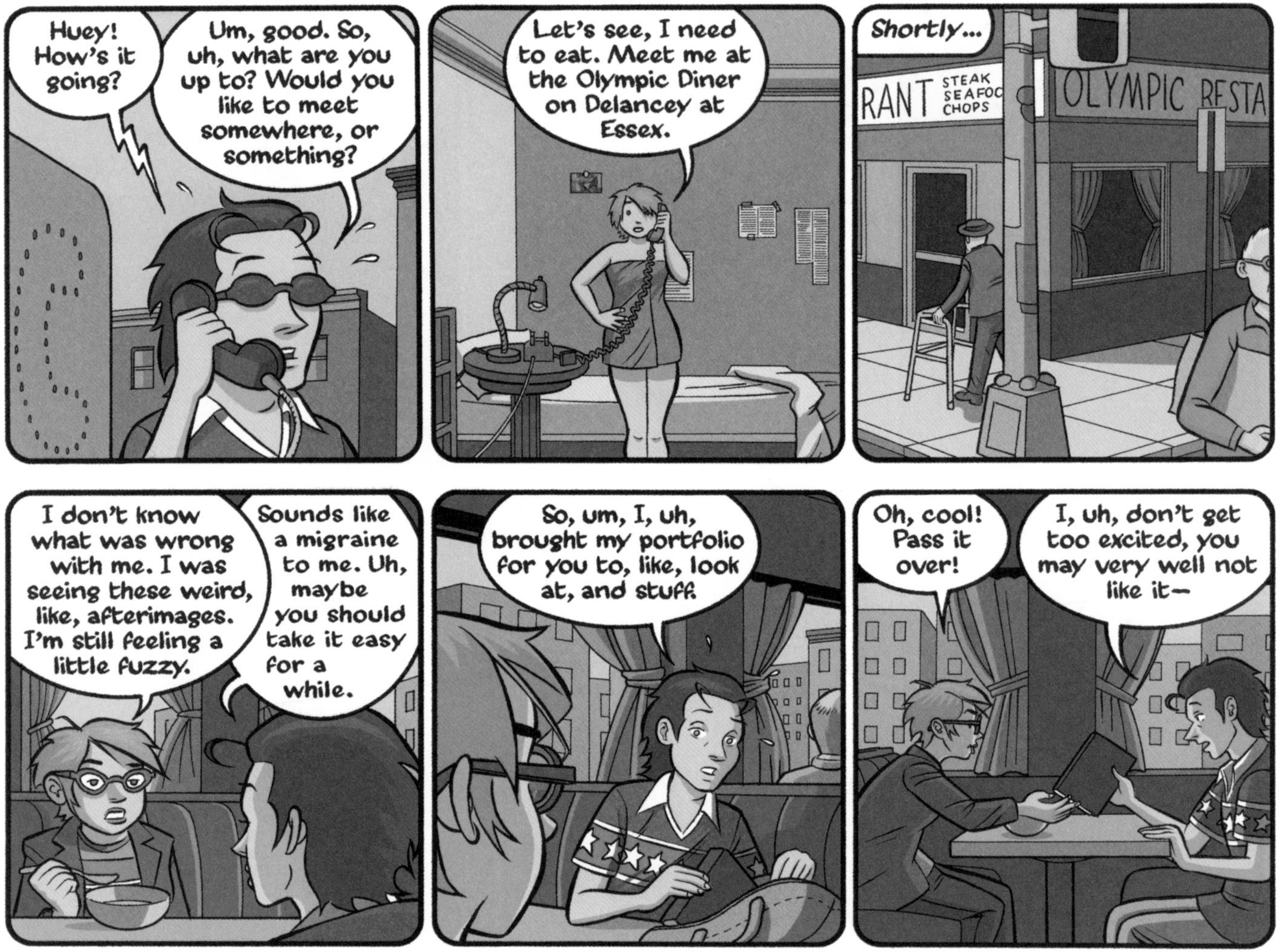
Huey! How's it going?
Um, good. So, uh, what are you up to? Would you like to meet somewhere, or something?
Let's see, I need to eat. Meet me at the Olympic Diner on Delancey at Essex.
Shortly...
RANT
STEAK SEAFOC CHOPS
OLYMPIC RESTA
I don't know what was wrong with me. I was seeing these weird, like, afterimages. I'm still feeling a little fuzzy.
Sounds like a migraine to me. Uh, maybe you should take it easy for a while.
So, um, I, uh, brought my portfolio for you to, like, look at, and stuff.
Oh, cool! Pass it over!
I, uh, don't get too excited, you may very well not like it—

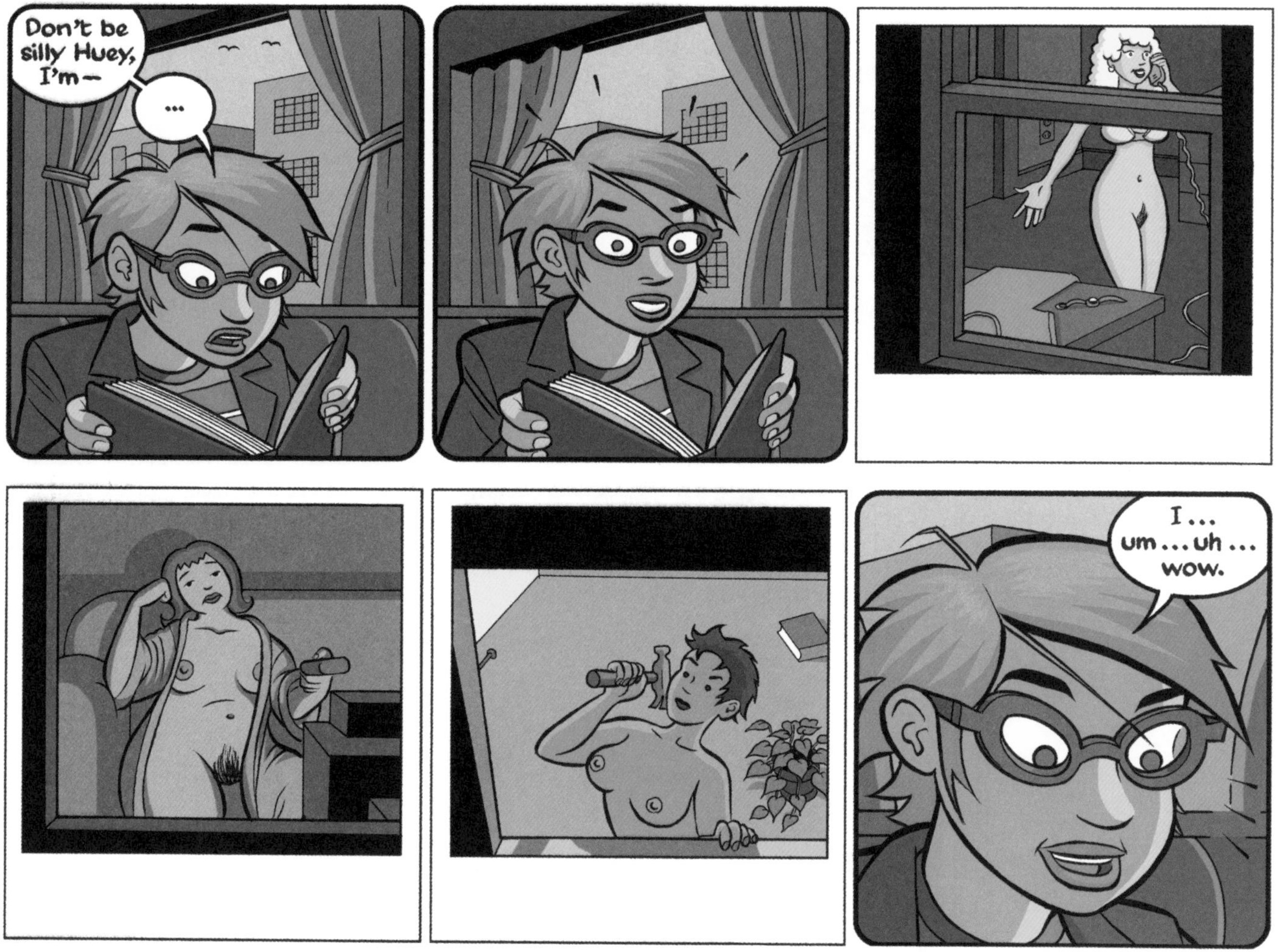
Don't be silly Huey, I'm—
...
I... um...uh... wow.

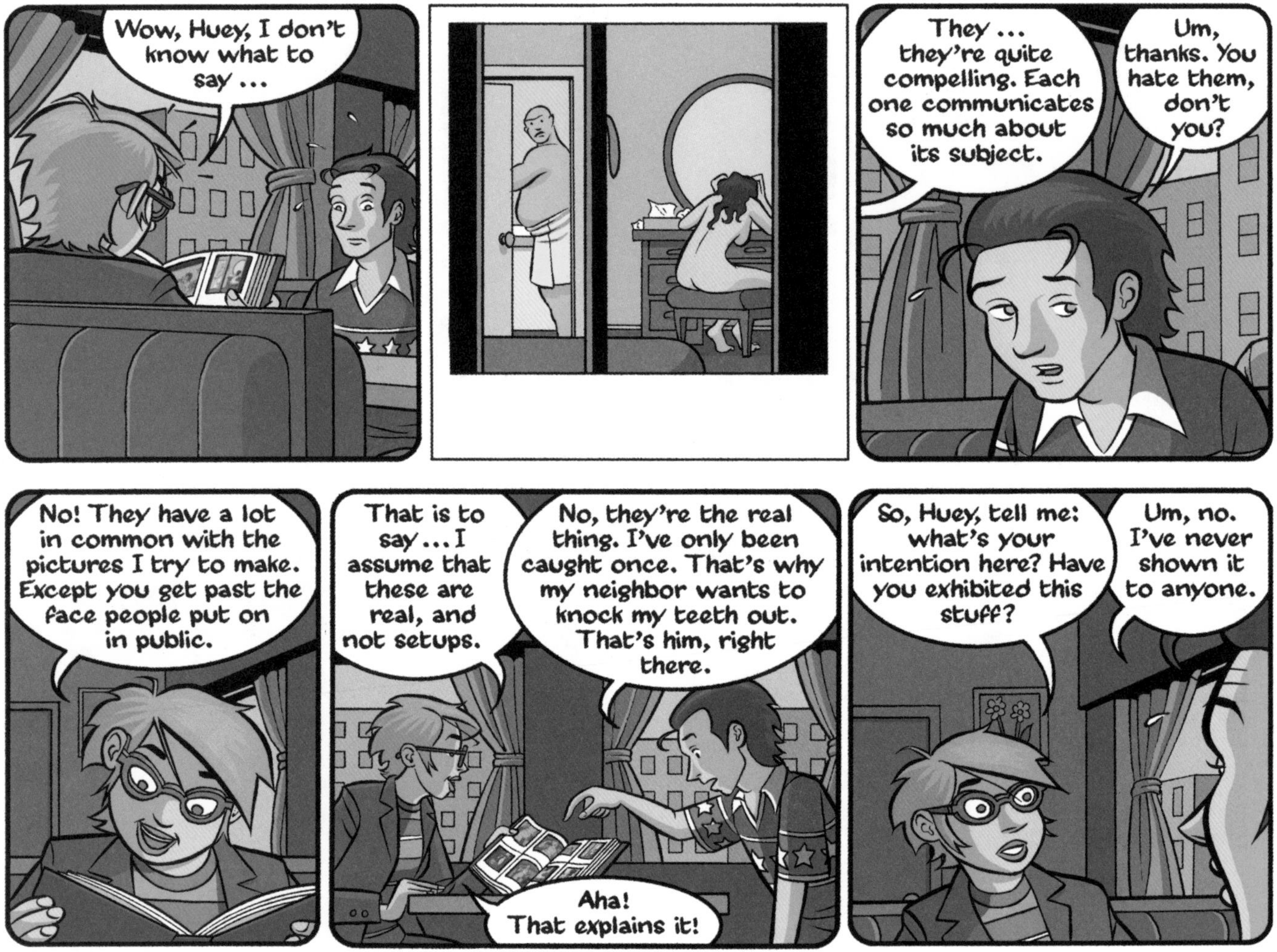
Wow, Huey, I don't know what to say ...
They ... they're quite compelling. Each one communicates so much about its subject.
Um, thanks. You hate them, don't you?
No! They have a lot in common with the pictures I try to make. Except you get past the face people put on in public.
That is to say ... I assume that these are real, and not setups.
No, they're the real thing. I've only been caught once. That's why my neighbor wants to knock my teeth out. That's him, right there.
Aha! That explains it!
So, Huey, tell me: what's your intention here? Have you exhibited this stuff?
Um, no. I've never shown it to anyone.

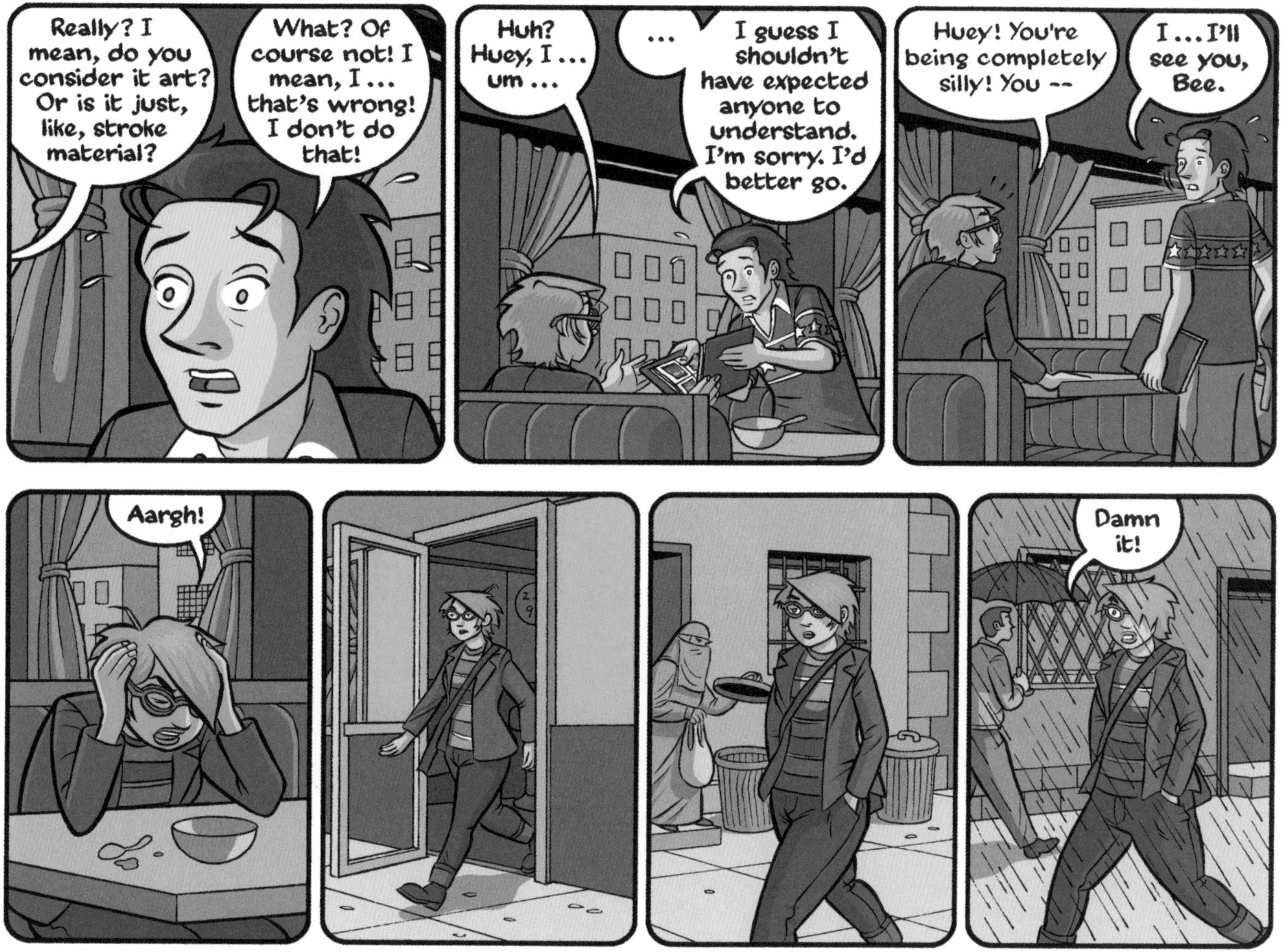
Really? I mean, do you consider it art? Or is it just, like, stroke material?
What? Of course not! I mean, I... that's wrong! I don't do that!
Huh? Huey, I... um...
...
I guess I shouldn't have expected anyone to understand. I'm sorry. I'd better go.
Huey! You're being completely silly! You --
I...I'll see you, Bee.
Aargh!
Damn it!

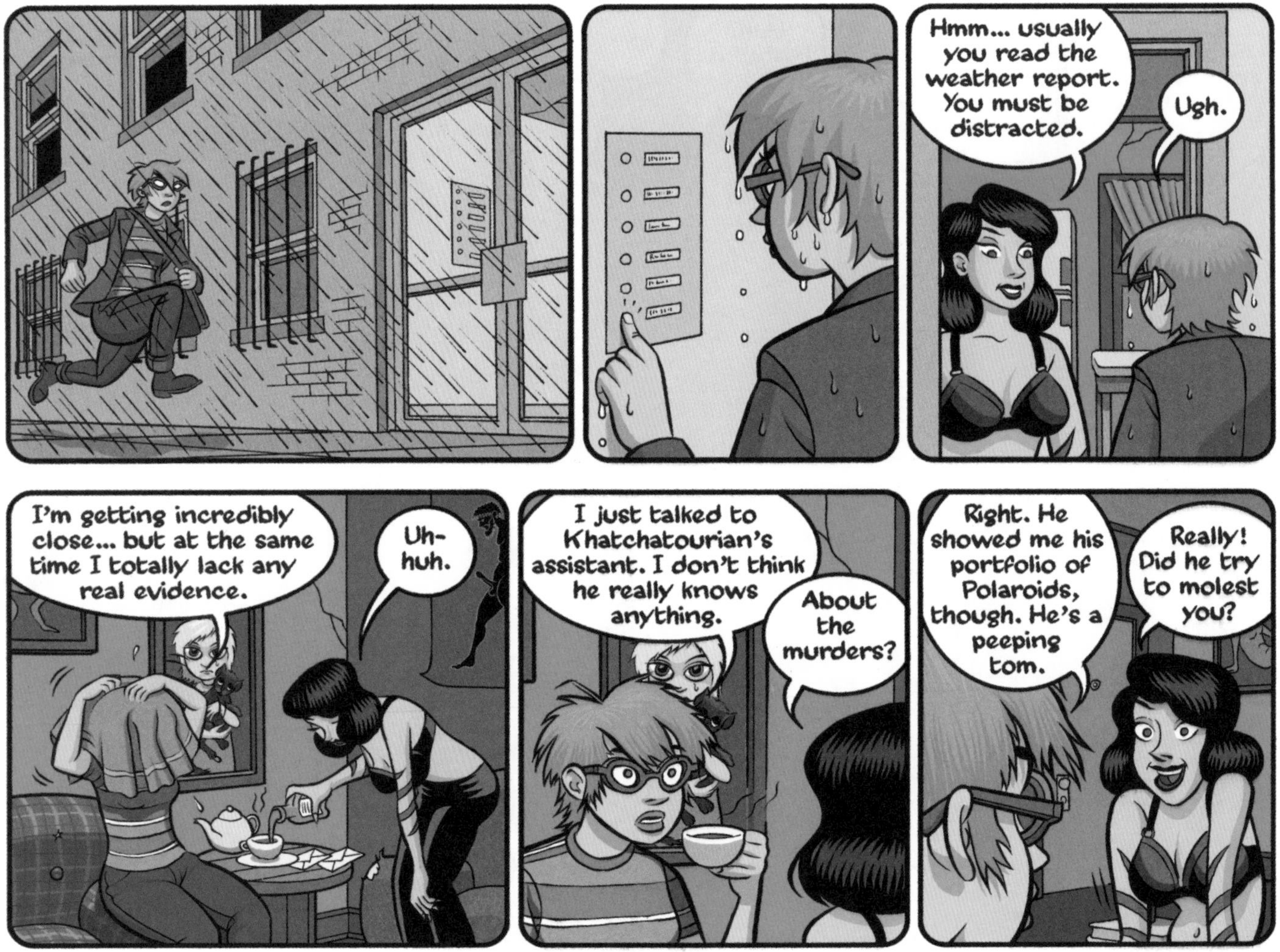
Hmm... usually you read the weather report. You must be distracted.
Ugh.
I'm getting incredibly close... but at the same time I totally lack any real evidence.
Uh-huh.
I just talked to Khatchatourian's assistant. I don't think he really knows anything.
About the murders?
Right. He showed me his portfolio of Polaroids, though. He's a peeping tom.
Really! Did he try to molest you?

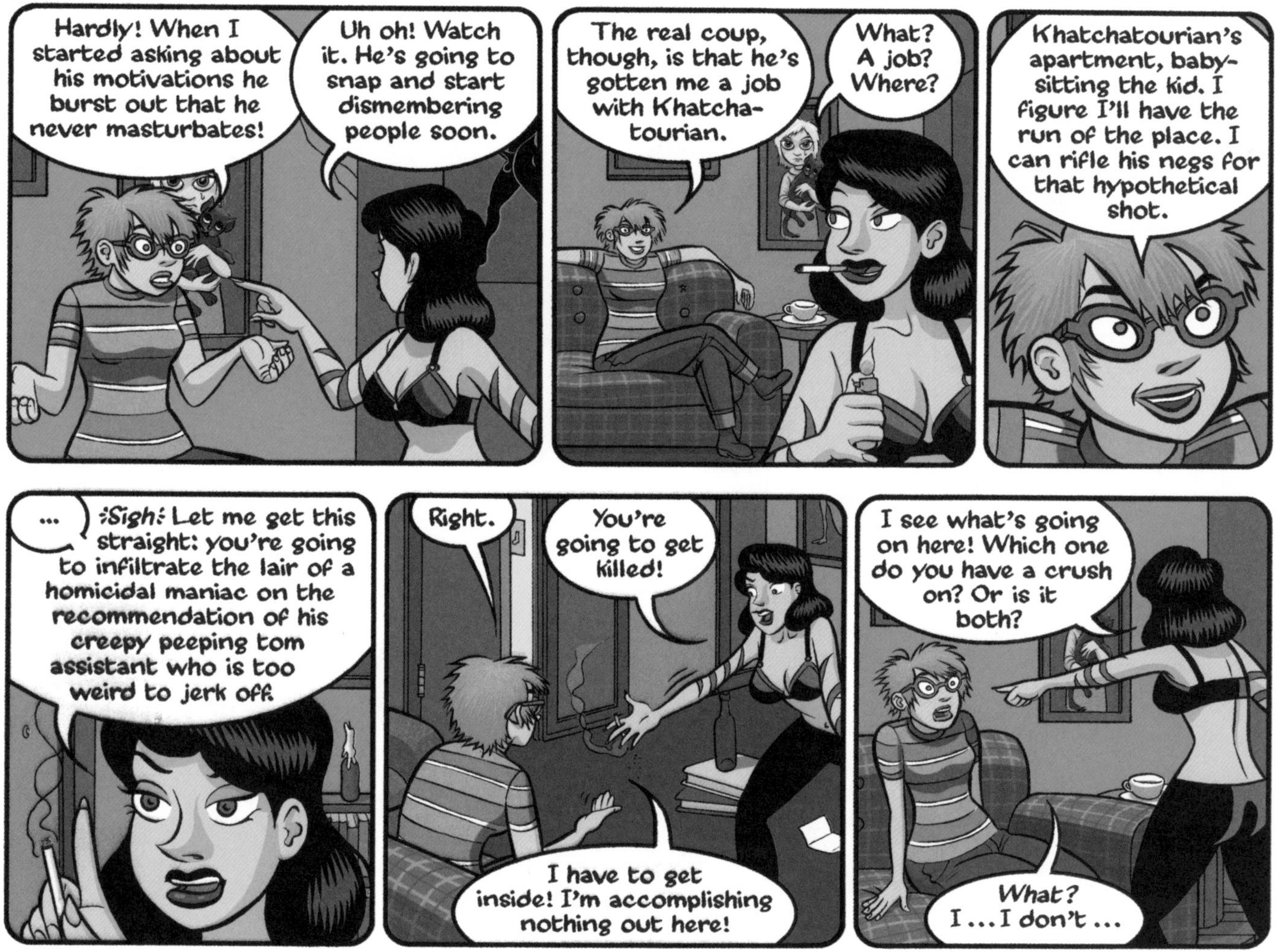

Hardly! When I started asking about his motivations he burst out that he never masturbates!
Uh oh! Watch it. He's going to snap and start dismembering people soon.
The real coup, though, is that he's gotten me a job with Khatcha-tourian.
What? A job? Where?
Khatchatourian's apartment, baby-sitting the kid. I figure I'll have the run of the place. I can rifle his negs for that hypothetical shot.
...
:Sigh: Let me get this straight: you're going to infiltrate the lair of a homicidal maniac on the recommendation of his creepy peeping tom assistant who is too weird to jerk off.
Right.
You're going to get killed!
I have to get inside! I'm accomplishing nothing out here!
I see what's going on here! Which one do you have a crush on? Or is it both?
What? I ... I don't ...

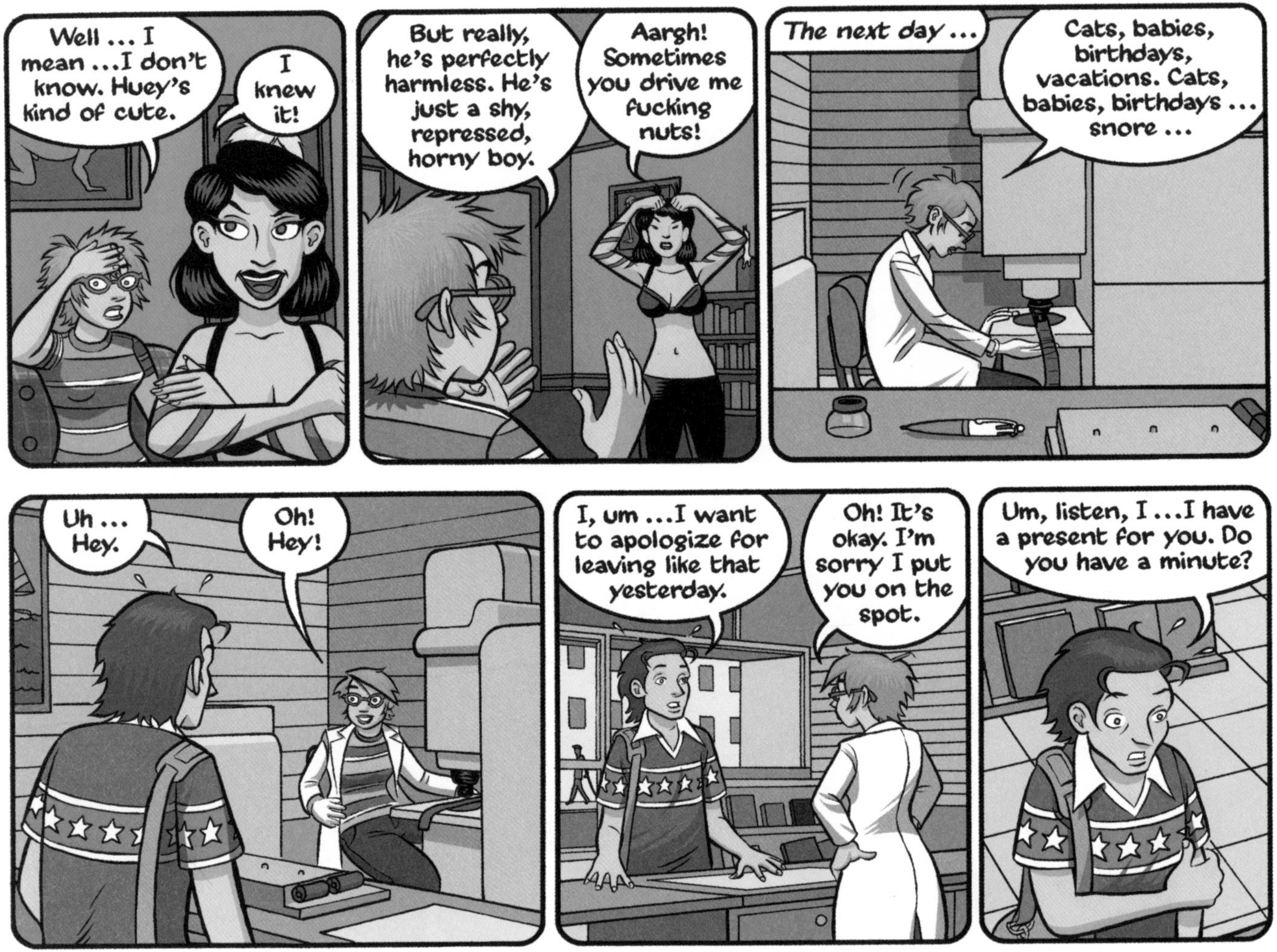
Well ... I mean ...I don't know. Huey's kind of cute.
I knew it!
But really, he's perfectly harmless. He's just a shy, repressed, horny boy.
Aargh! Sometimes you drive me fucking nuts!
The next day ...
Cats, babies, birthdays, vacations. Cats, babies, birthdays ... snore ...
Uh ... Hey.
Oh! Hey!
I, um ...I want to apologize for leaving like that yesterday.
Oh! It's okay. I'm sorry I put you on the spot.
Um, listen, I ...I have a present for you. Do you have a minute?

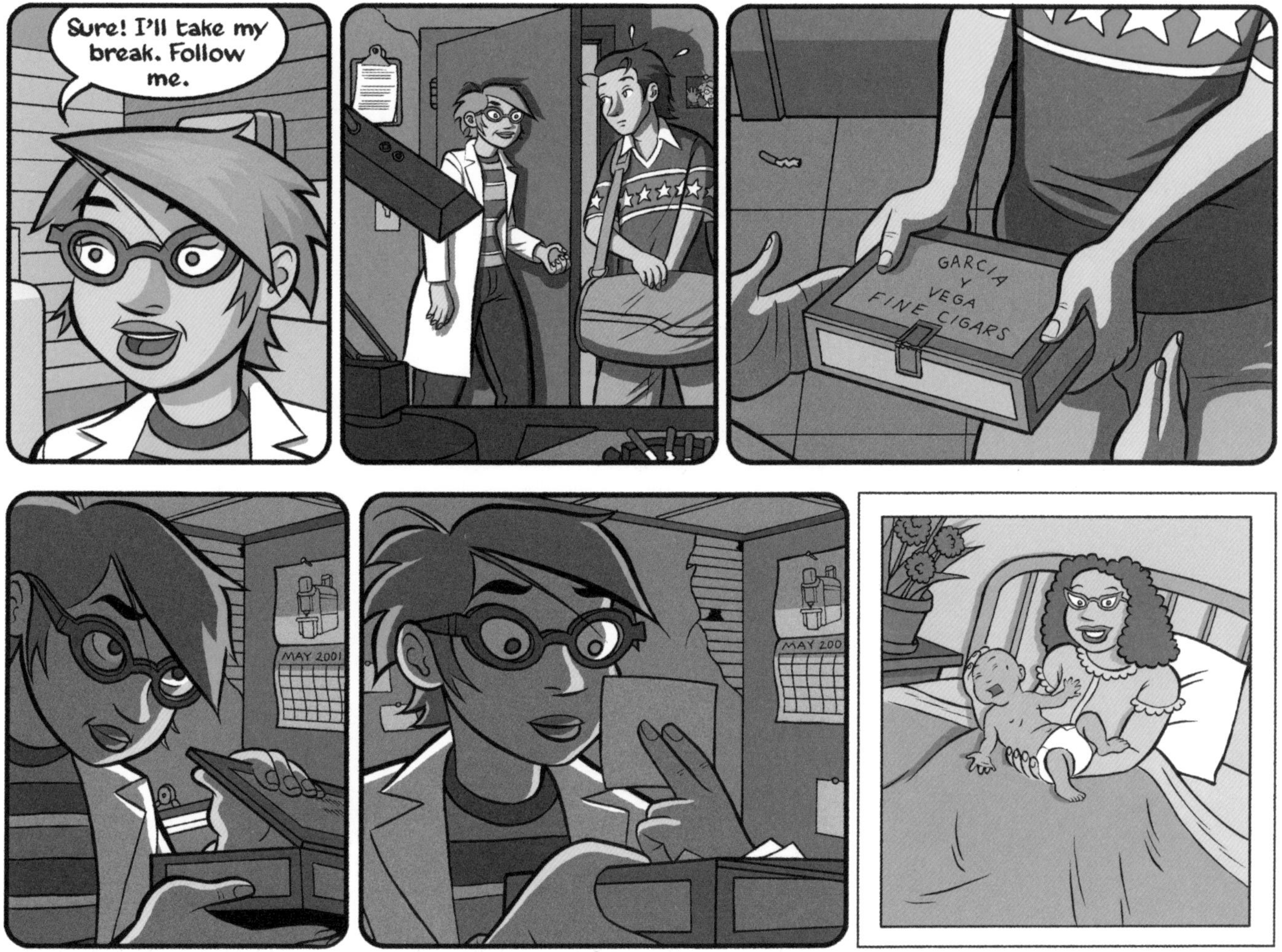
Sure! I'll take my break. Follow me.
GARCIA Y VEGA FINE CIGARS
MAY 2001

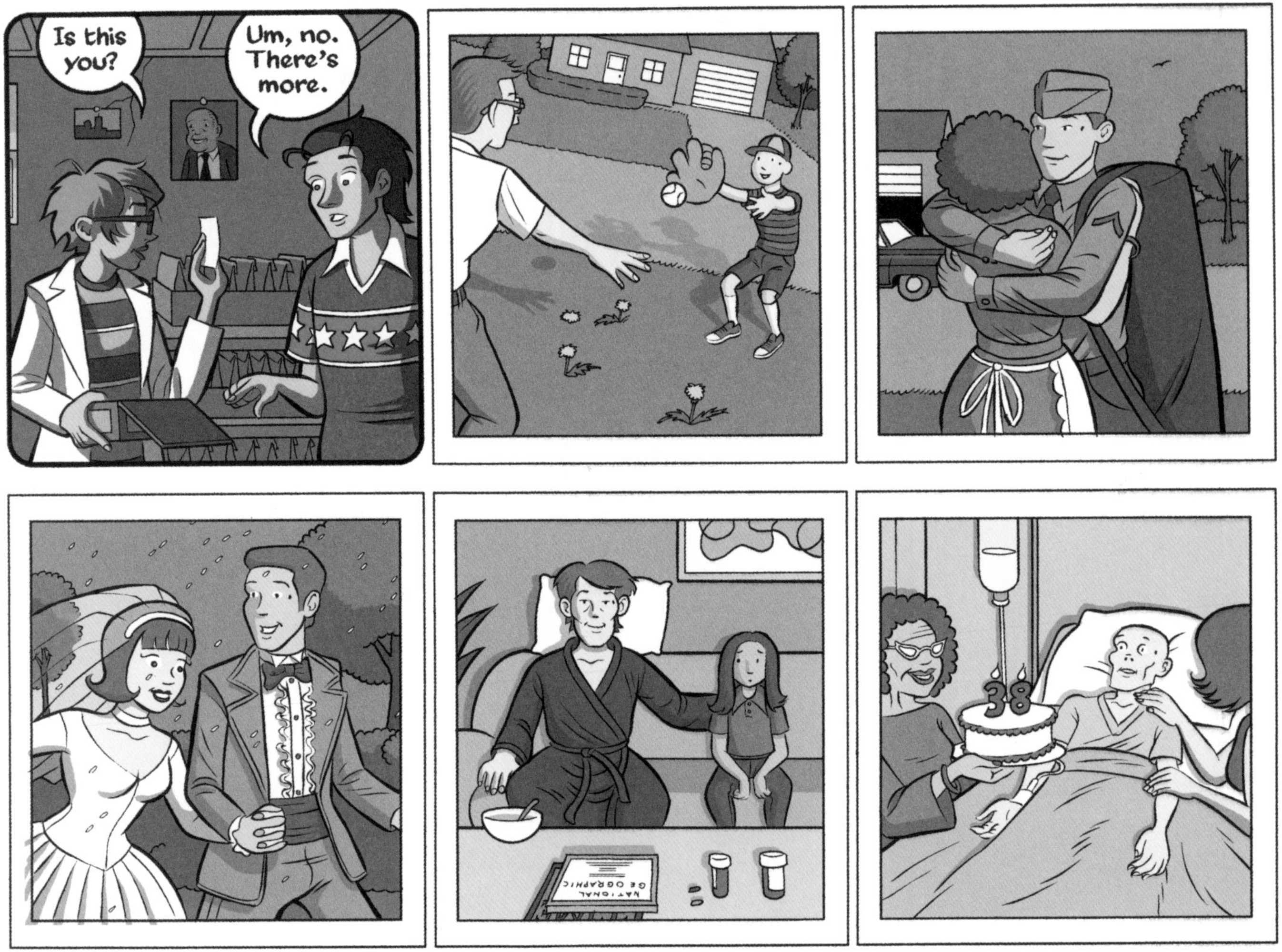
Is this you?
Um, no. There's more.
38

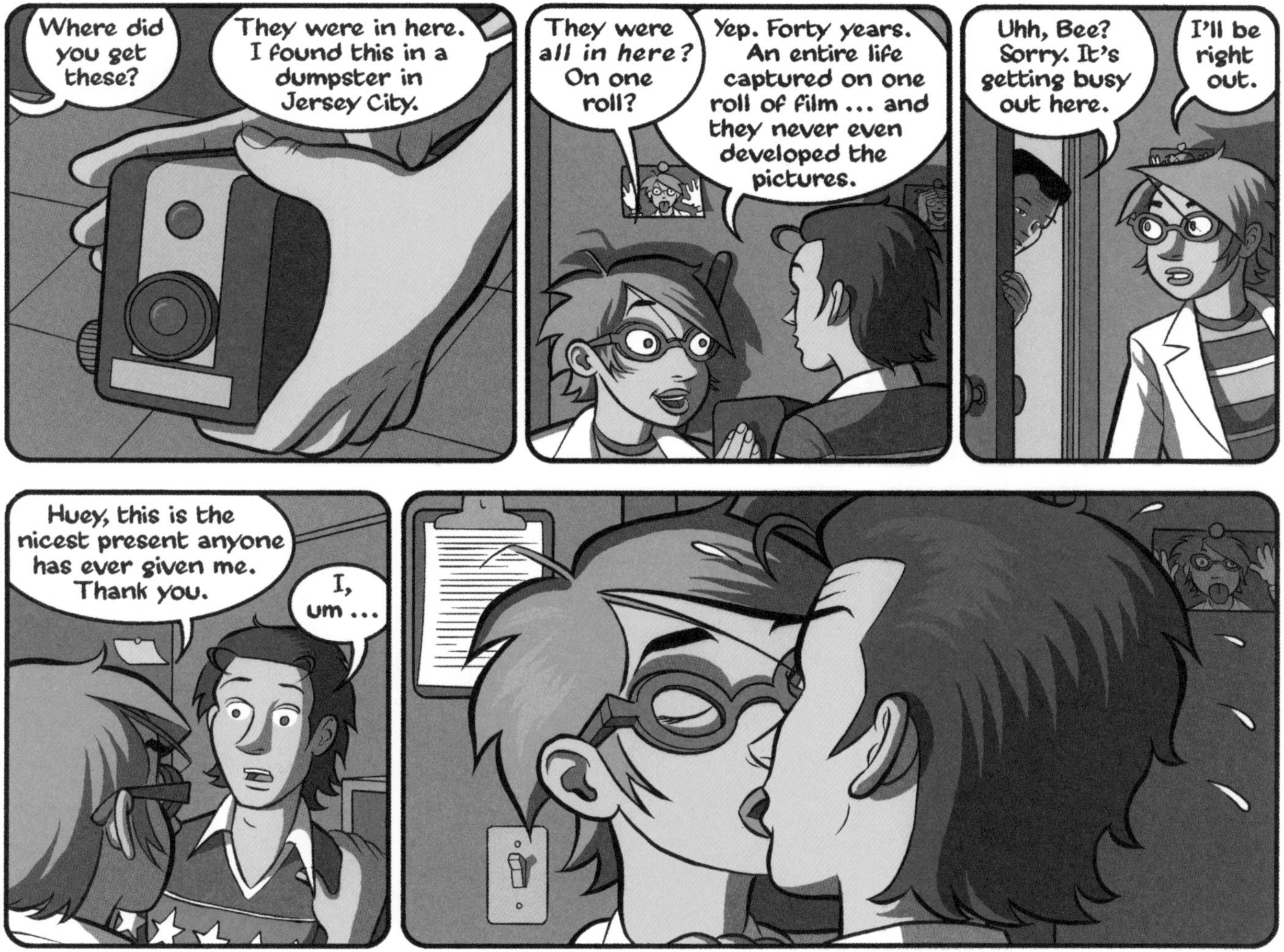
Where did you get these?
They were in here. I found this in a dumpster in Jersey City.
They were *all in here?* On one roll?
Yep. Forty years. An entire life captured on one roll of film ... and they never even developed the pictures.
Uhh, Bee? Sorry. It's getting busy out here.
I'll be right out.
Huey, this is the nicest present anyone has ever given me. Thank you.
I, um ...

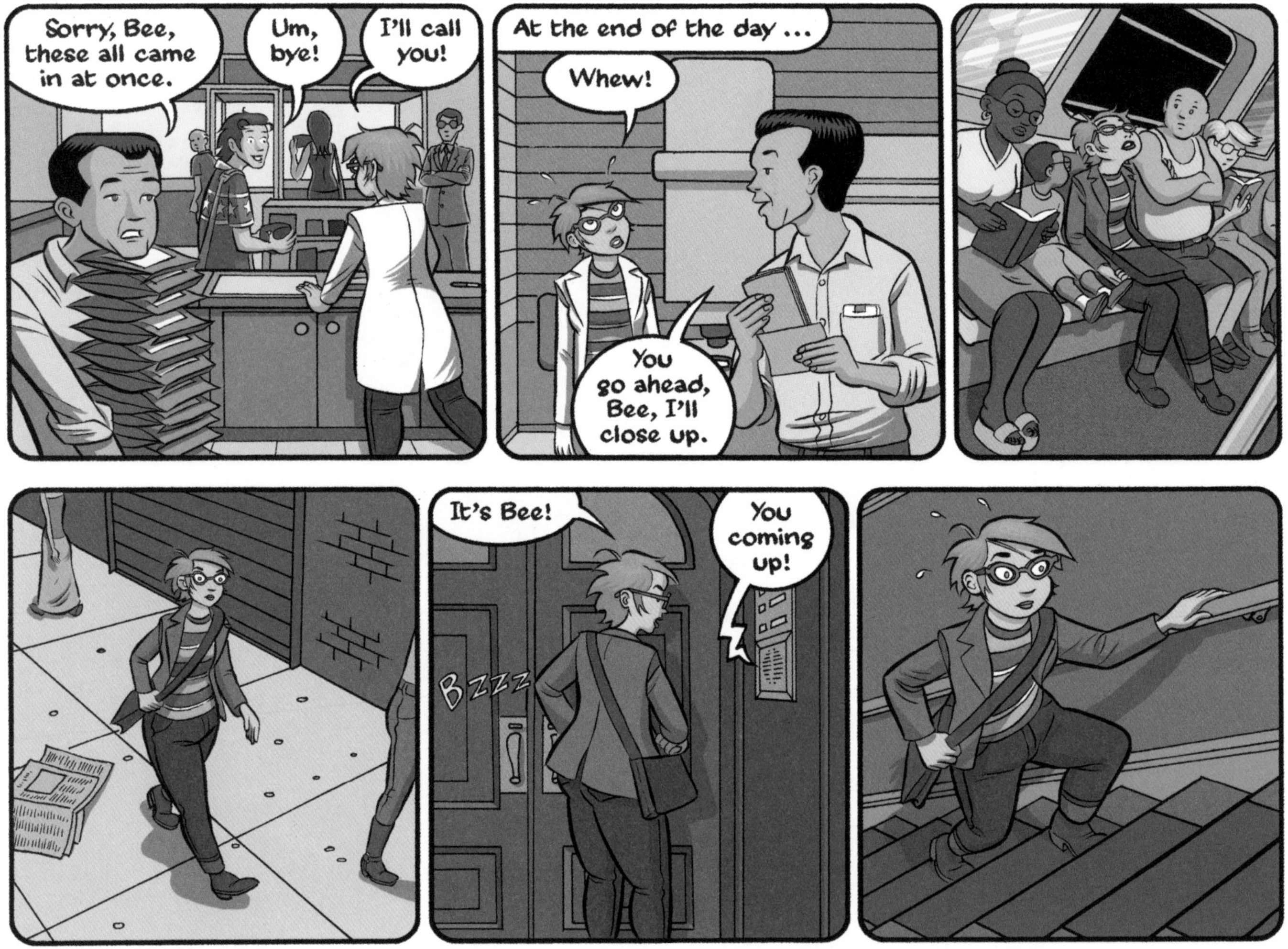
Sorry, Bee, these all came in at once.
Um, bye!
I'll call you!
At the end of the day ...
Whew!
You go ahead, Bee, I'll close up.
It's Bee!
You coming up!
Bzzz

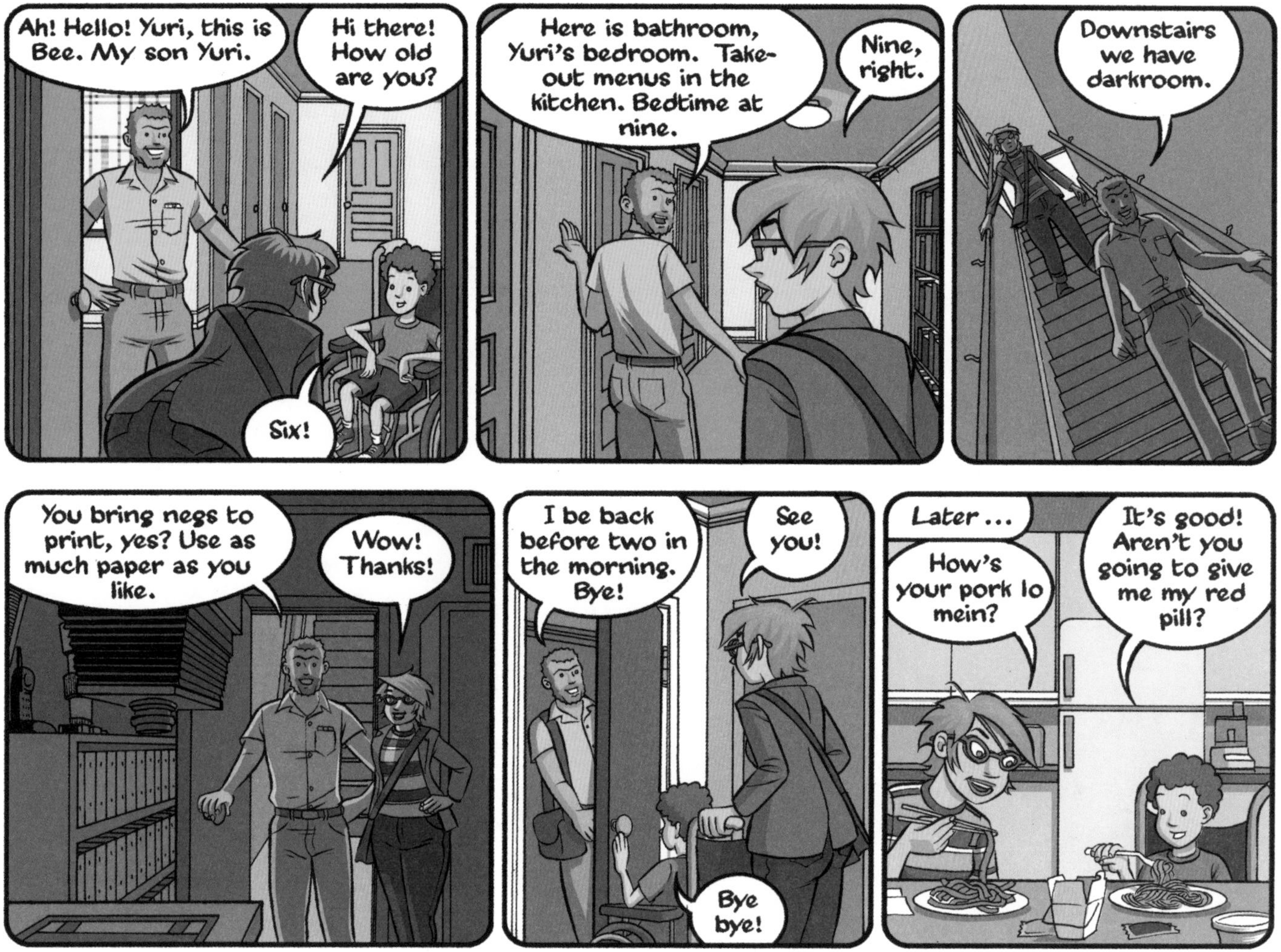
Ah! Hello! Yuri, this is Bee. My son Yuri.
Hi there! How old are you?
Six!
Here is bathroom, Yuri's bedroom. Take-out menus in the kitchen. Bedtime at nine.
Nine, right.
Downstairs we have darkroom.
You bring negs to print, yes? Use as much paper as you like.
Wow! Thanks!
I be back before two in the morning. Bye!
See you!
Bye bye!
Later...
How's your pork lo mein?
It's good! Aren't you going to give me my red pill?

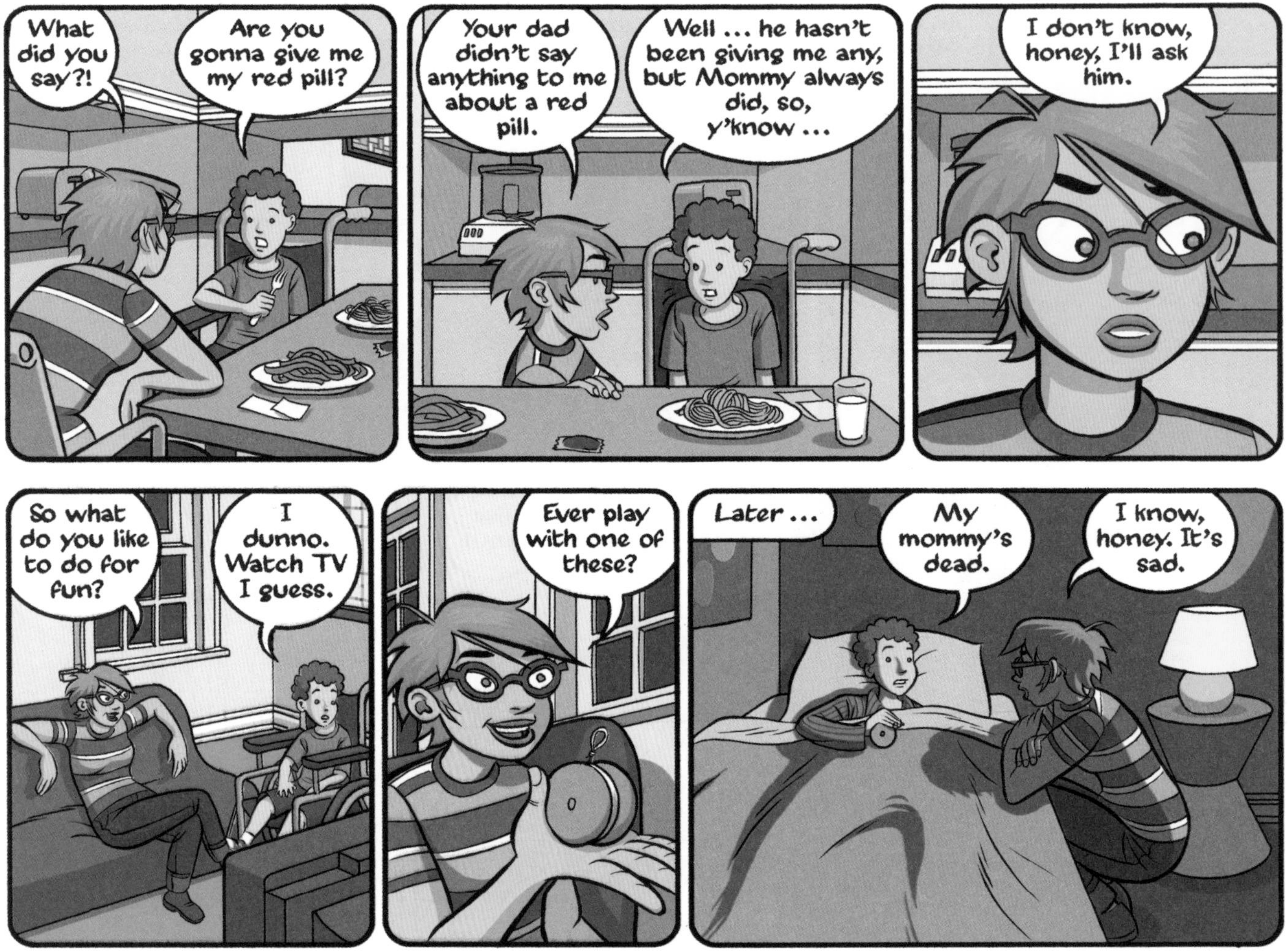
What did you say?!
Are you gonna give me my red pill?
Your dad didn't say anything to me about a red pill.
Well ... he hasn't been giving me any, but Mommy always did, so, y'know ...
I don't know, honey, I'll ask him.
So what do you like to do for fun?
I dunno. Watch TV I guess.
Ever play with one of these?
Later ...
My mommy's dead.
I know, honey. It's sad.

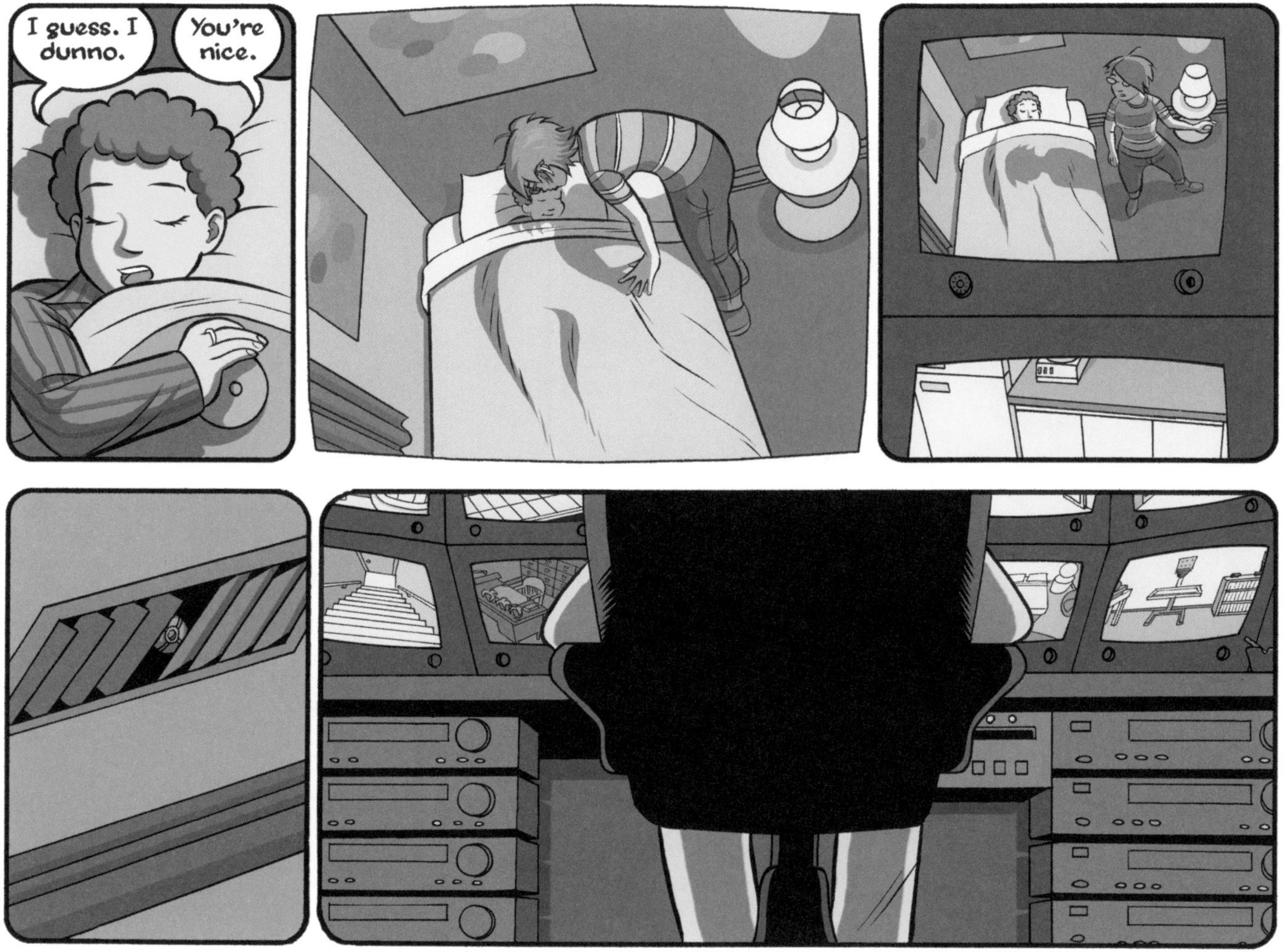
I guess. I dunno.
You're nice.

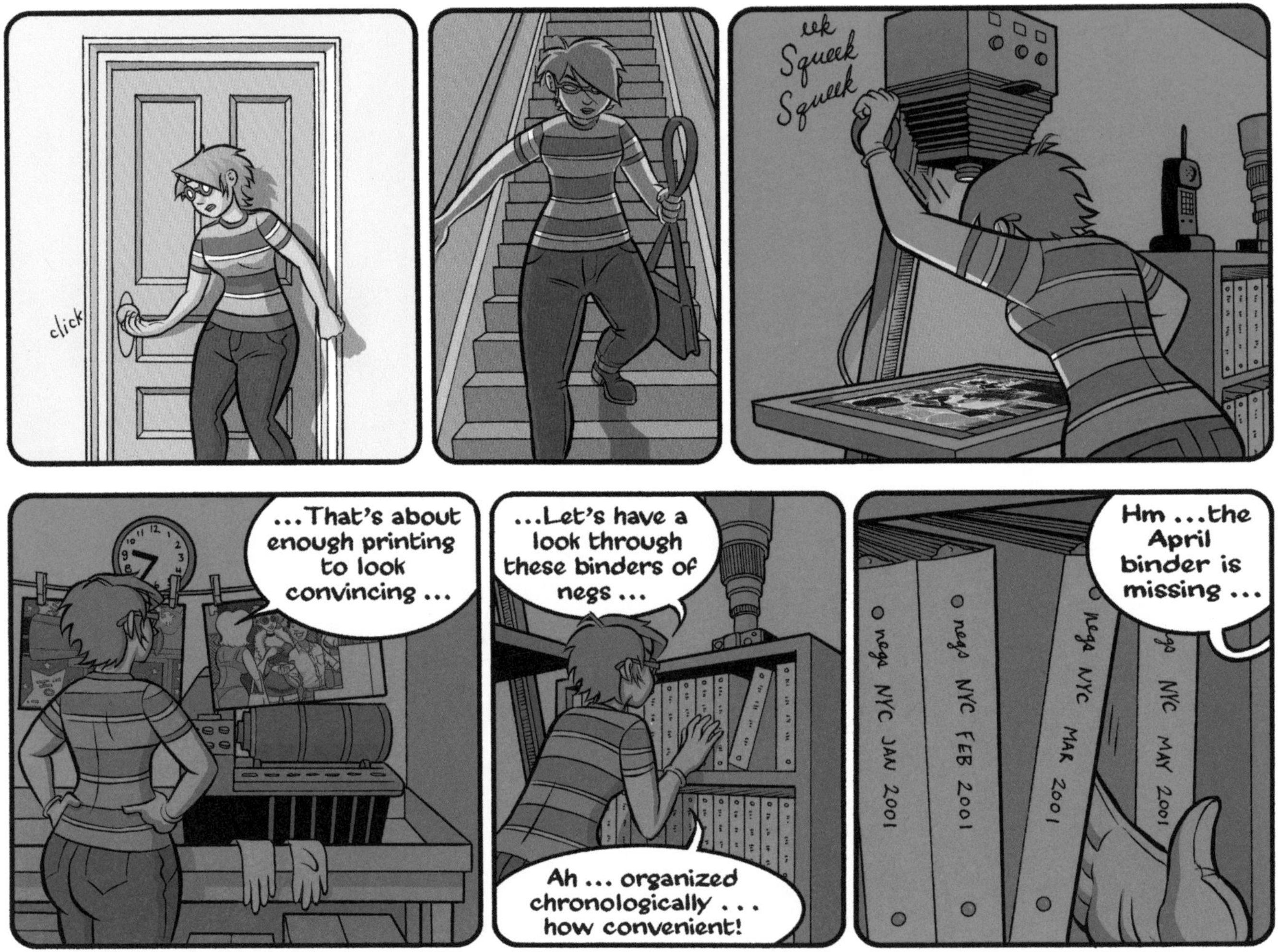
click
Squeek
Squeek
...That's about enough printing to look convincing ...
...Let's have a look through these binders of negs ...
Ah ... organized chronologically . . . how convenient!
negs NYC JAN 2001
negs NYC FEB 2001
negs NYC MAR 2001
NYC MAY 2001
Hm ...the April binder is missing ...

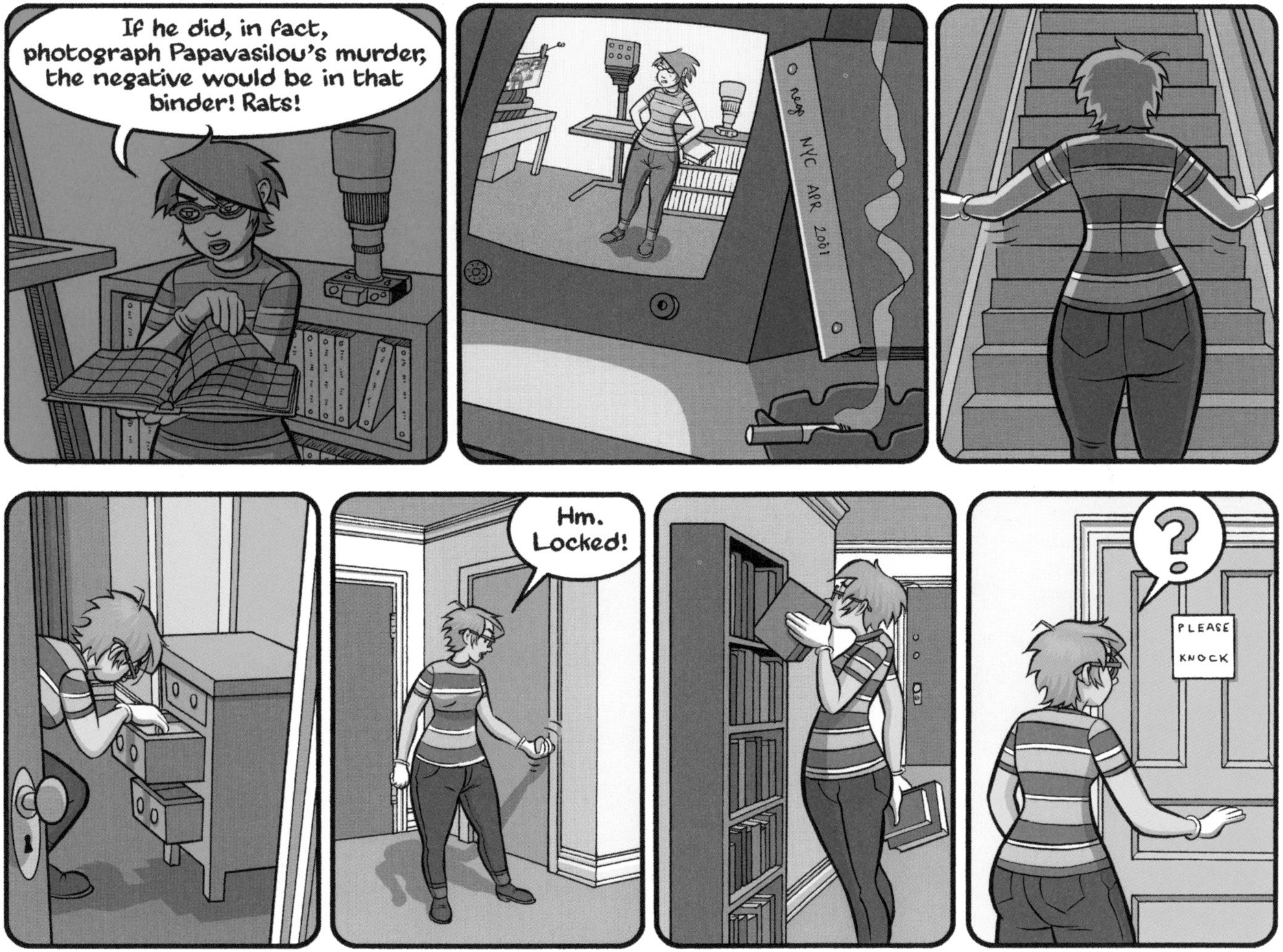
If he did, in fact, photograph Papavasilou's murder, the negative would be in that binder! Rats!
neg NYC APR 2001
Hm. Locked!
?
PLEASE KNOCK

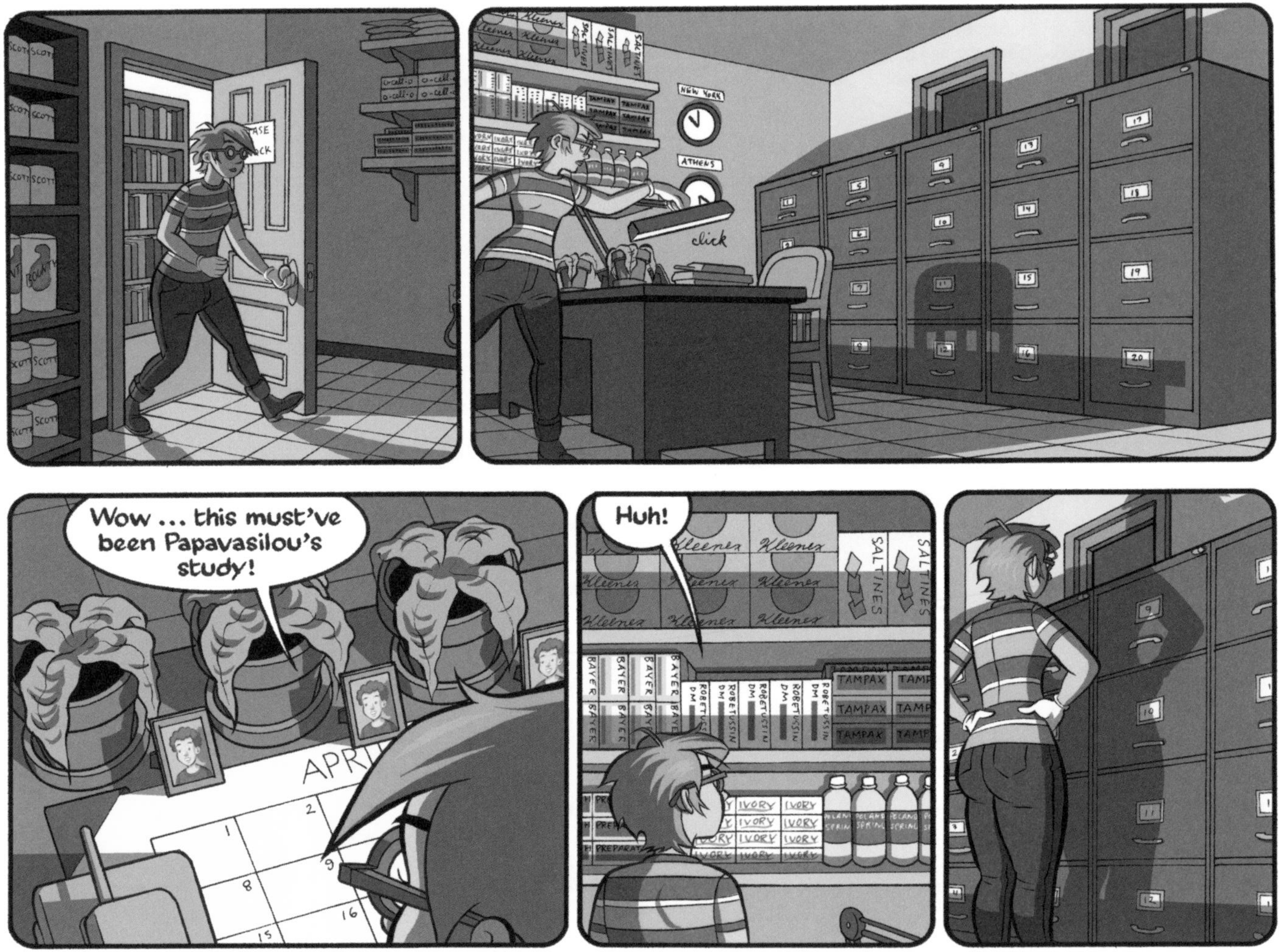
NEW YORK
ATHENS
click
Wow ... this must've been Papavasilou's study!
APRIL
Huh!
Kleenex
SALTINES
BAYER
ROBETUSSIN DM
TAMPAX
IVORY

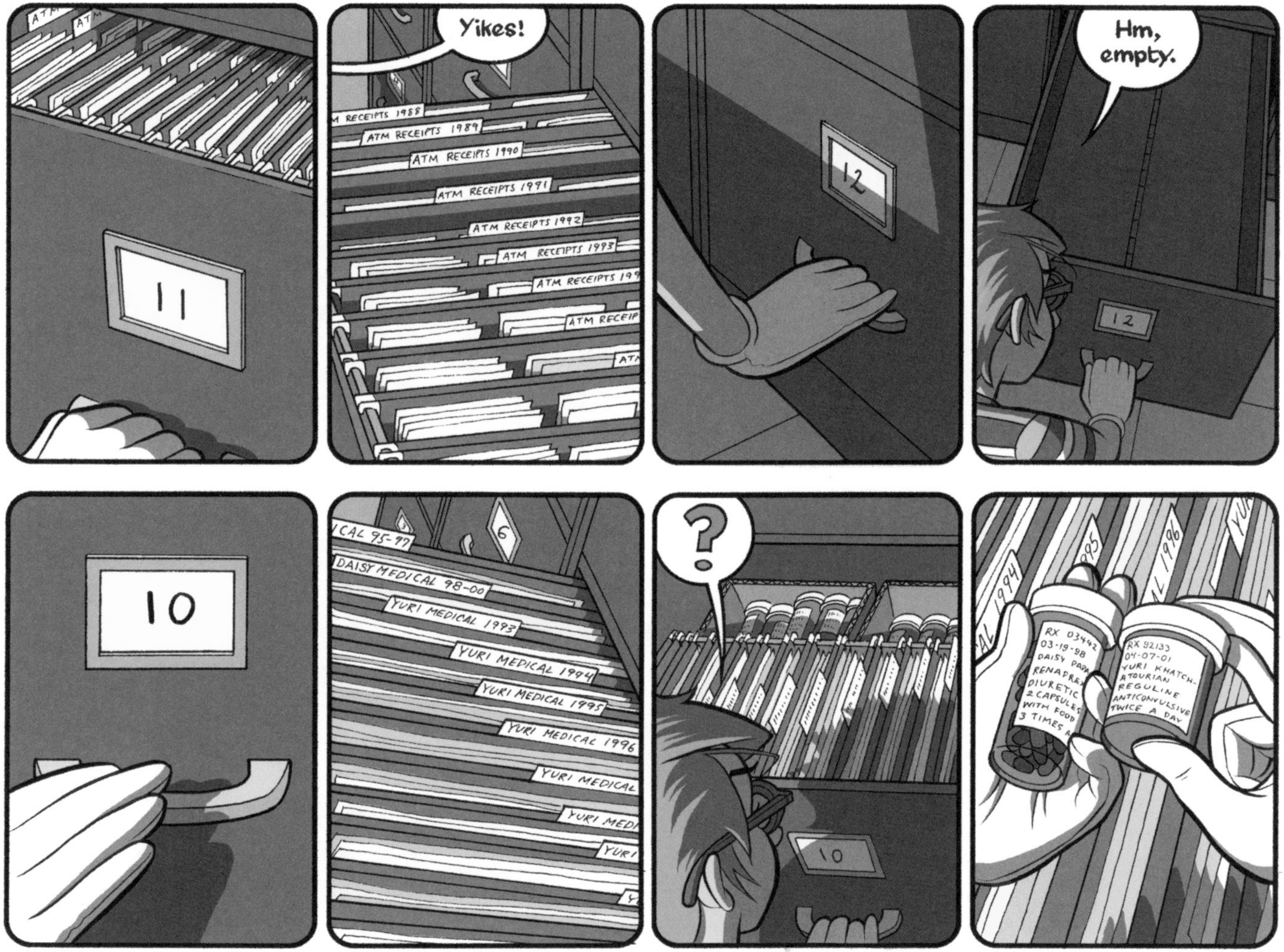
11
Yikes!
ATM RECEIPTS 1988
ATM RECEIPTS 1989
ATM RECEIPTS 1990
ATM RECEIPTS 1991
ATM RECEIPTS 1992
ATM RECEIPTS 1993
12
Hm, empty.
12
10
DAISY MEDICAL 98-00
YURI MEDICAL 1993
YURI MEDICAL 1994
YURI MEDICAL 1995
YURI MEDICAL 1996
?
10
RX 03442
03-19-98
RX 92133
04-07-01
YURI KHATCH-
ATOURIAN
REGULINE
ANTICONVULSIVE
TWICE A DAY
DIURETIC
2 CAPSULES
WITH FOOD

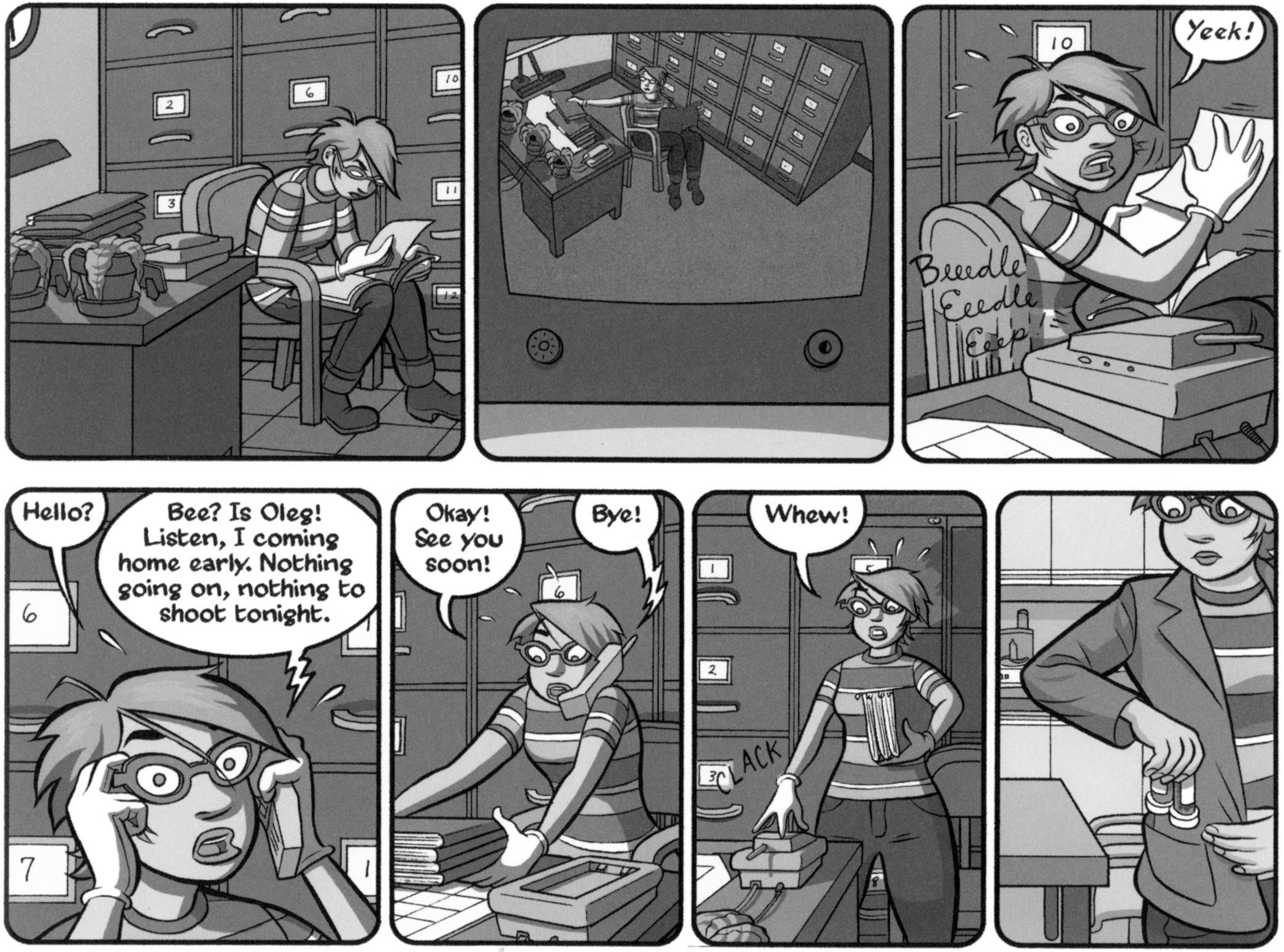
Yeek!
Beedle Eeedle Eeep!
Hello?
Bee? Is Oleg! Listen, I coming home early. Nothing going on, nothing to shoot tonight.
Okay! See you soon!
Bye!
Whew!
CLACK

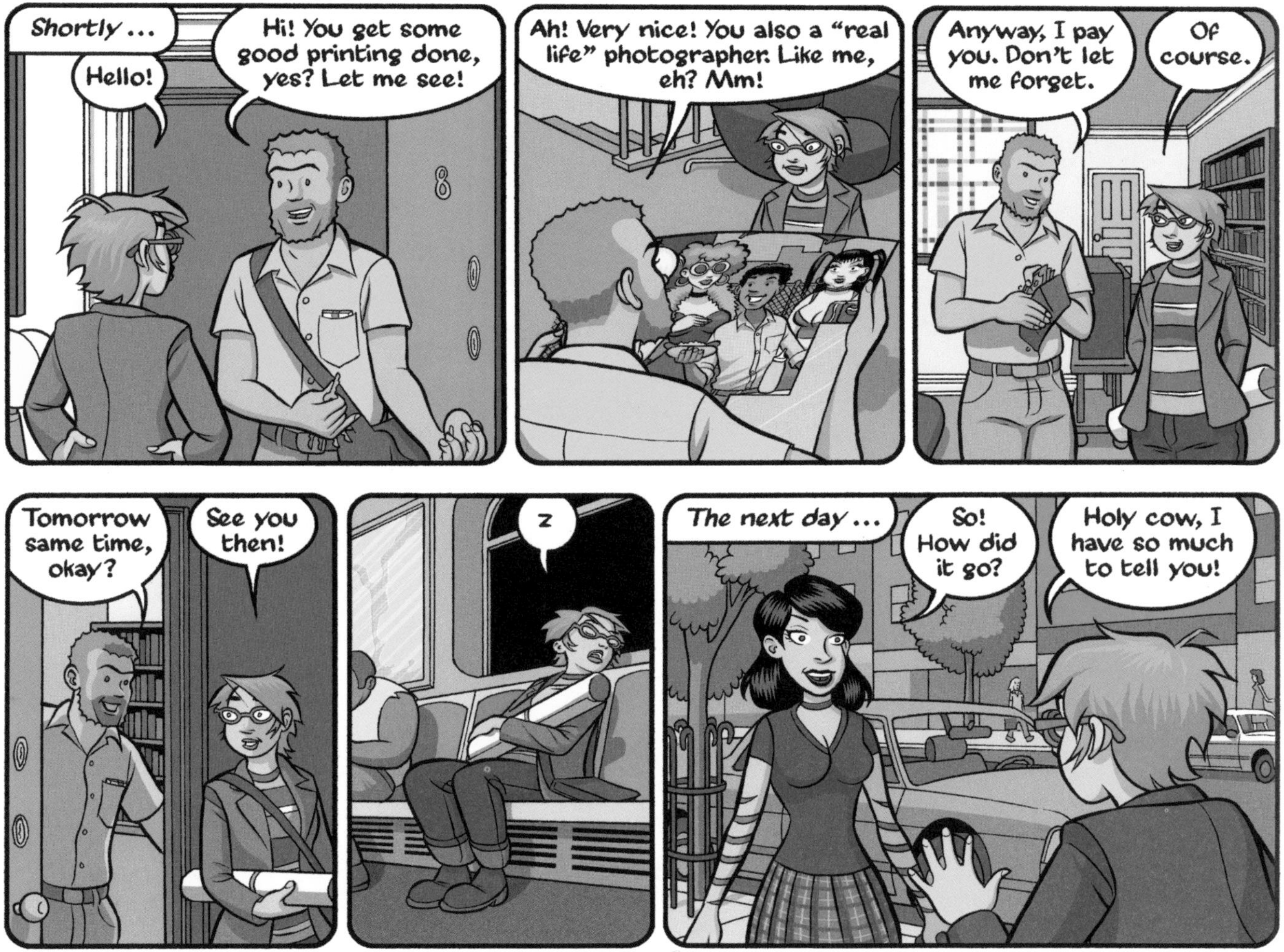
Shortly ...
Hello!
Hi! You get some good printing done, yes? Let me see!
Ah! Very nice! You also a "real life" photographer. Like me, eh? Mm!
Anyway, I pay you. Don't let me forget.
Of course.
Tomorrow same time, okay?
See you then!
z
The next day ...
So! How did it go?
Holy cow, I have so much to tell you!

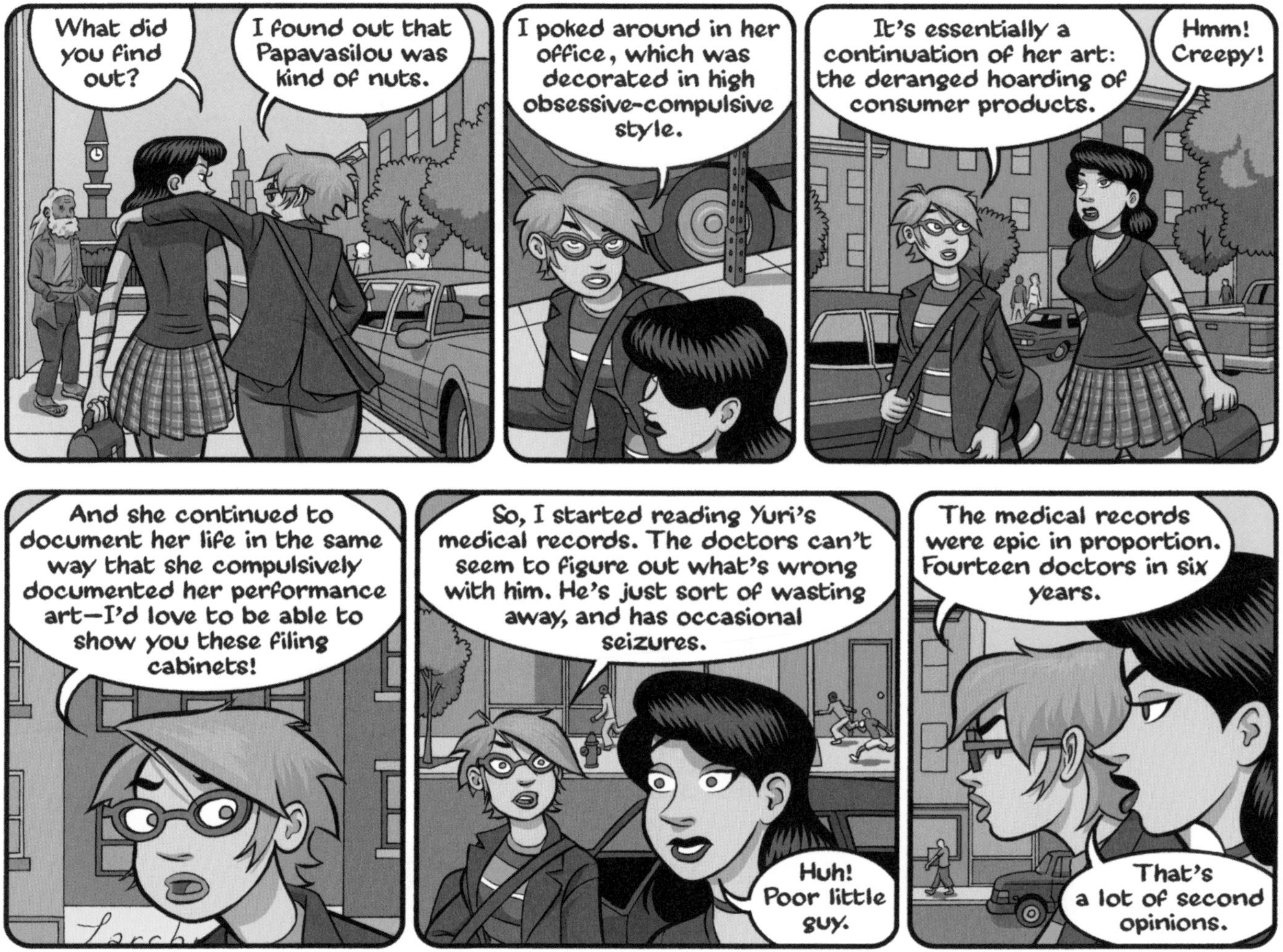
What did you find out?
I found out that Papavasilou was kind of nuts.
I poked around in her office, which was decorated in high obsessive-compulsive style.
It's essentially a continuation of her art: the deranged hoarding of consumer products.
Hmm! Creepy!
And she continued to document her life in the same way that she compulsively documented her performance art—I'd love to be able to show you these filing cabinets!
So, I started reading Yuri's medical records. The doctors can't seem to figure out what's wrong with him. He's just sort of wasting away, and has occasional seizures.
Huh! Poor little guy.
The medical records were epic in proportion. Fourteen doctors in six years.
That's a lot of second opinions.

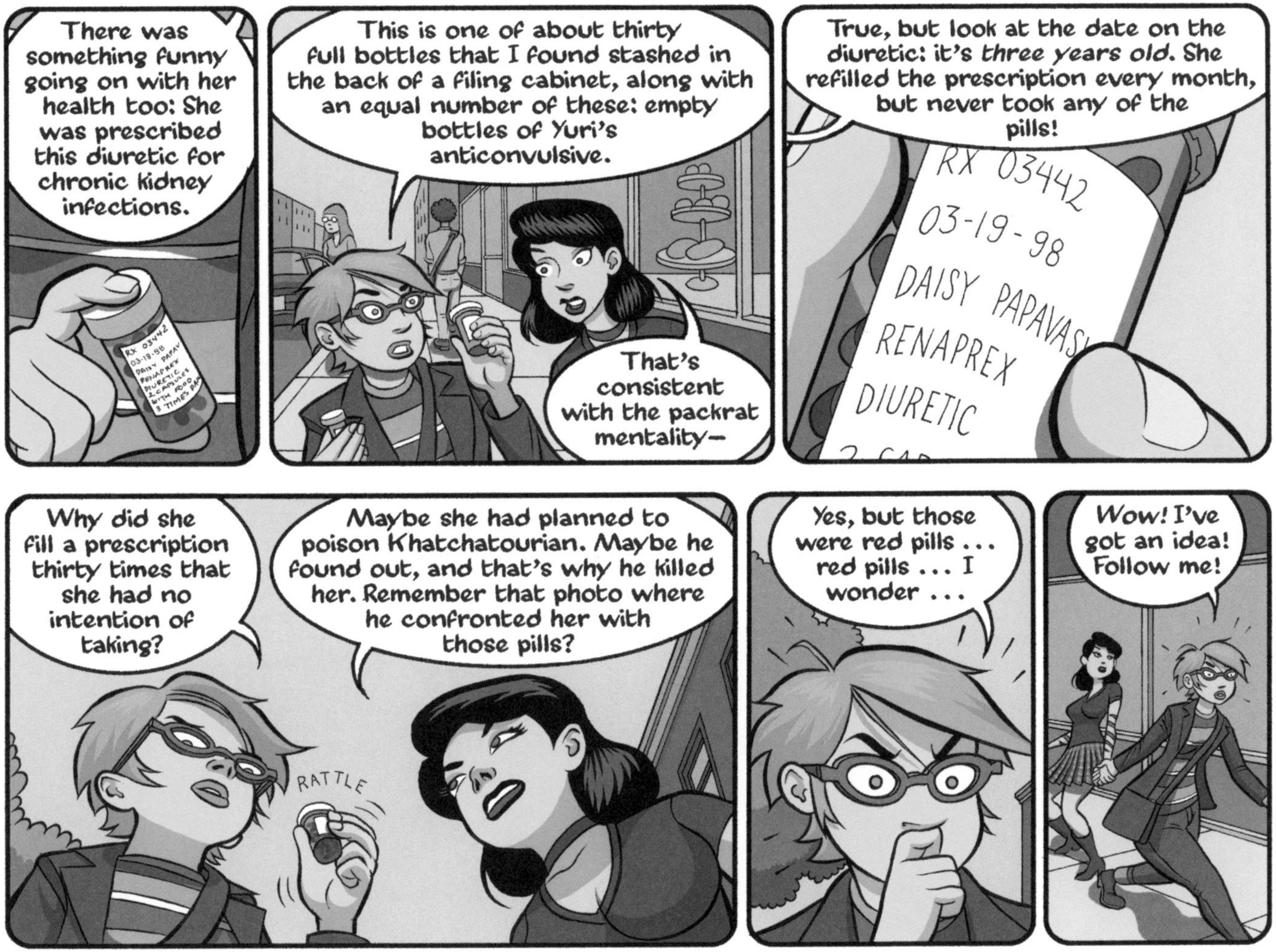
There was something funny going on with her health too: She was prescribed this diuretic for chronic kidney infections.
This is one of about thirty full bottles that I found stashed in the back of a filing cabinet, along with an equal number of these: empty bottles of Yuri's anticonvulsive.
That's consistent with the packrat mentality—
True, but look at the date on the diuretic: it's *three years old*. She refilled the prescription every month, but never took any of the pills!
RX 03442
03-19-98
RENAPREX
DIURETIC
Why did she fill a prescription thirty times that she had no intention of taking?
Maybe she had planned to poison Khatchatourian. Maybe he found out, and that's why he killed her. Remember that photo where he confronted her with those pills?
RATTLE
Yes, but those were red pills . . . red pills . . . I wonder . . .
Wow! I've got an idea! Follow me!

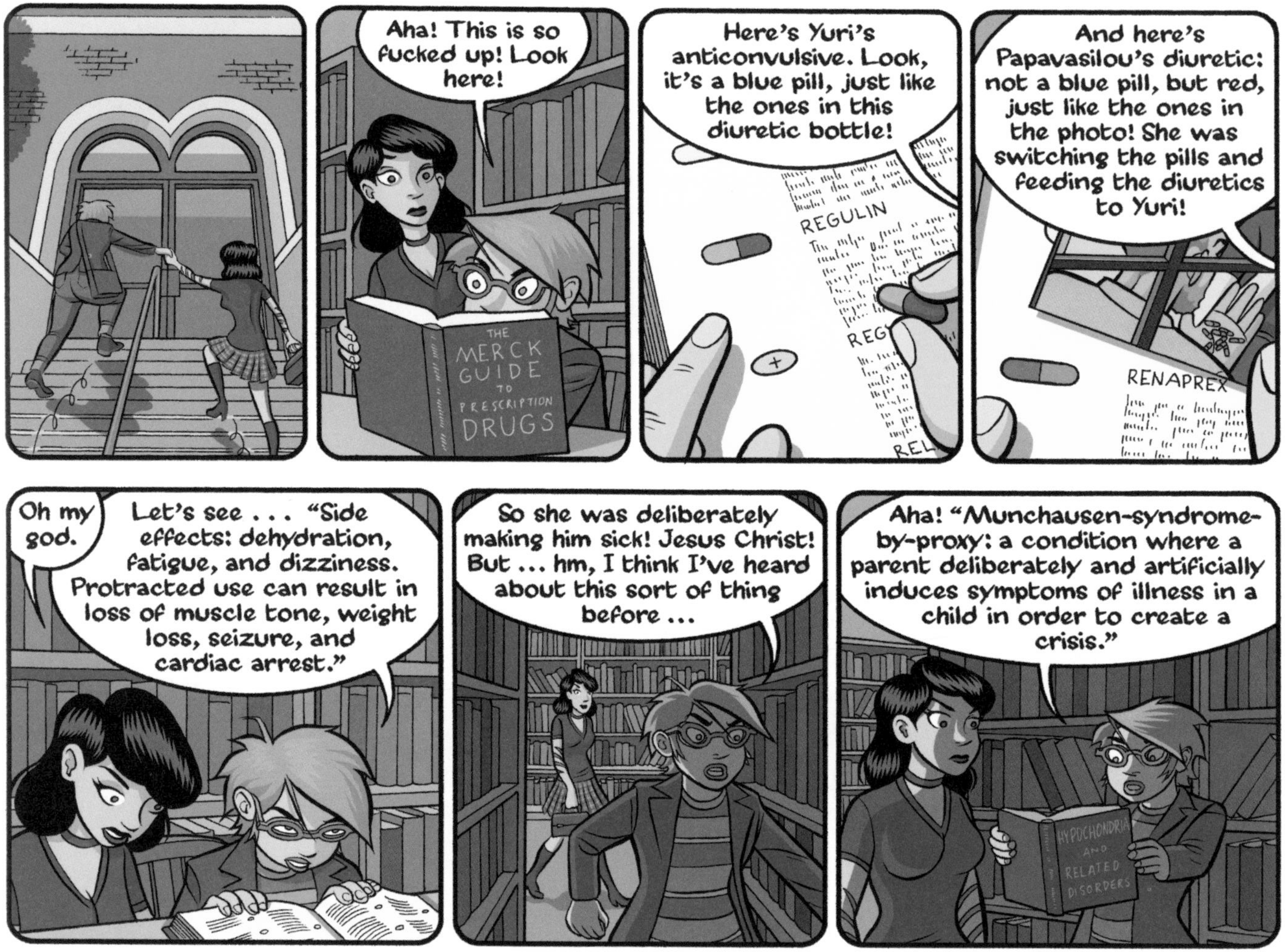
Aha! This is so fucked up! Look here!
THE MERCK GUIDE TO PRESCRIPTION DRUGS
Here's Yuri's anticonvulsive. Look, it's a blue pill, just like the ones in this diuretic bottle!
REGULIN
And here's Papavasilou's diuretic: not a blue pill, but red, just like the ones in the photo! She was switching the pills and feeding the diuretics to Yuri!
RENAPREX
Oh my god.
Let's see . . . "Side effects: dehydration, fatigue, and dizziness. Protracted use can result in loss of muscle tone, weight loss, seizure, and cardiac arrest."
So she was deliberately making him sick! Jesus Christ! But ... hm, I think I've heard about this sort of thing before ...
Aha! "Munchausen-syndrome-by-proxy: a condition where a parent deliberately and artificially induces symptoms of illness in a child in order to create a crisis."
HYPOCHONDRIA AND RELATED DISORDERS

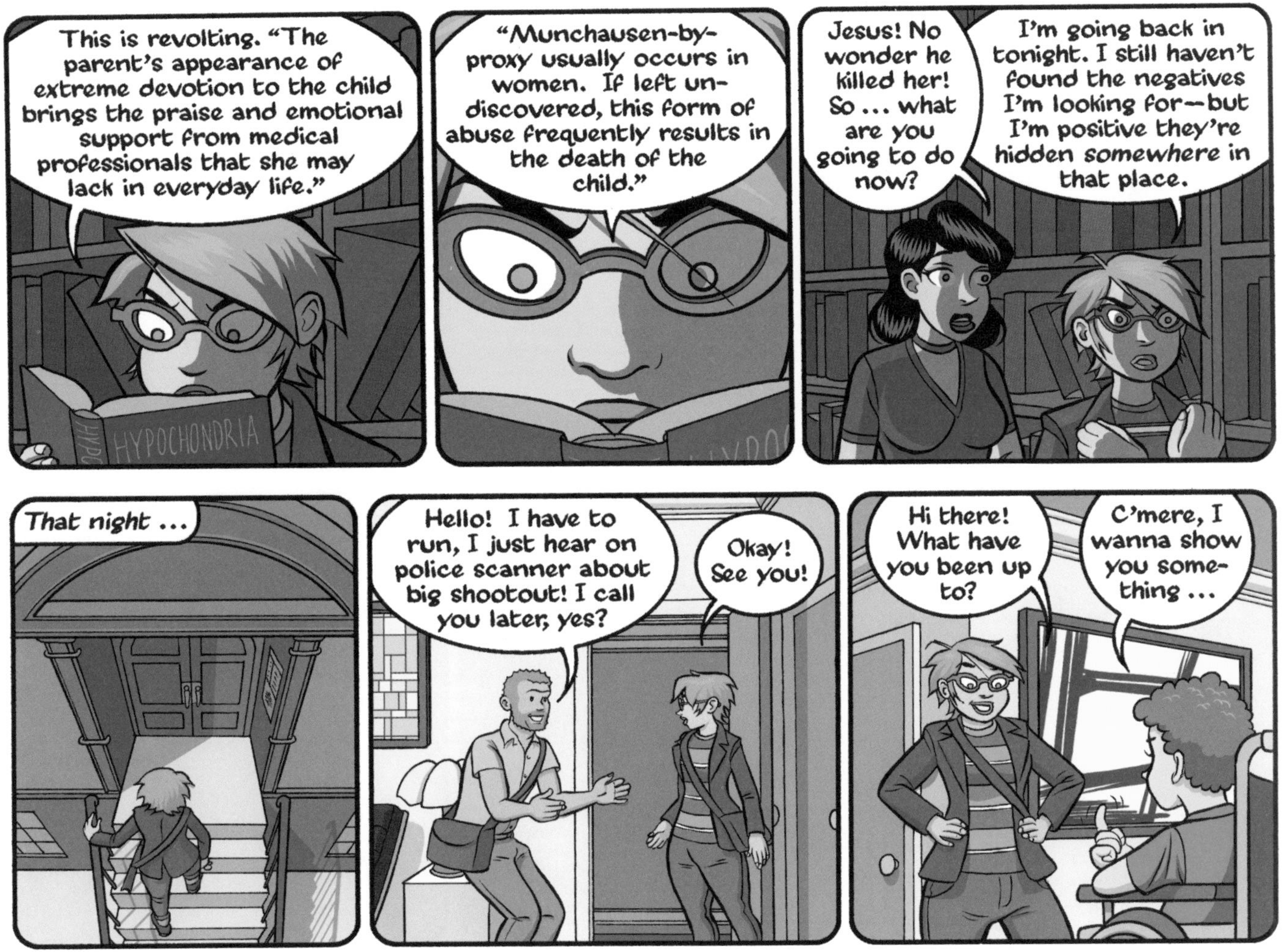
This is revolting. "The parent's appearance of extreme devotion to the child brings the praise and emotional support from medical professionals that she may lack in everyday life."
HYPOCHONDRIA
"Munchausen-by-proxy usually occurs in women. If left un-discovered, this form of abuse frequently results in the death of the child."
Jesus! No wonder he killed her! So ... what are you going to do now?
I'm going back in tonight. I still haven't found the negatives I'm looking for—but I'm positive they're hidden *somewhere* in that place.
That night ...
Hello! I have to run, I just hear on police scanner about big shootout! I call you later, yes?
Okay! See you!
Hi there! What have you been up to?
C'mere, I wanna show you some-thing ...

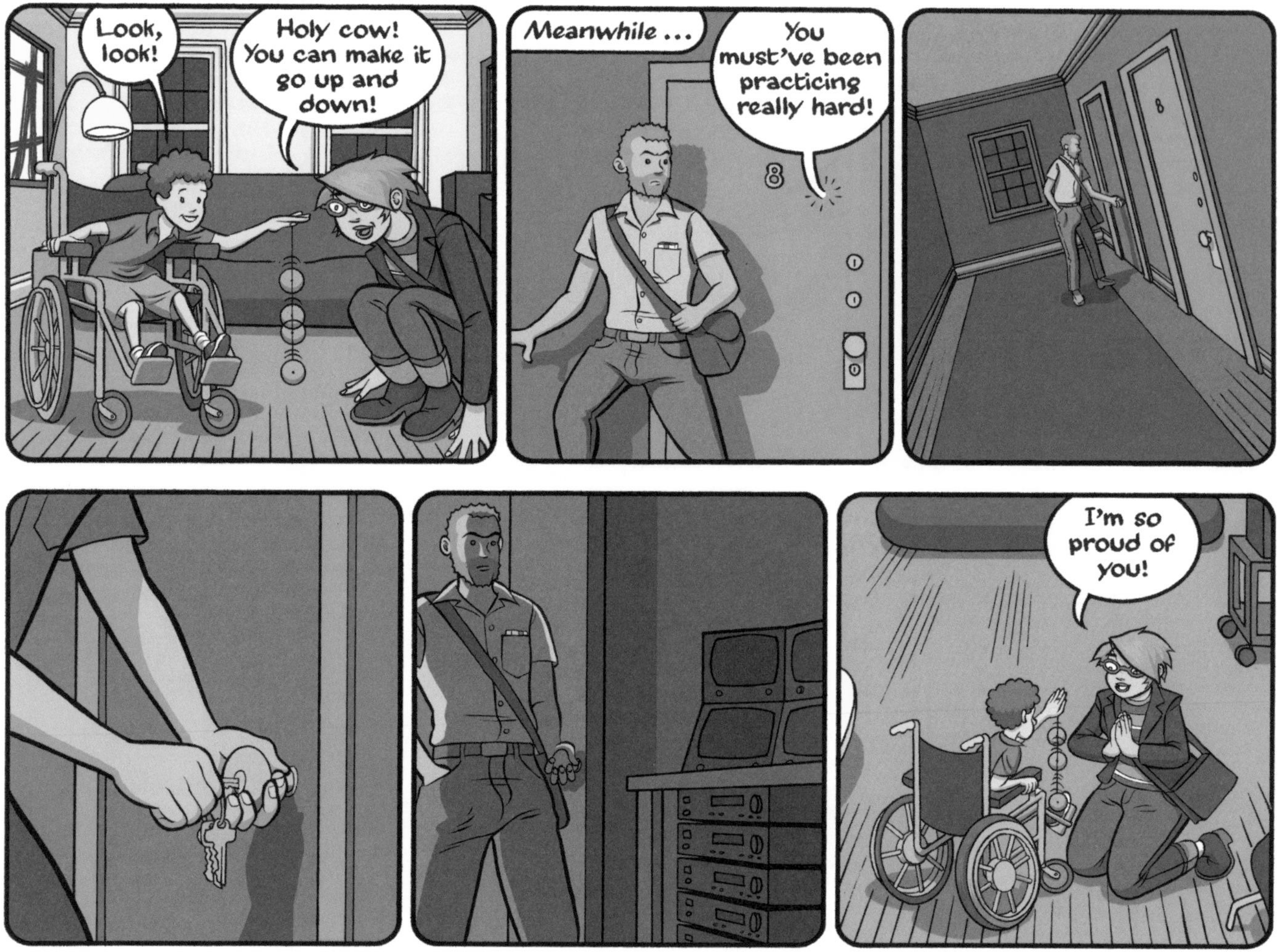
Look, look!
Holy cow! You can make it go up and down!
Meanwhile ...
You must've been practicing really hard!
8
8
I'm so proud of you!

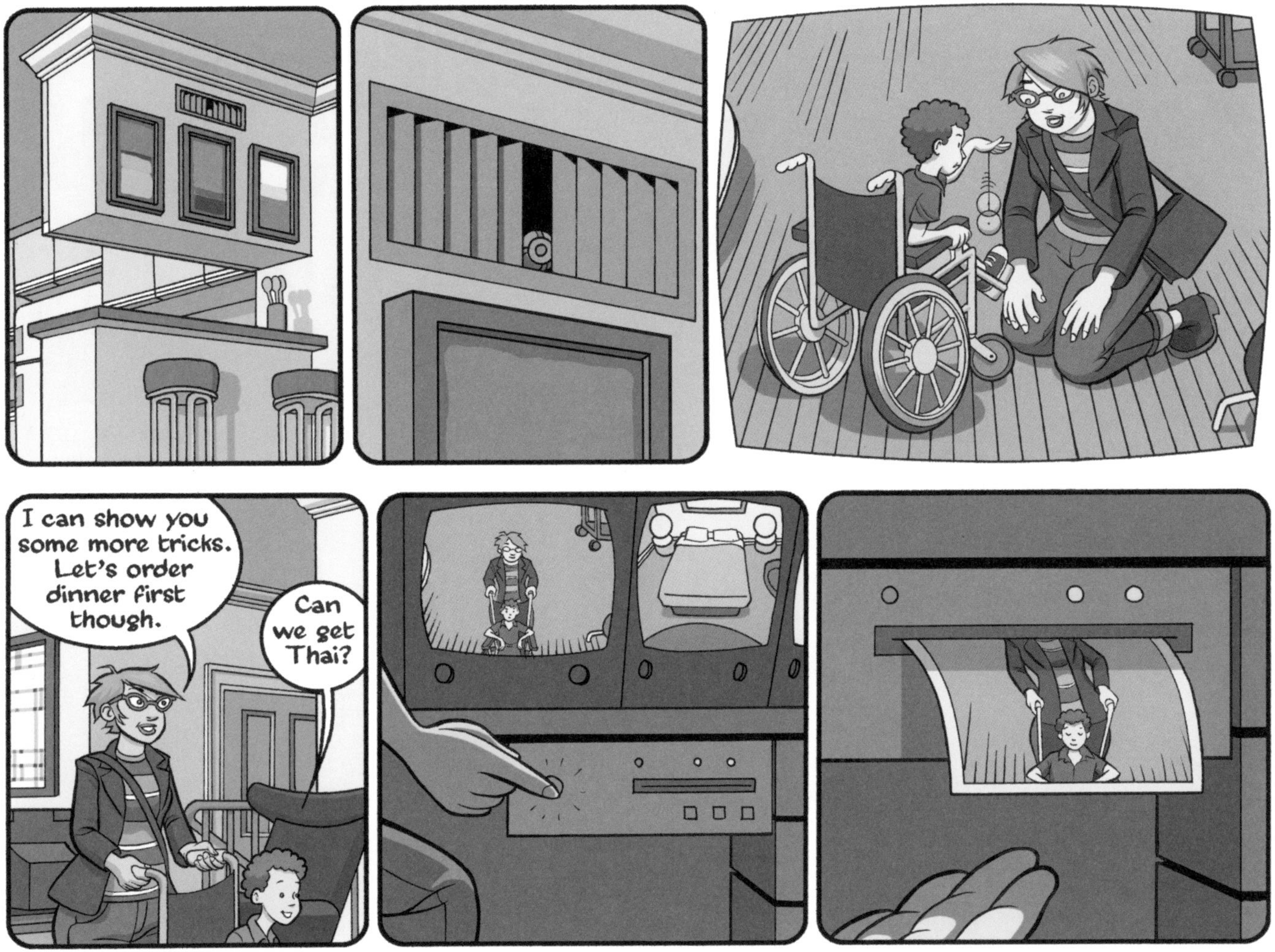
I can show you some more tricks. Let's order dinner first though.
Can we get Thai?

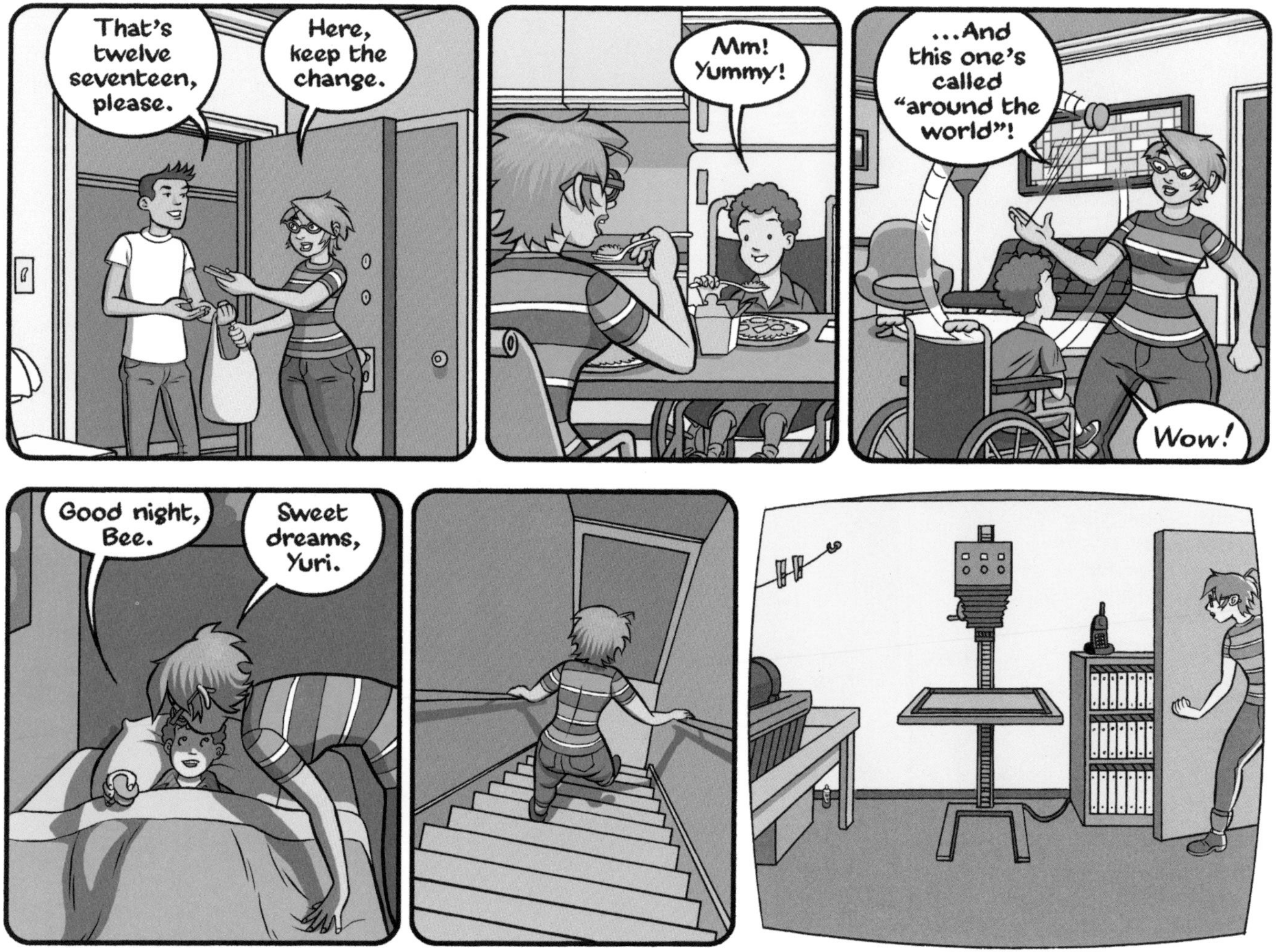
That's twelve seventeen, please.
Here, keep the change.
Mm! Yummy!
...And this one's called "around the world"!
Wow!
Good night, Bee.
Sweet dreams, Yuri.

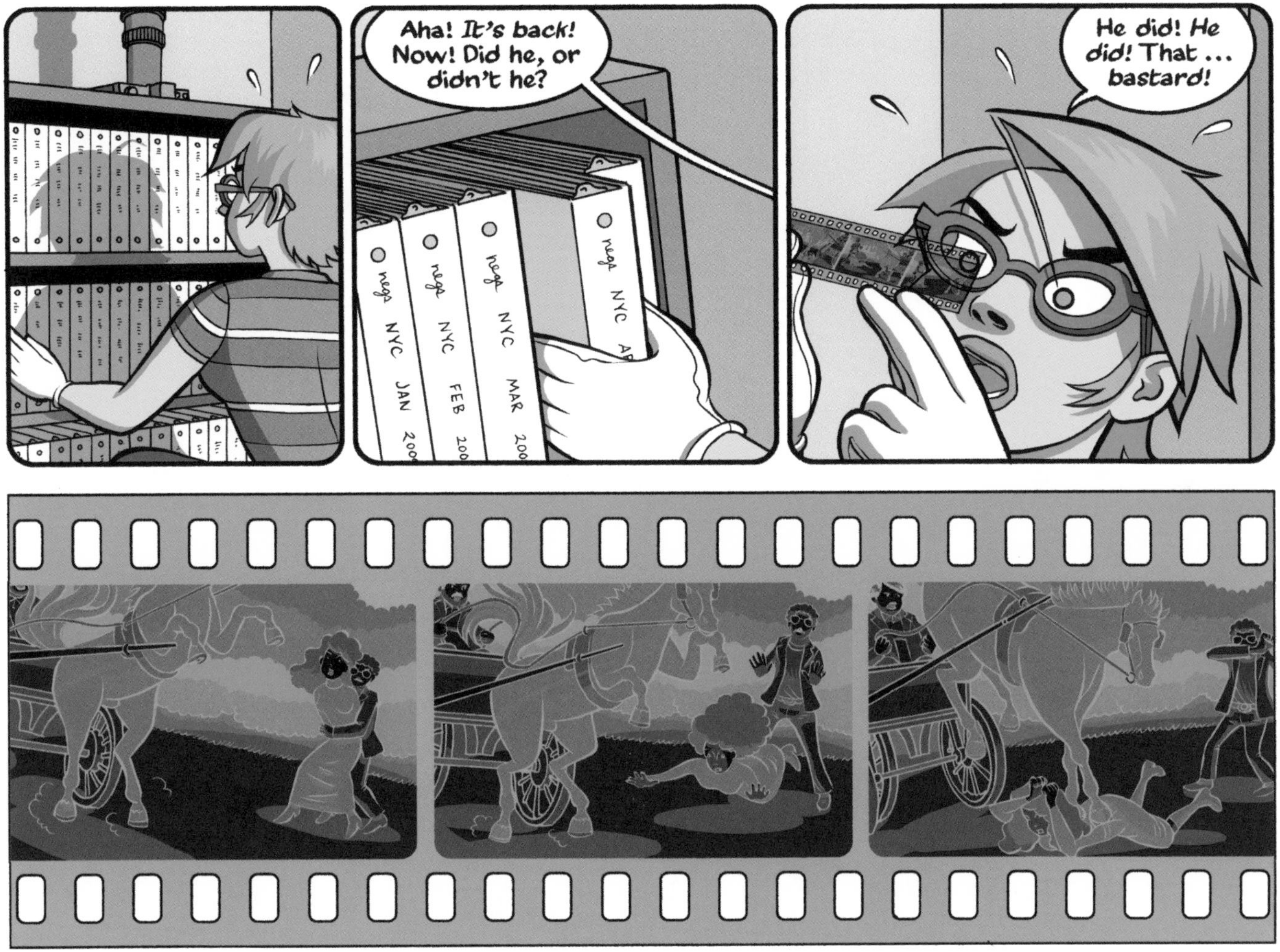
Aha! It's back! Now! Did he, or didn't he?
negs NYC JAN
negs NYC FEB
negs NYC MAR
He did! He did! That ... bastard!

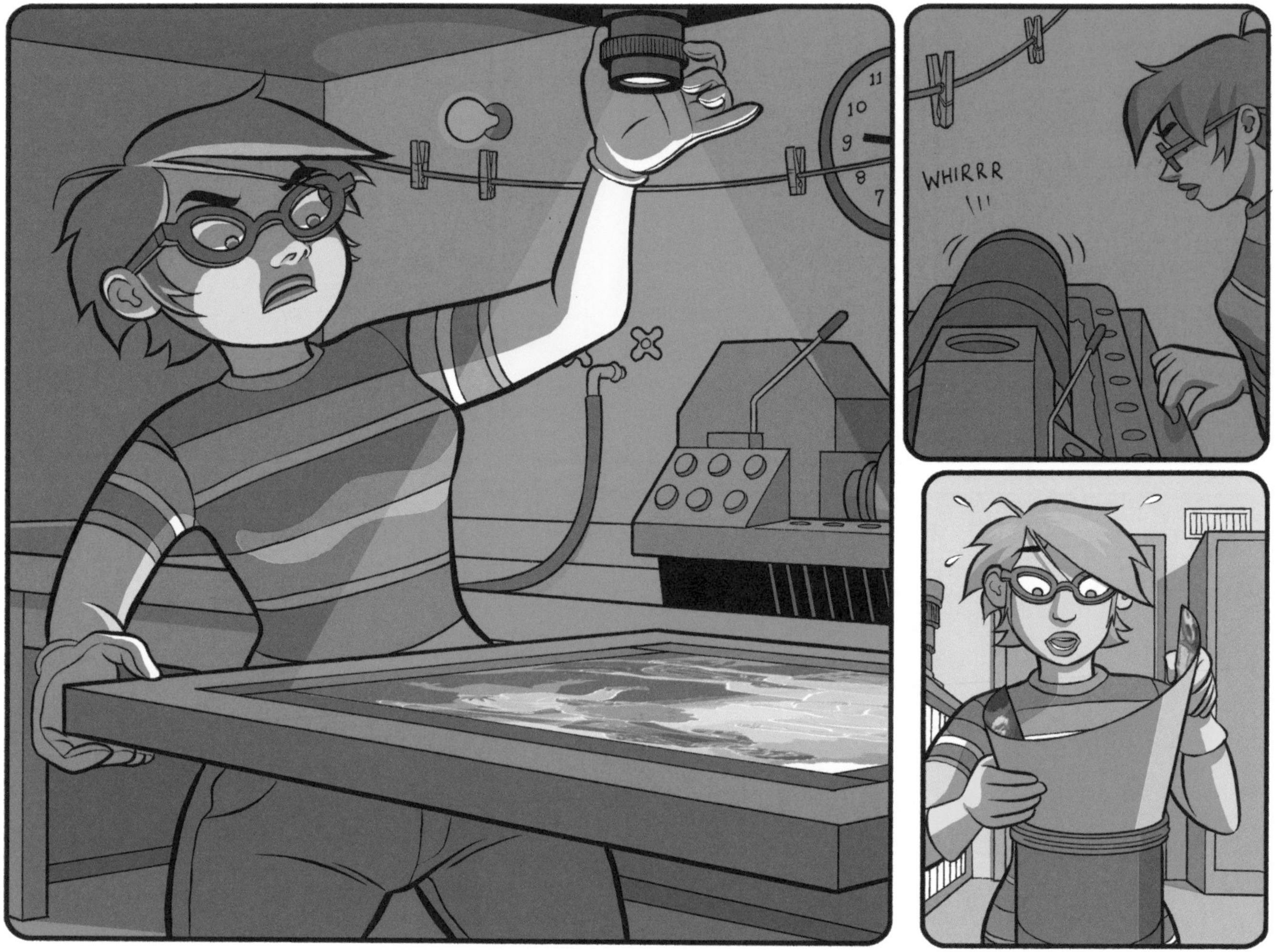
WHIRRR

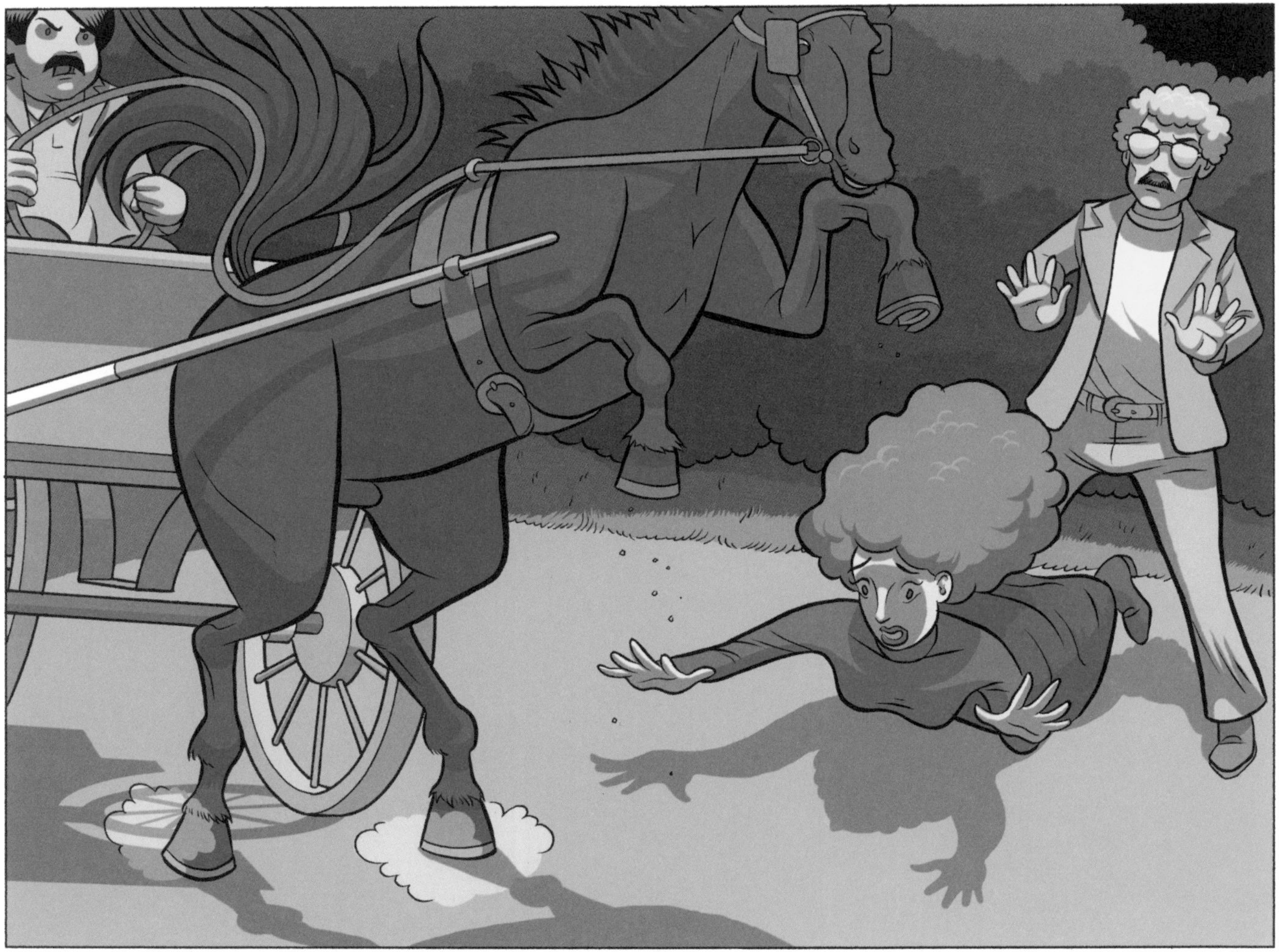

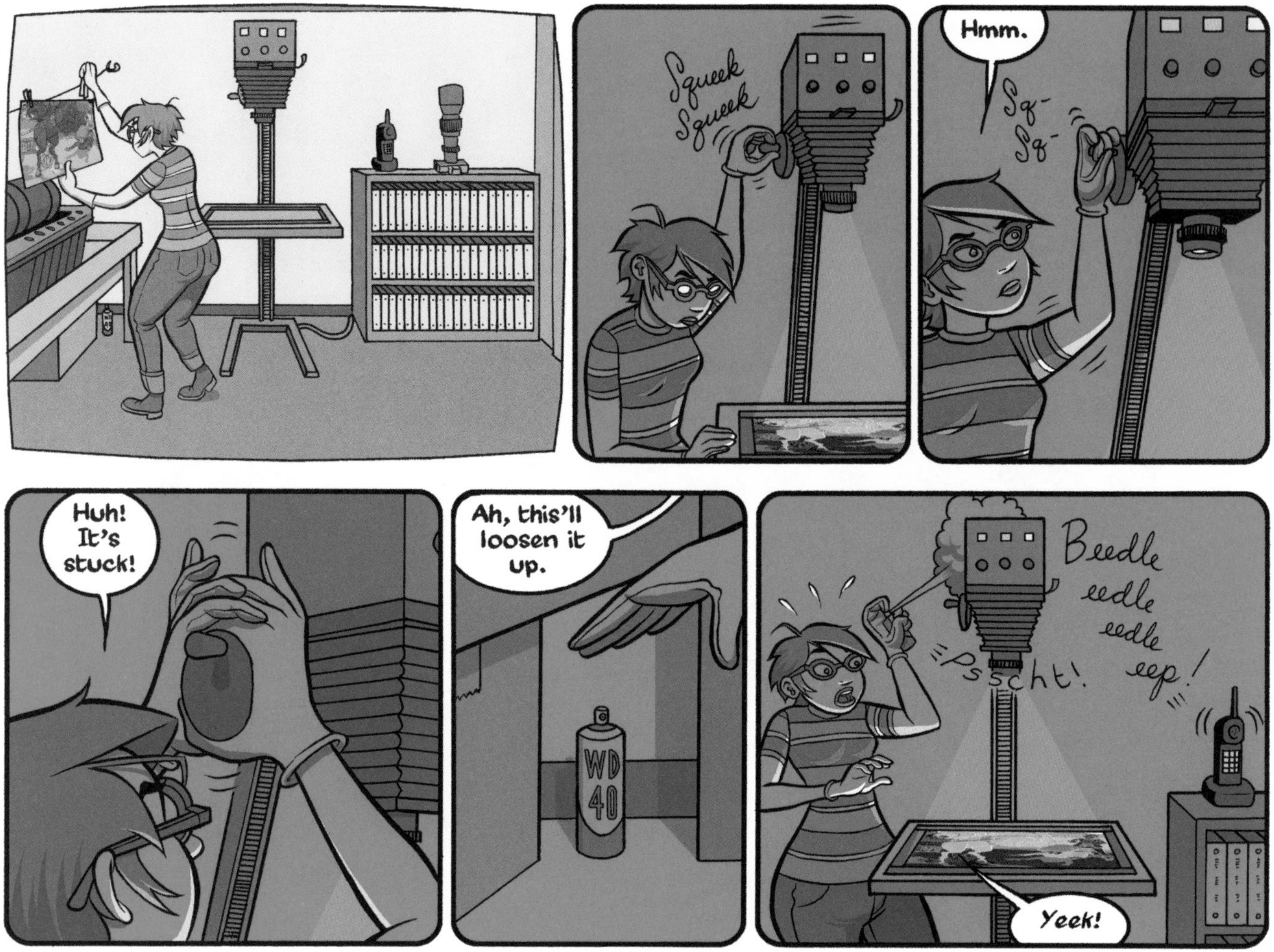
Squeek
Squeek
Hmm.
Sq-
Sq-
Huh! It's stuck!
Ah, this'll loosen it up.
WD 40
Beedle eedle eedle eep!
Psscht!
Yeek!

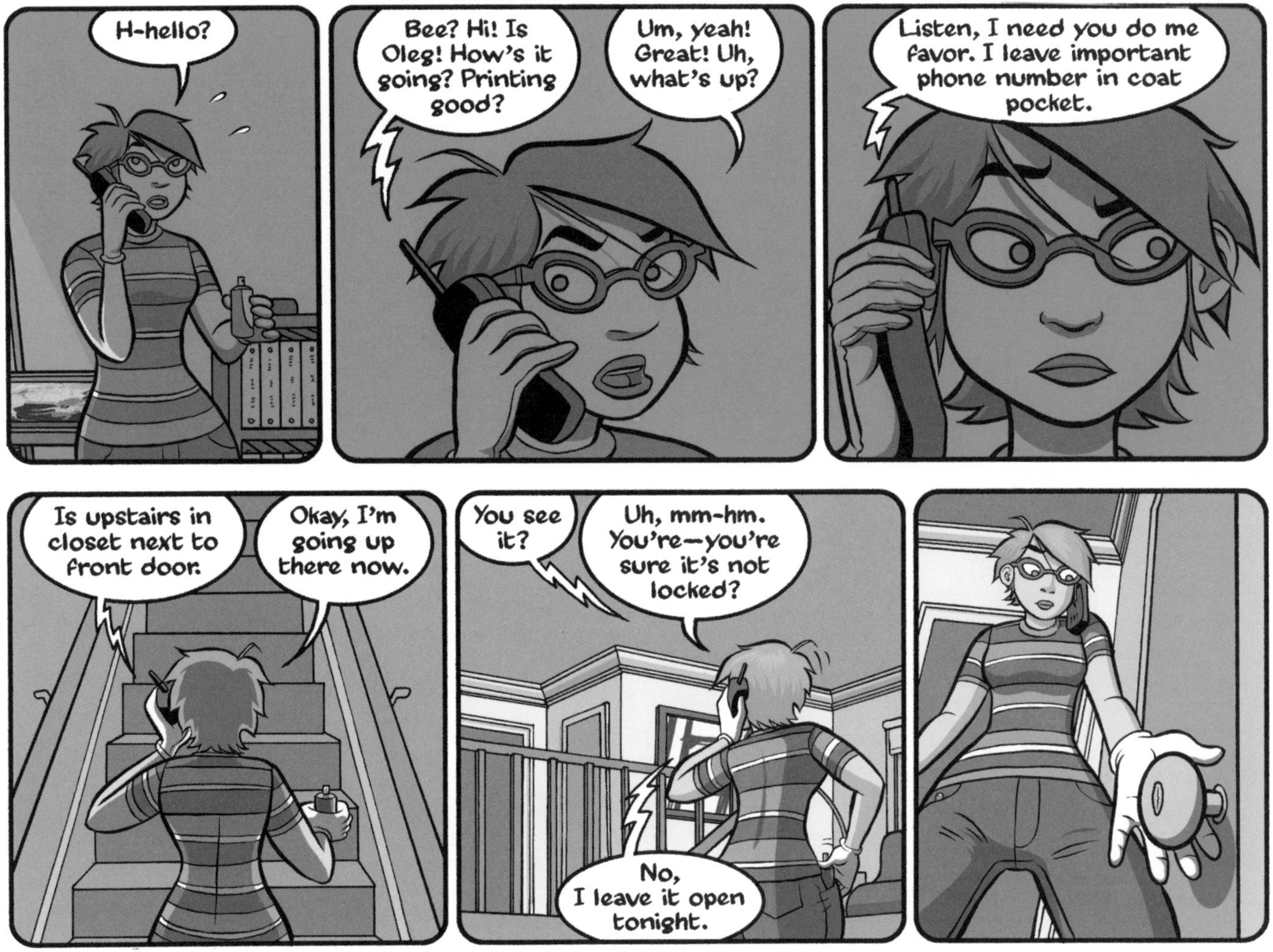
H-hello?
Bee? Hi! Is Oleg! How's it going? Printing good?
Um, yeah! Great! Uh, what's up?
Listen, I need you do me favor. I leave important phone number in coat pocket.
Is upstairs in closet next to front door.
Okay, I'm going up there now.
You see it?
Uh, mm-hm. You're—you're sure it's not locked?
No, I leave it open tonight.

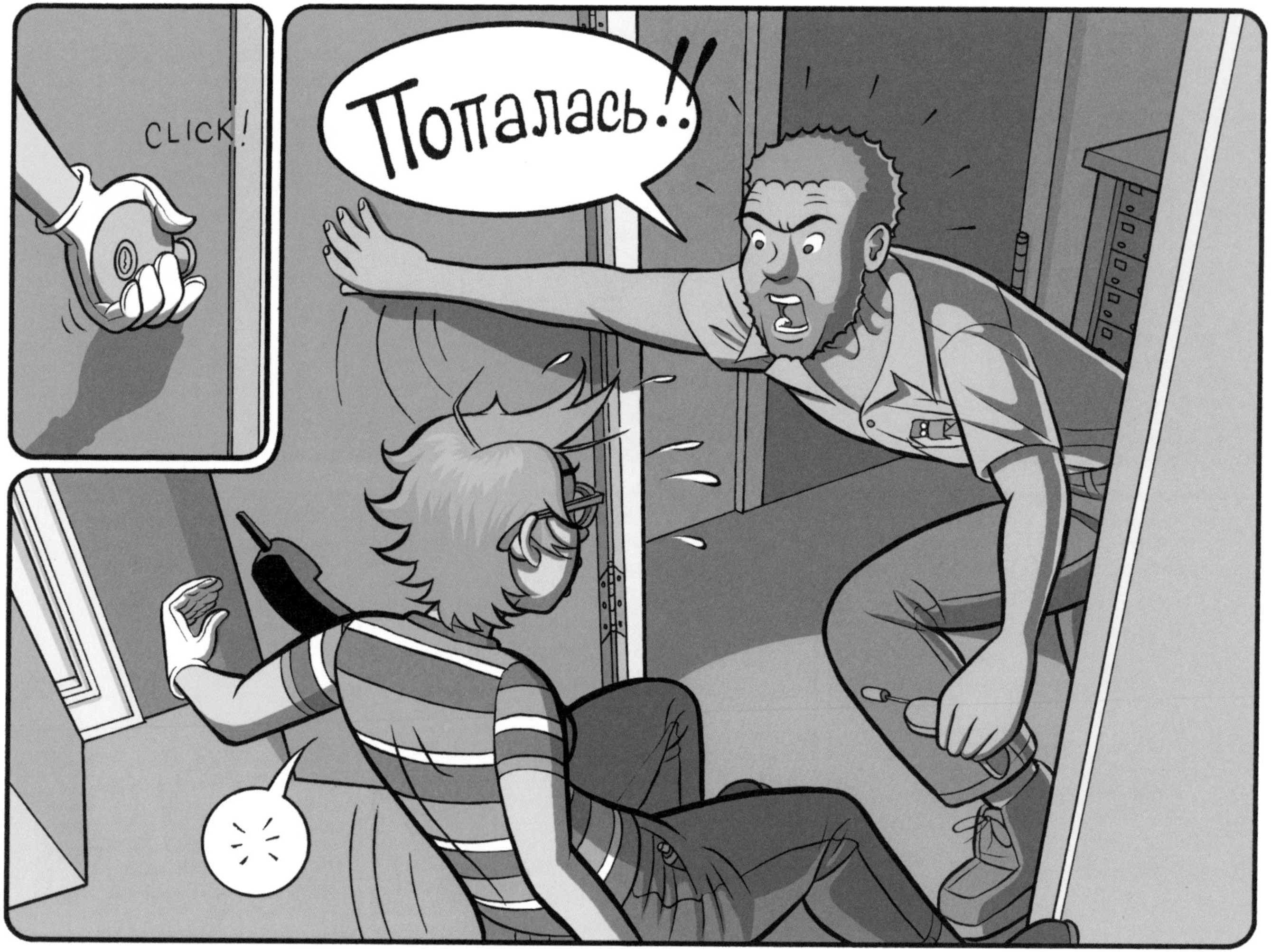
CLICK!
Попалась!!

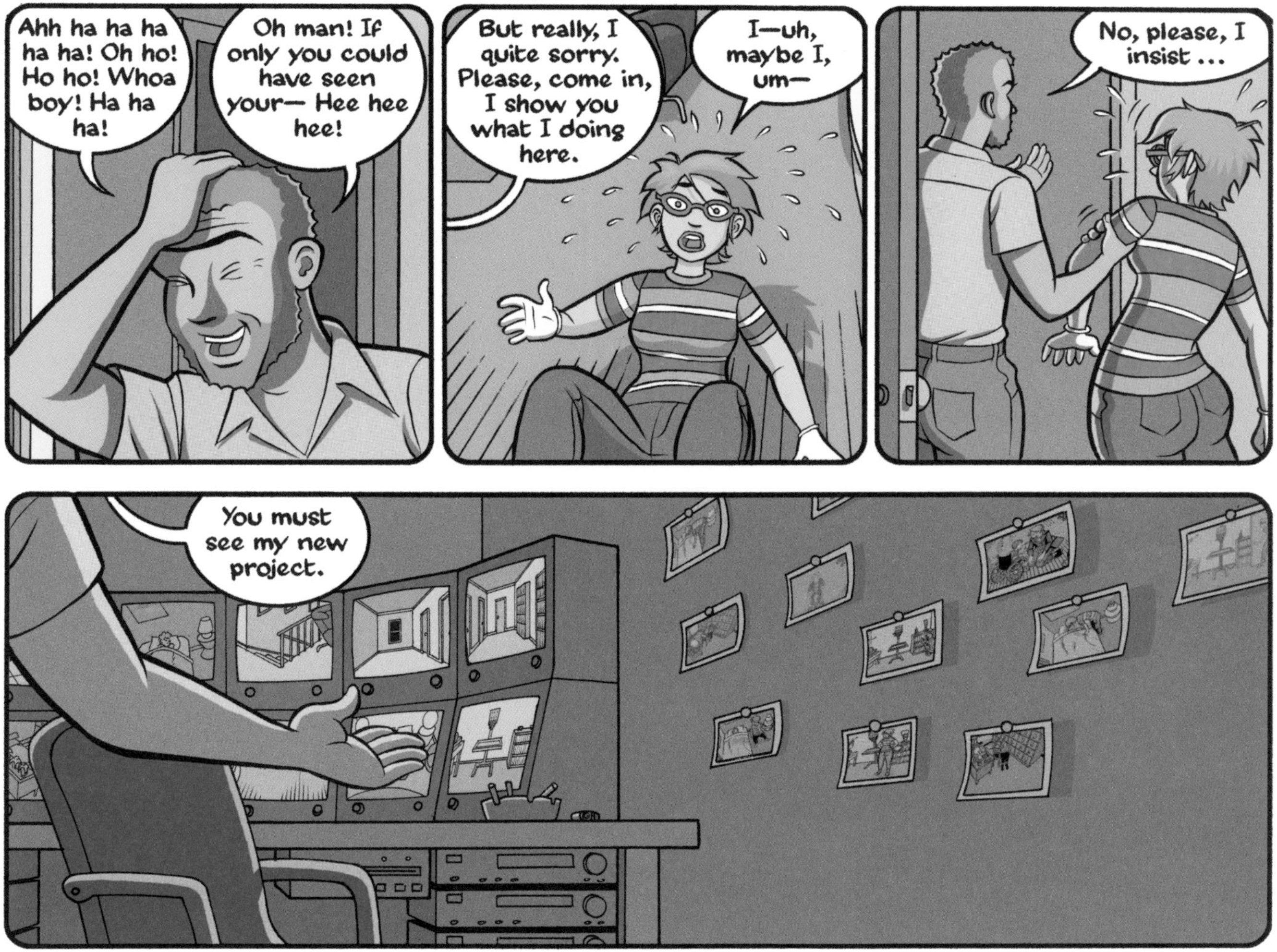
Ahh ha ha ha ha ha! Oh ho! Ho ho! Whoa boy! Ha ha ha!
Oh man! If only you could have seen your— Hee hee hee!
But really, I quite sorry. Please, come in, I show you what I doing here.
I—uh, maybe I, um—
No, please, I insist ...
You must see my new project.

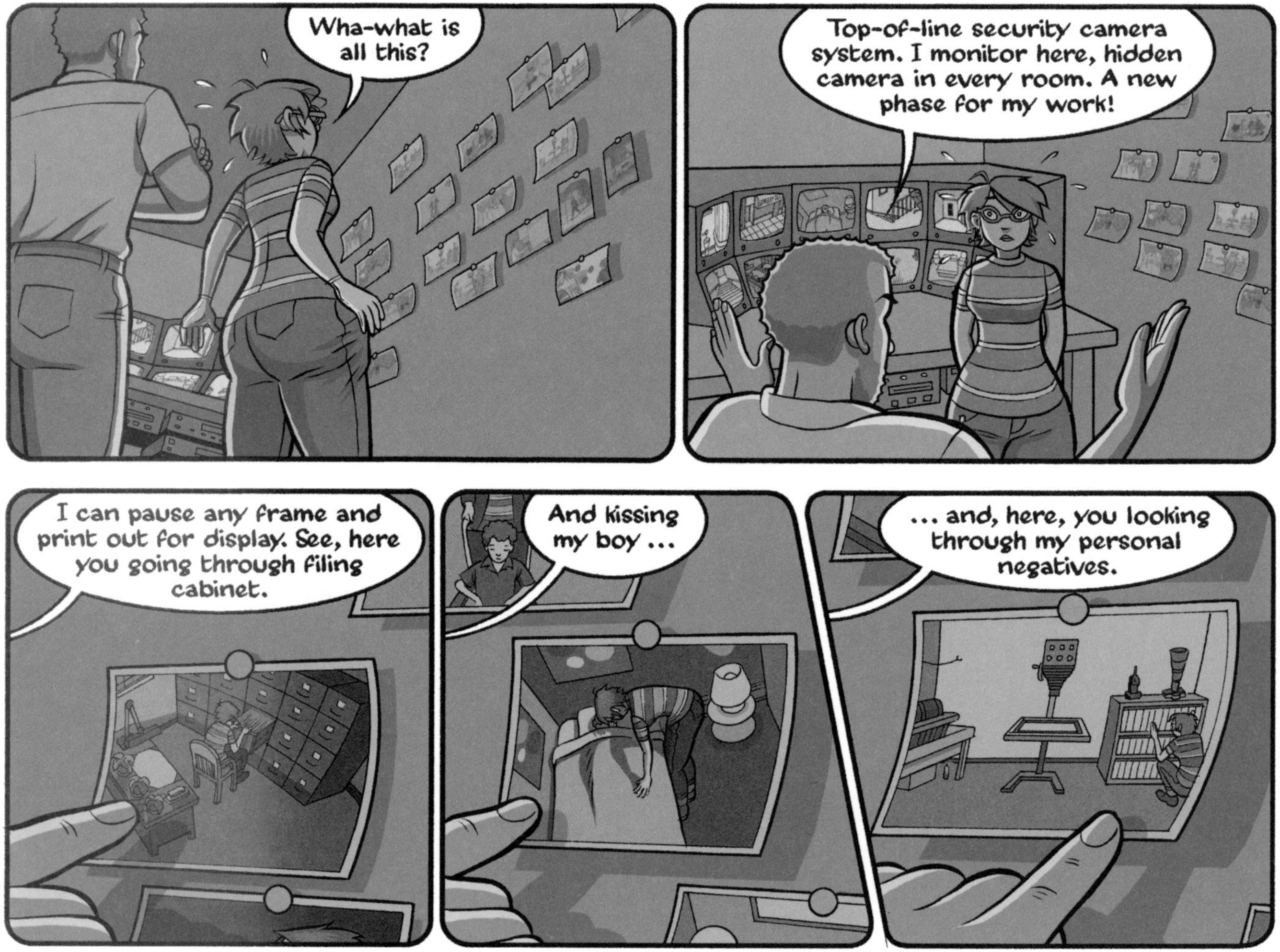
Wha-what is all this?
Top-of-line security camera system. I monitor here, hidden camera in every room. A new phase for my work!
I can pause any frame and print out for display. See, here you going through filing cabinet.
And kissing my boy ...
... and, here, you looking through my personal negatives.

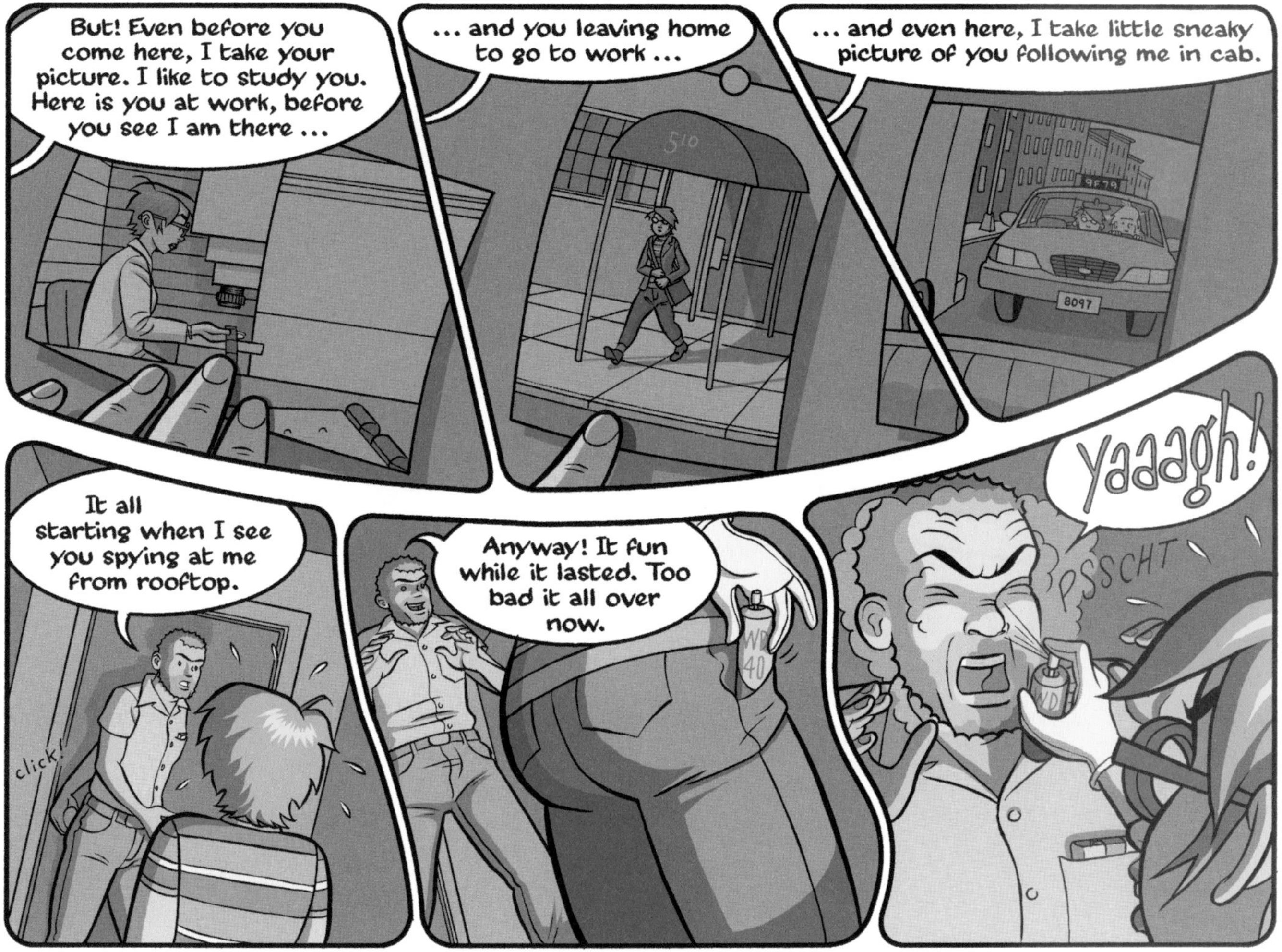

But! Even before you come here, I take your picture. I like to study you. Here is you at work, before you see I am there . . .
. . . and you leaving home to go to work . . .
510
. . . and even here, I take little sneaky picture of you following me in cab.
9F79
8097
It all starting when I see you spying at me from rooftop.
click!
Anyway! It fun while it lasted. Too bad it all over now.
WD 40
yaaagh!
PSSCHT

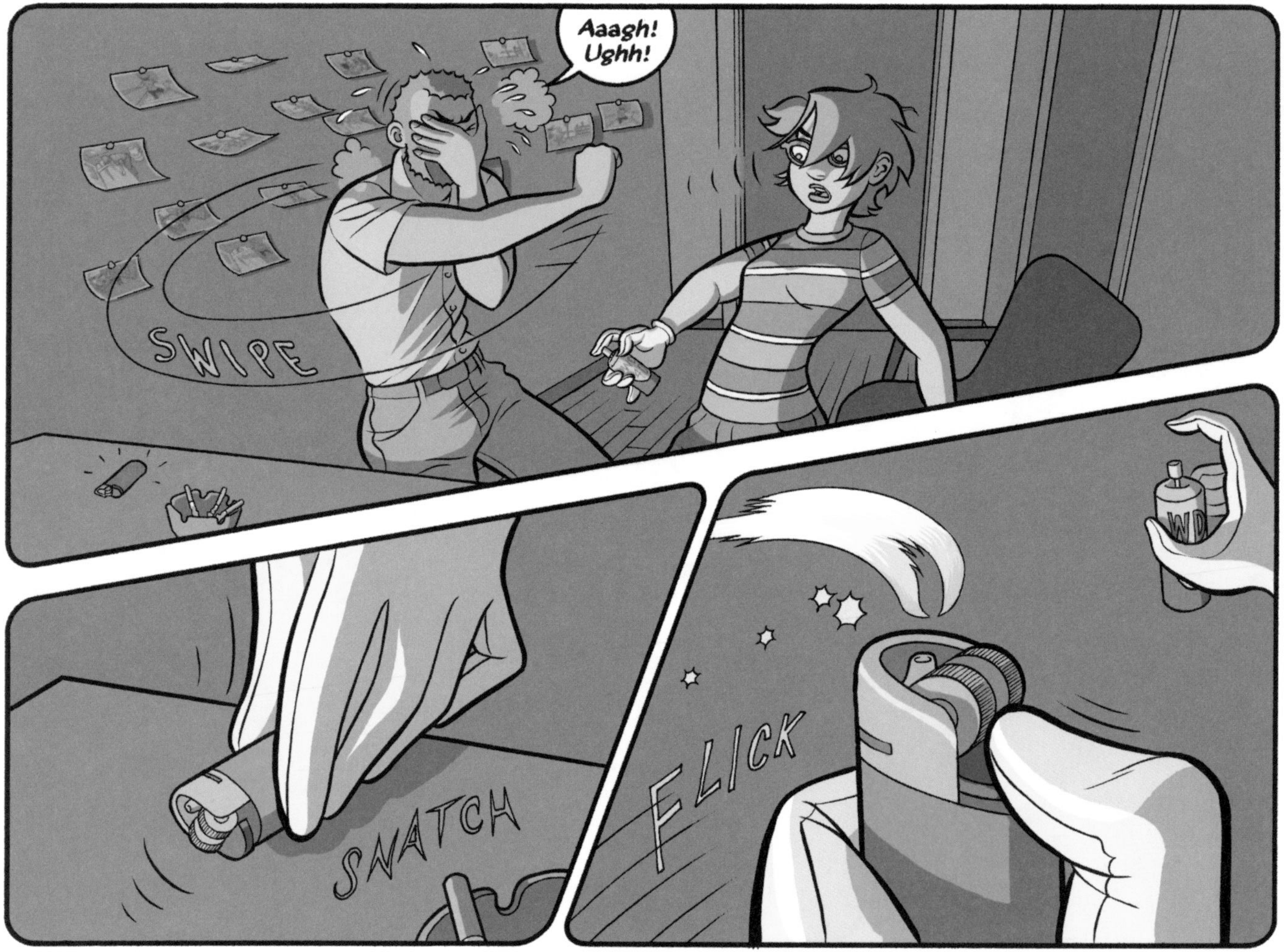
Aaagh!
Ughh!
SWIPE
SNATCH
FLICK
WD

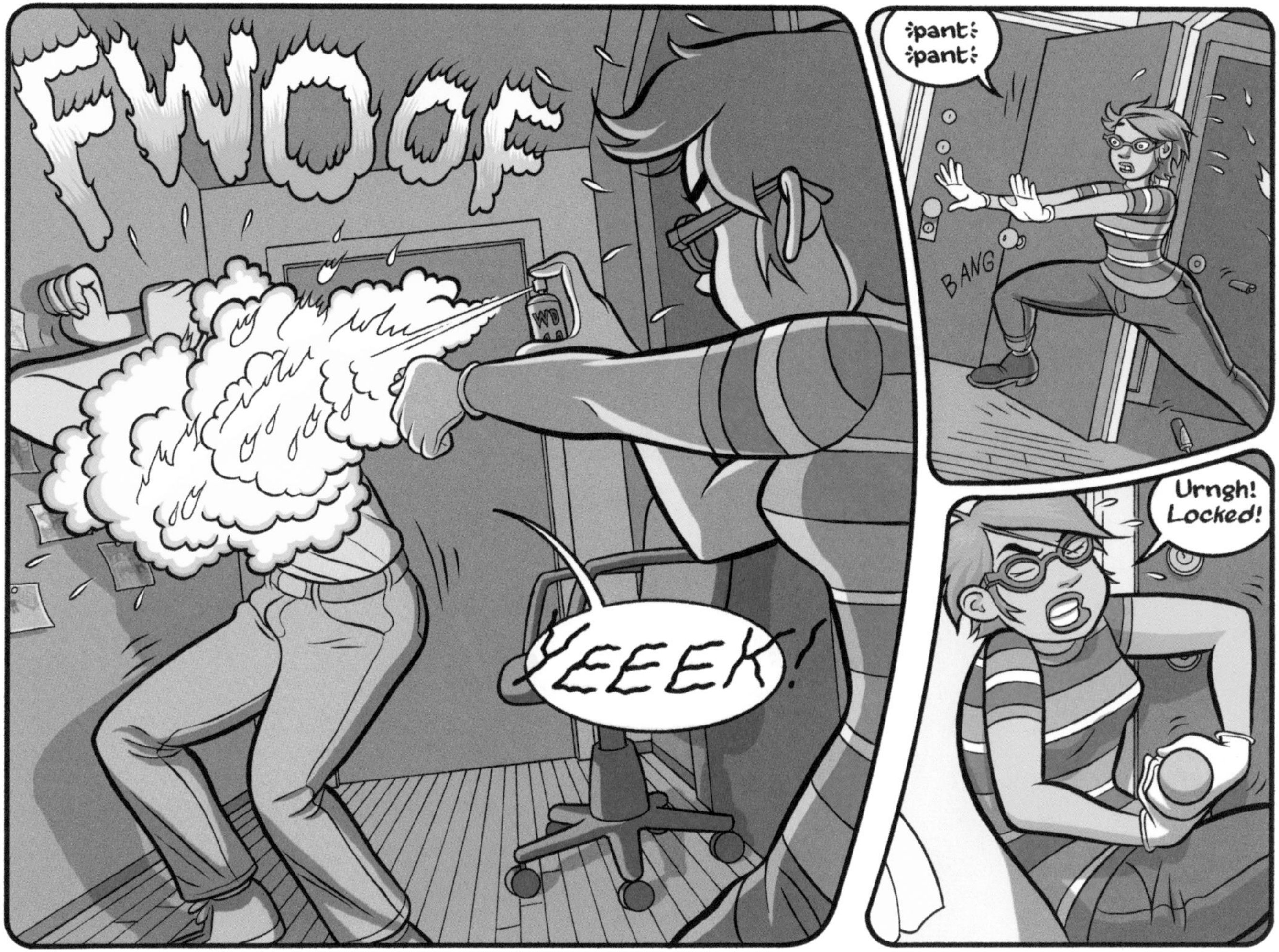
FWOOF
WD
YEEEK!
pant pant
BANG
Urngh! Locked!

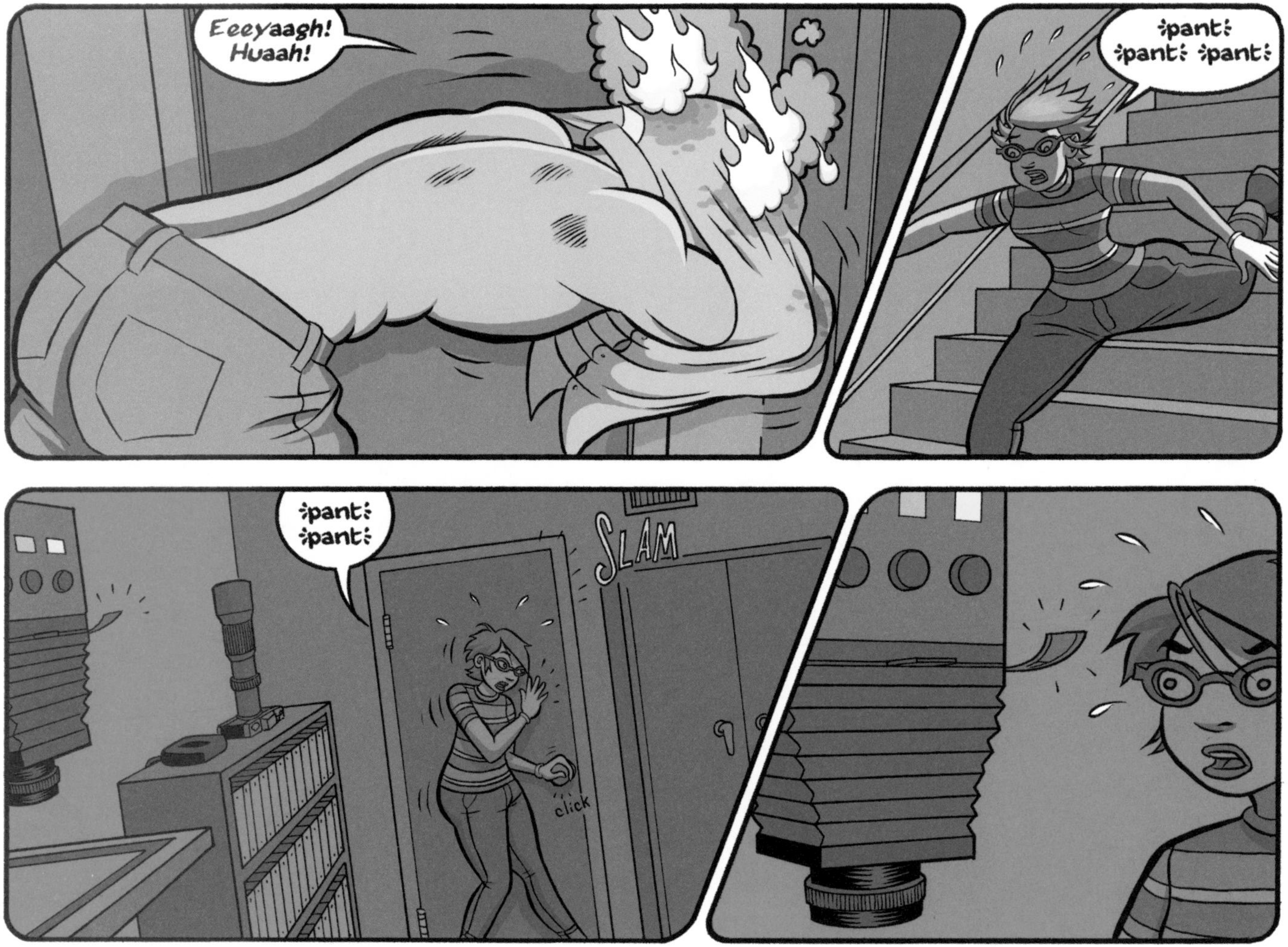
Eeeyaagh!
Huaah!
pant
pant pant
pant
pant
SLAM
click

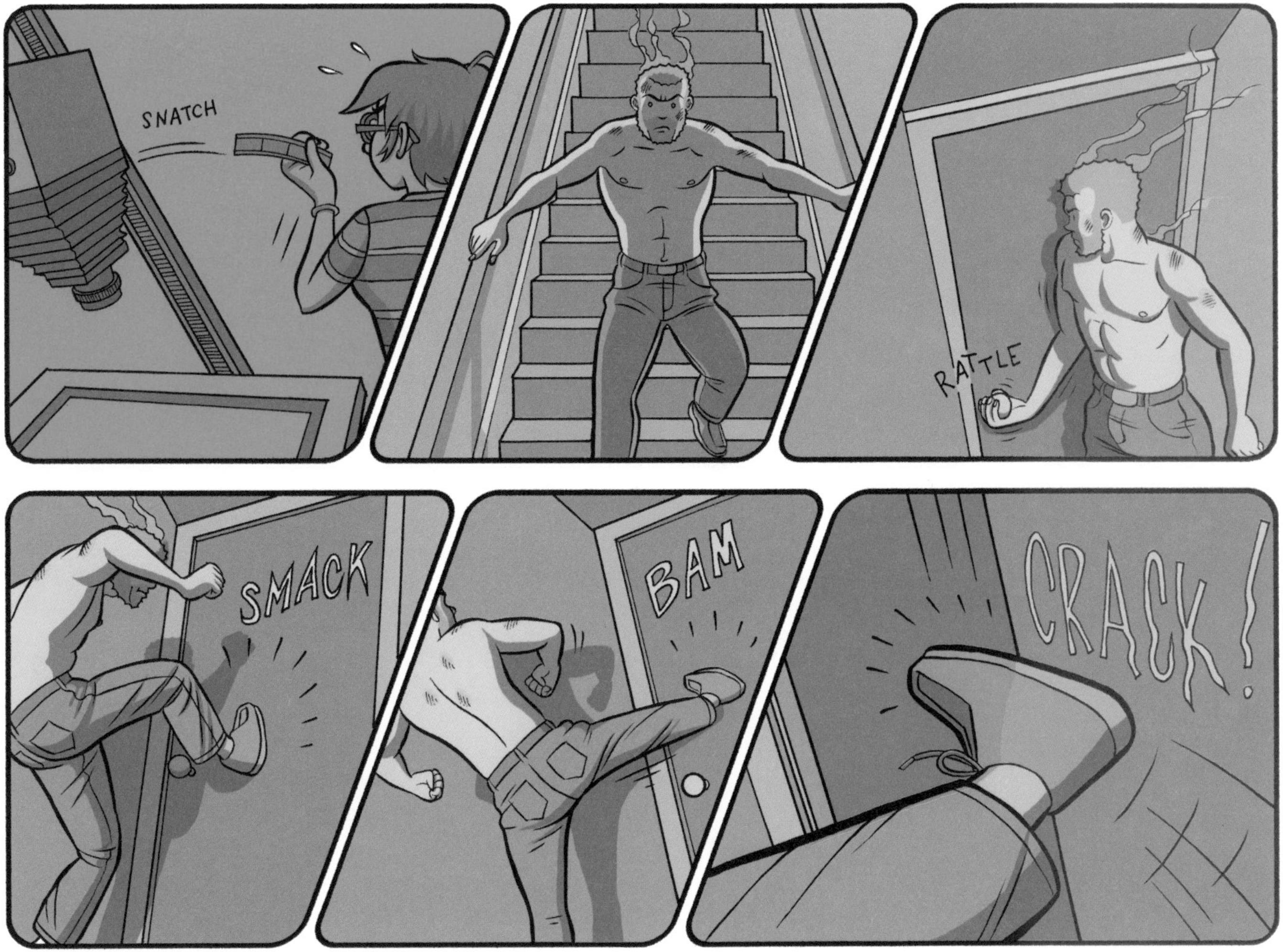
SNATCH
RATTLE
SMACK
BAM
CRACK!

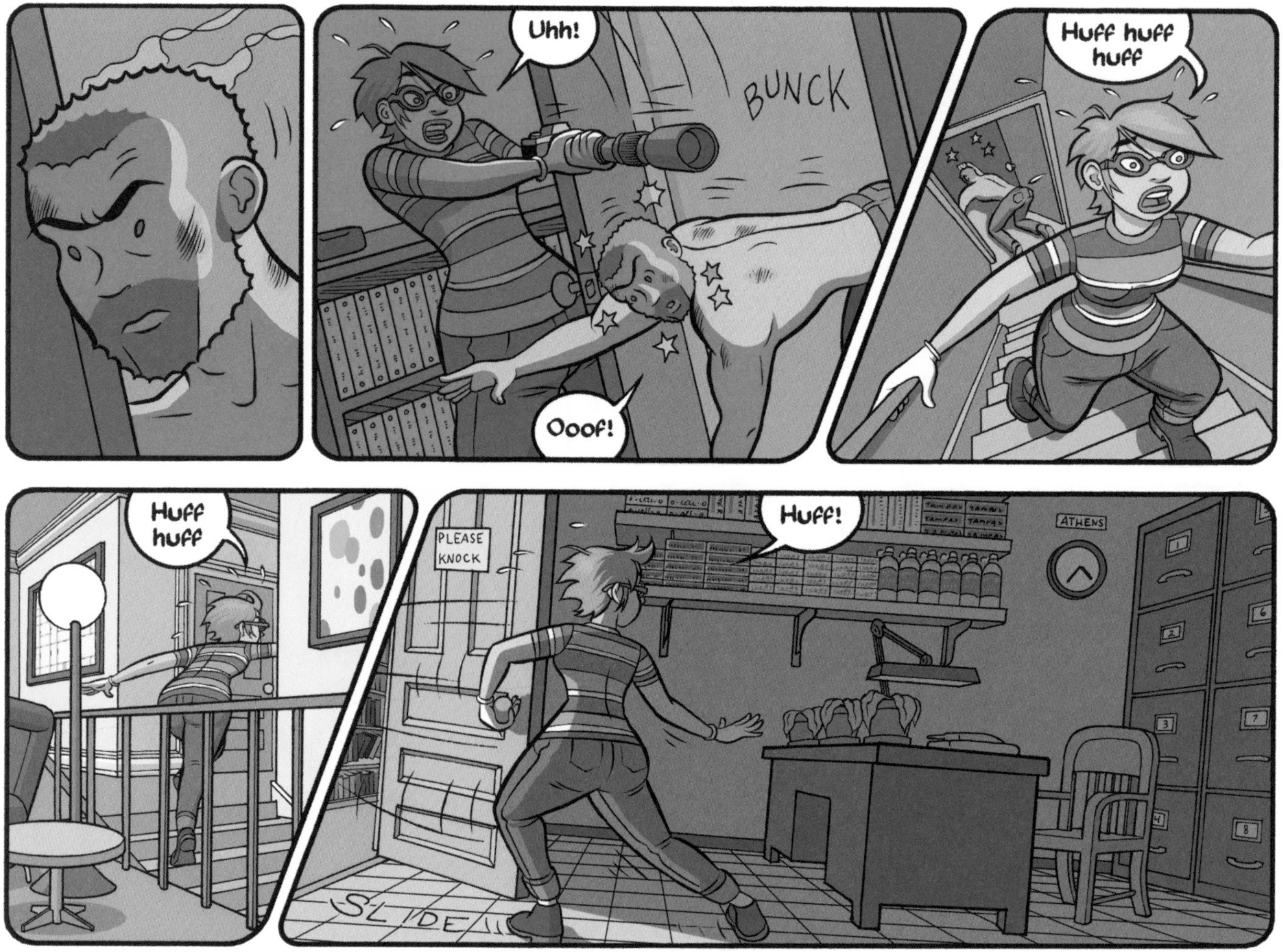
Uhh!
BUNCK
Ooof!
Huff huff huff
Huff huff
PLEASE KNOCK
Huff!
ATHENS
SLIDE

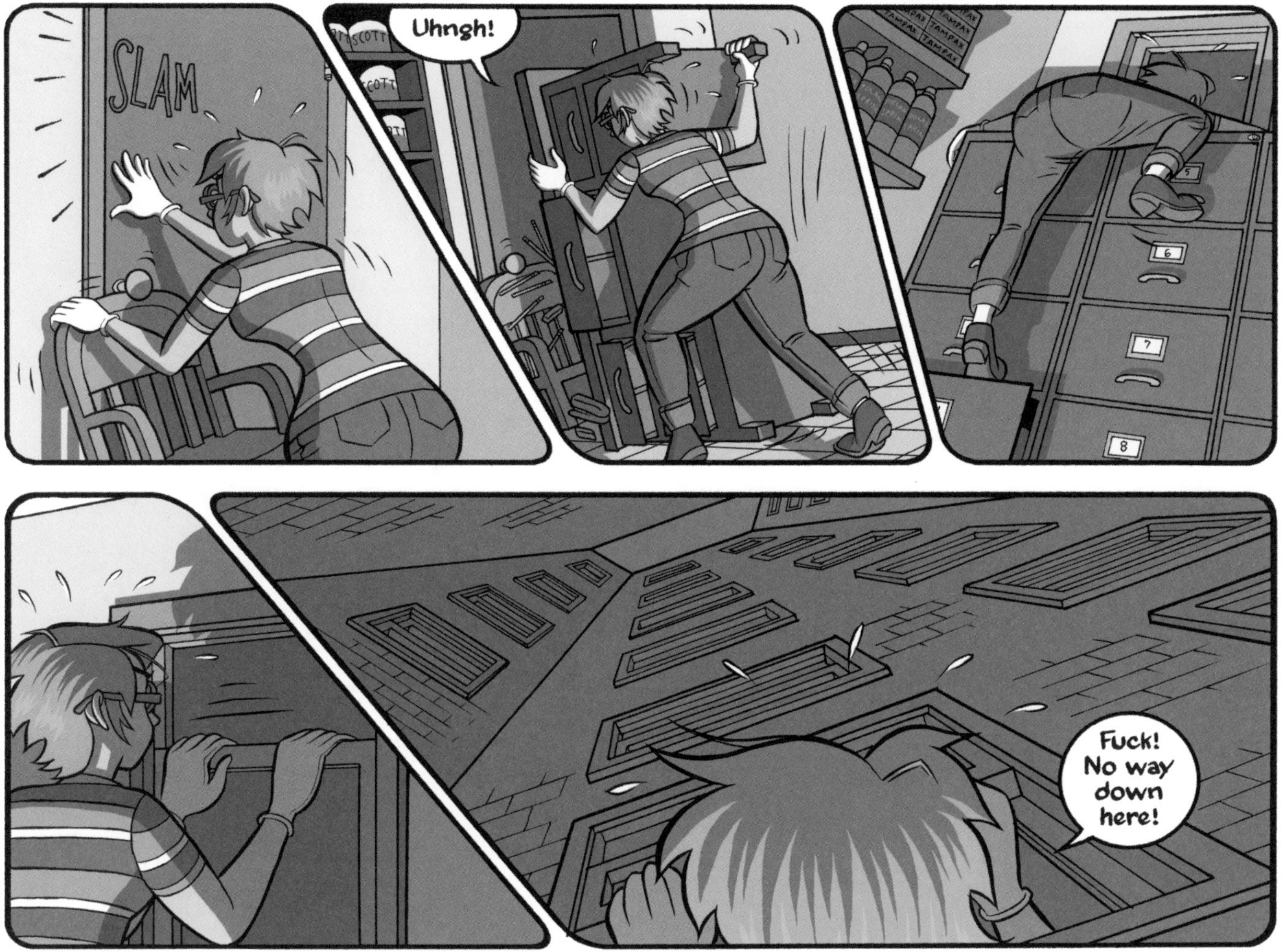
SLAM
Uhngh!
TAMPAX
SCOTT
5
6
7
8
Fuck! No way down here!

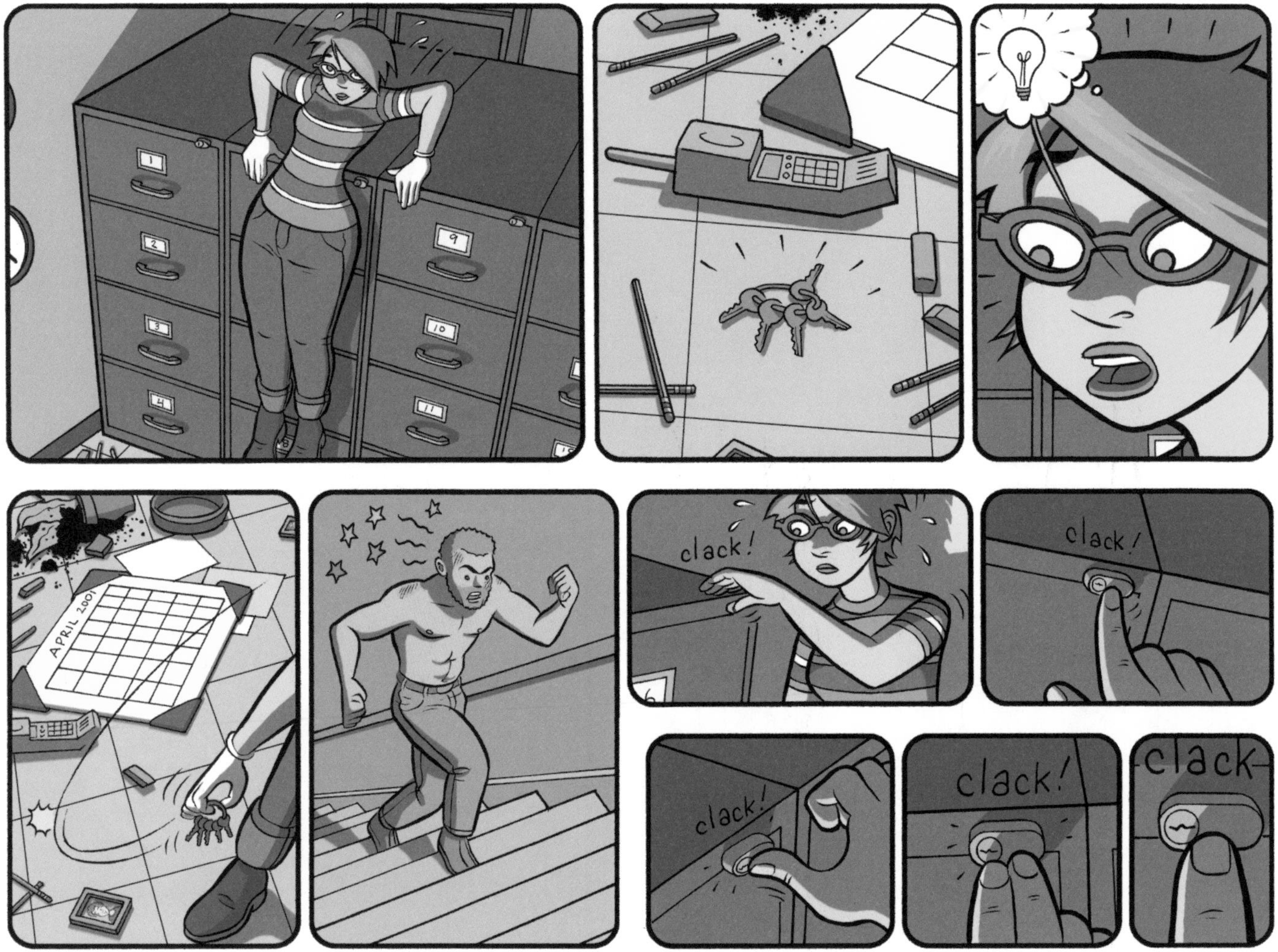
APRIL 2001
clack!
clack!
clack!
clack!
clack

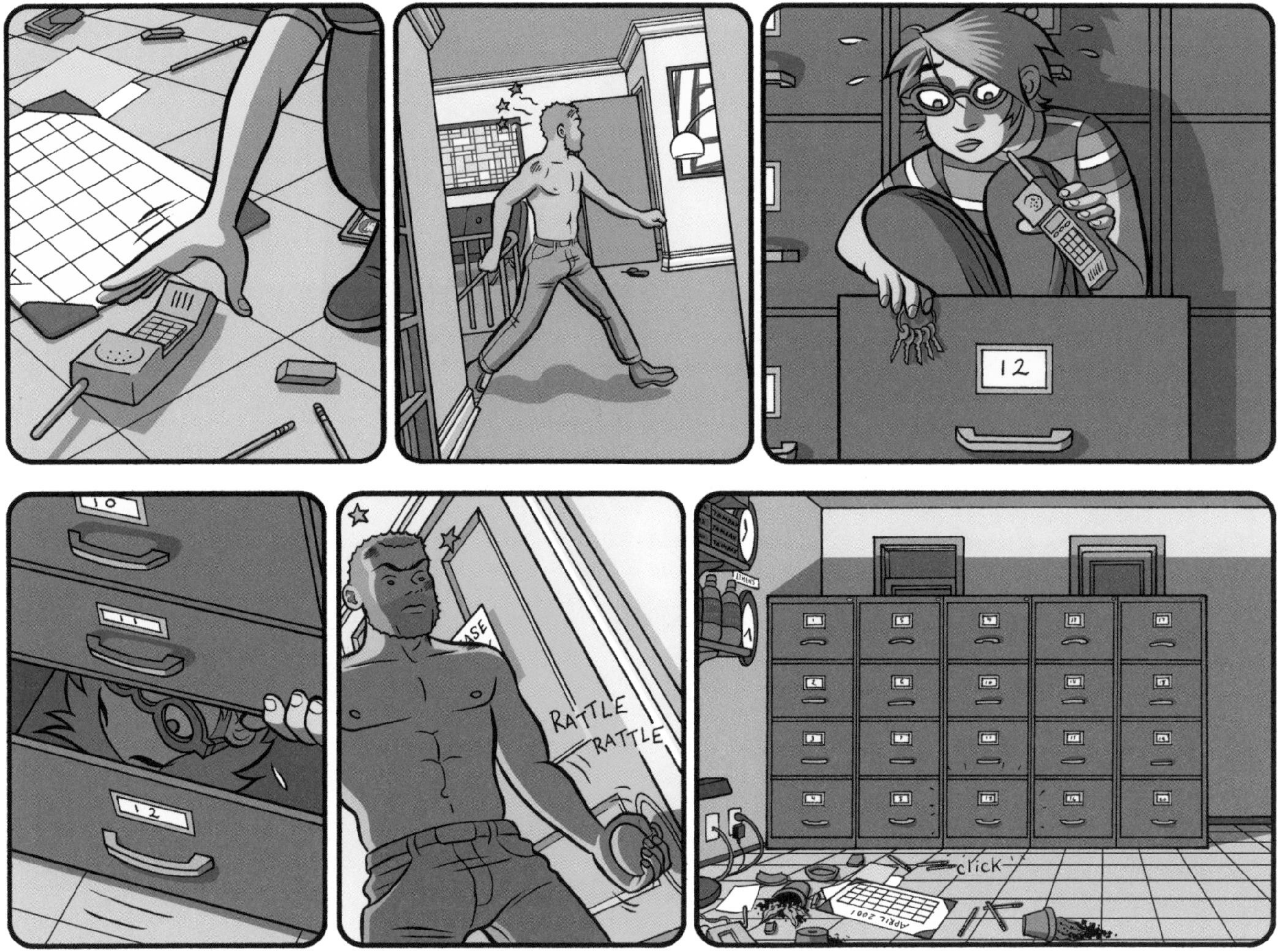
12
12
RATTLE
RATTLE
click
APRIL 2001

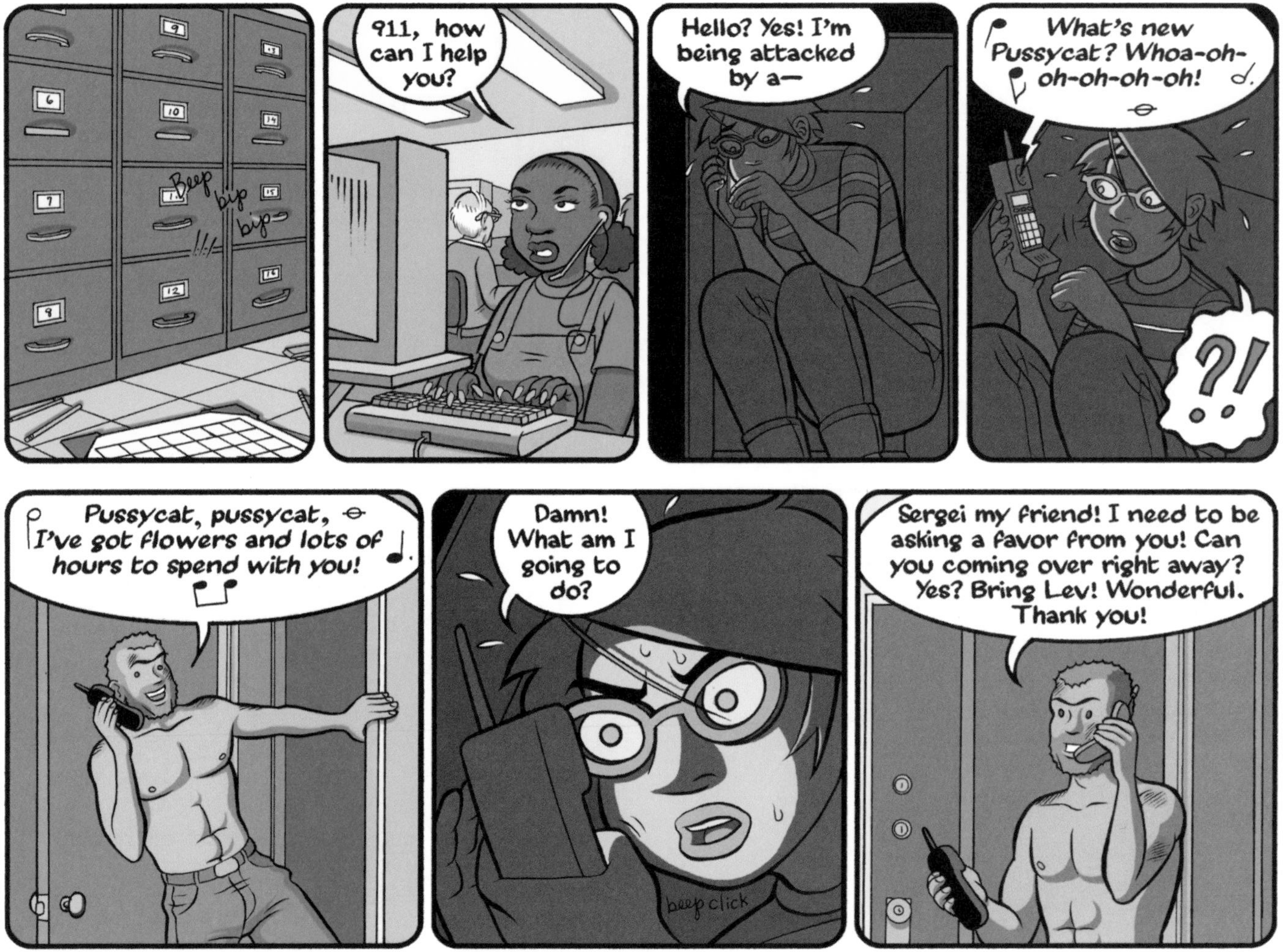
Beep bip bip
911, how can I help you?
Hello? Yes! I'm being attacked by a—
What's new Pussycat? Whoa-oh-oh-oh-oh-oh!
?!
Pussycat, pussycat, I've got flowers and lots of hours to spend with you!
Damn! What am I going to do?
beep click
Sergei my friend! I need to be asking a favor from you! Can you coming over right away? Yes? Bring Lev! Wonderful. Thank you!

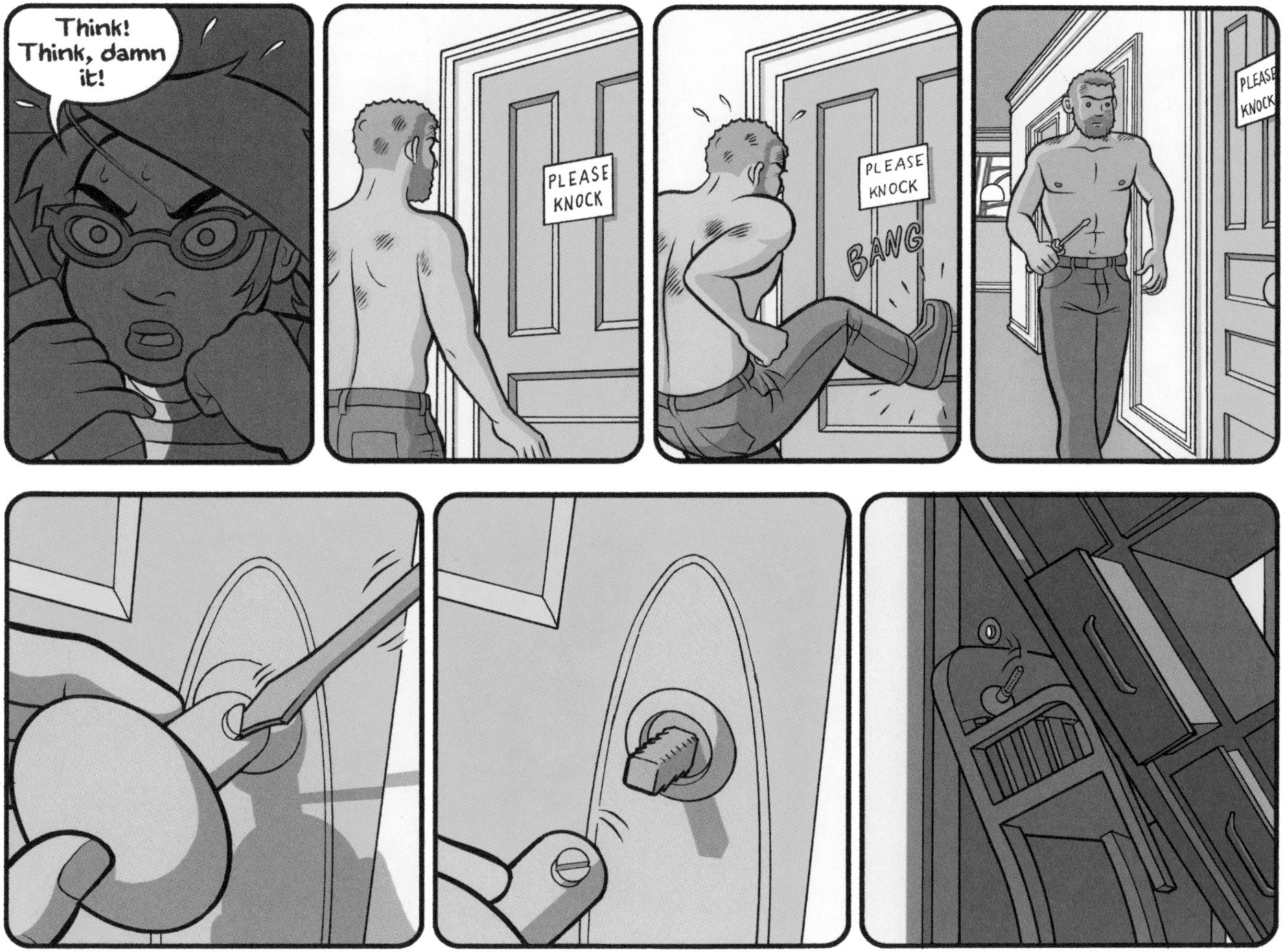
Think! Think, damn it!
PLEASE KNOCK
PLEASE KNOCK
BANG
PLEASE KNOCK

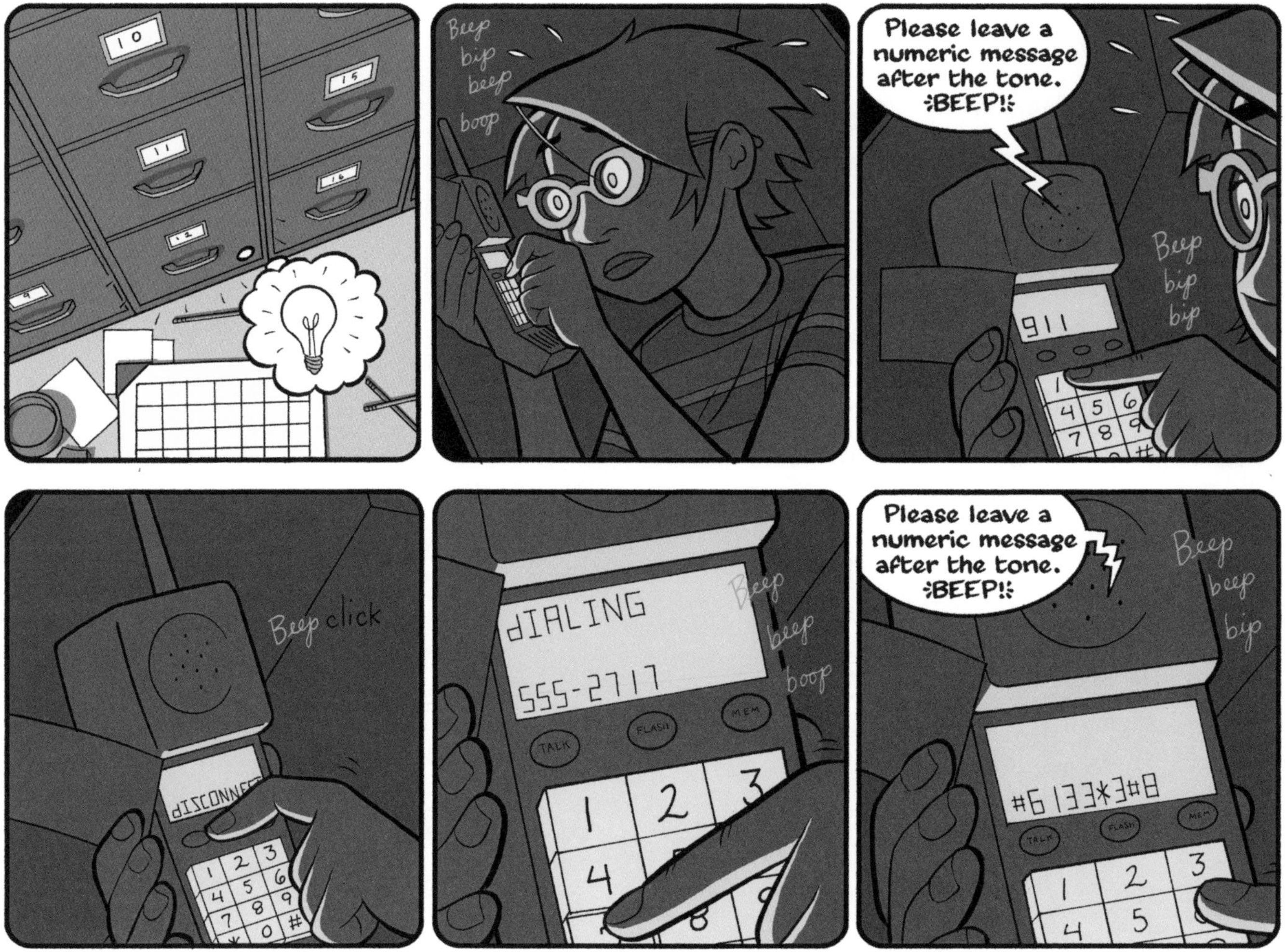
Beep
bip
beep
boop
Please leave a numeric message after the tone. ⁑BEEP!⁑
Beep
bip
bip
911
Beep click
DIALING
555-2717
TALK
FLASH
MEM
Beep
beep
boop
Please leave a numeric message after the tone. ⁑BEEP!⁑
Beep
beep
bip
#6133*3#8

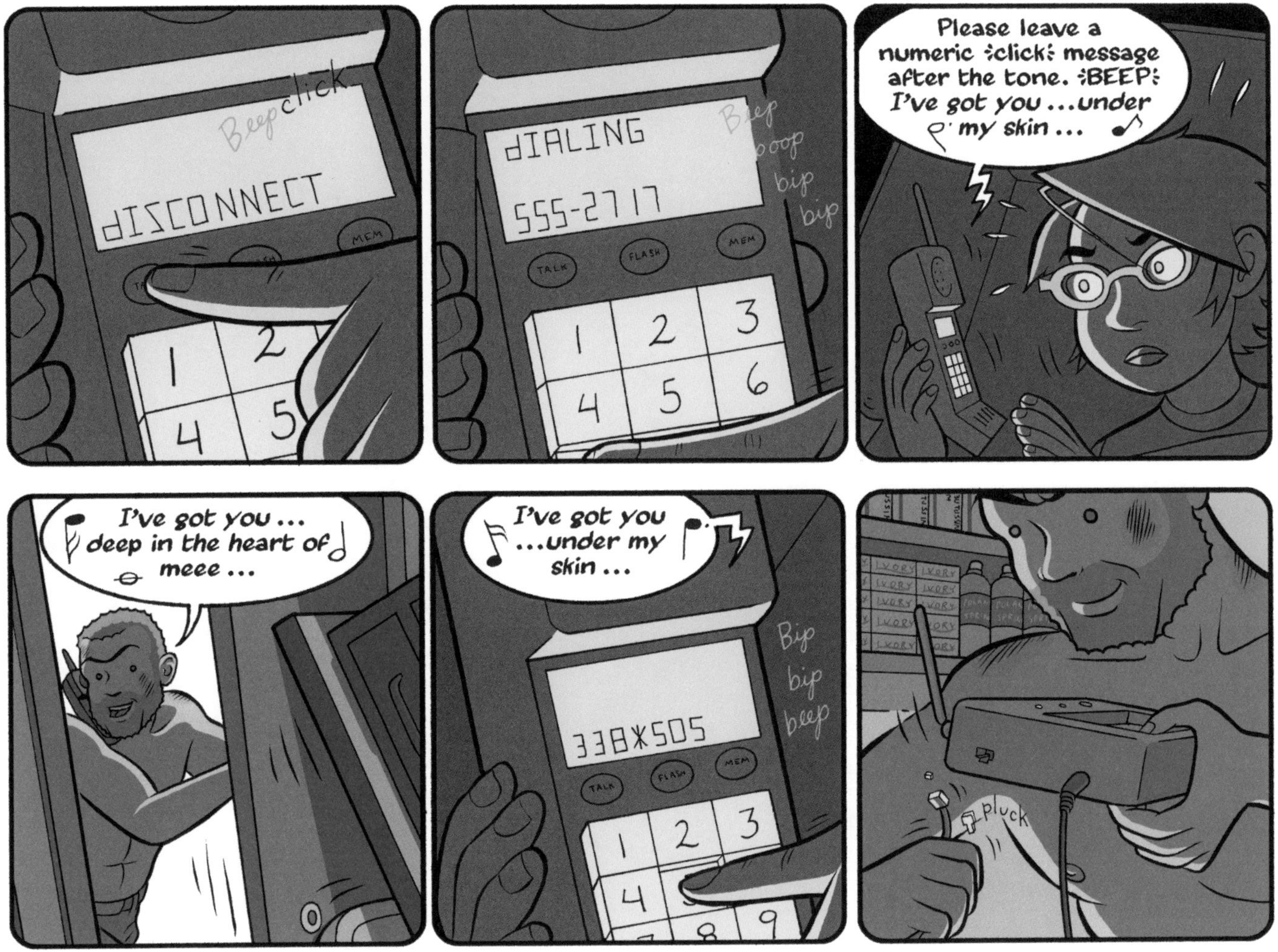
Beep click
DISCONNECT
DIALING
555-2717
Beep boop bip bip
Please leave a numeric :click: message after the tone. :BEEP: I've got you ...under my skin ...
I've got you ... deep in the heart of meee ...
I've got you ...under my skin ...
338*505
Bip bip beep
pluck

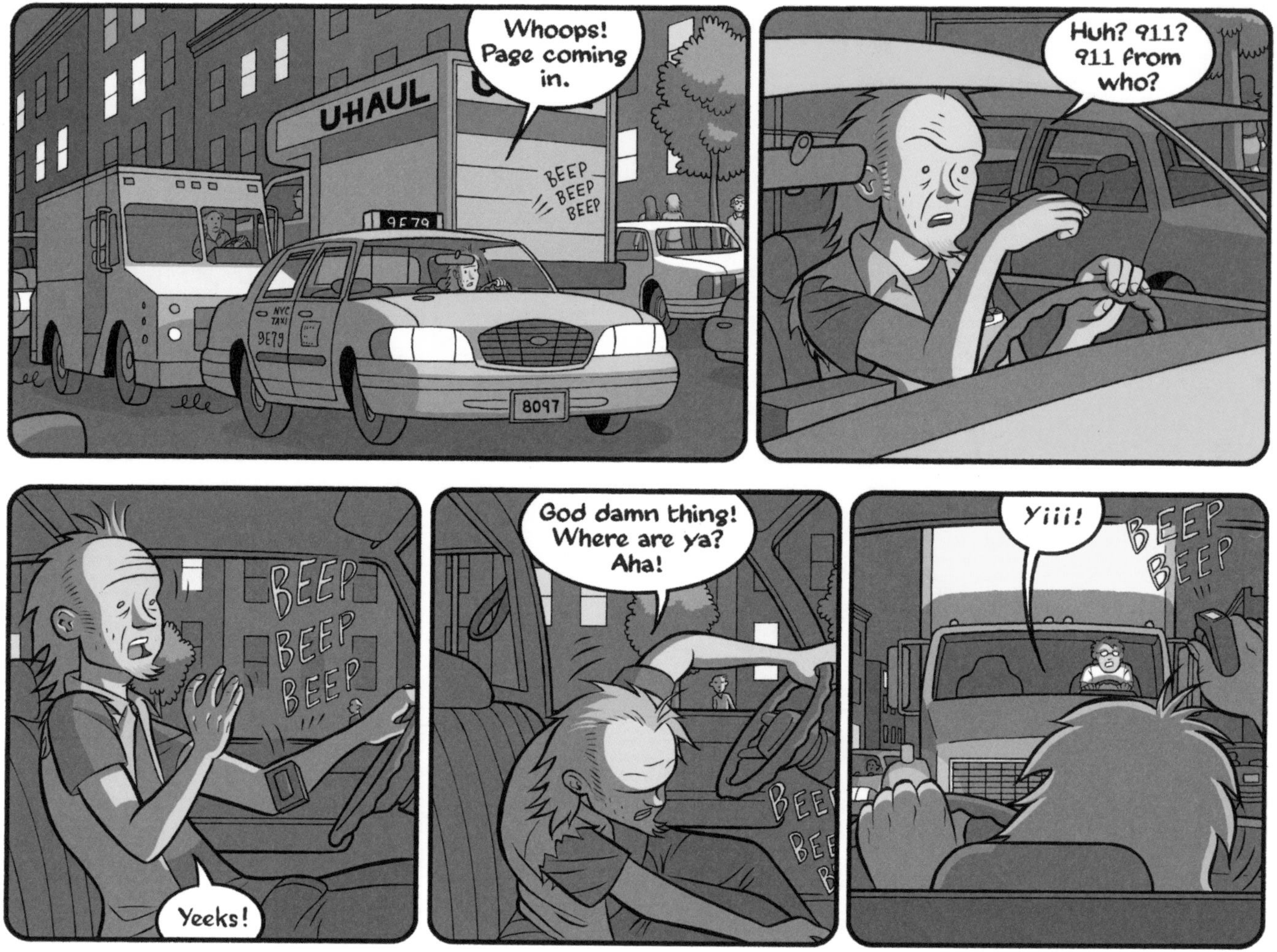
Whoops! Page coming in.
U-HAUL
BEEP BEEP BEEP
9E79
NYC TAXI
9E79
8097
Huh? 911? 911 from who?
BEEP BEEP BEEP
Yeeks!
God damn thing! Where are ya? Aha!
Yiii!
BEEP BEEP

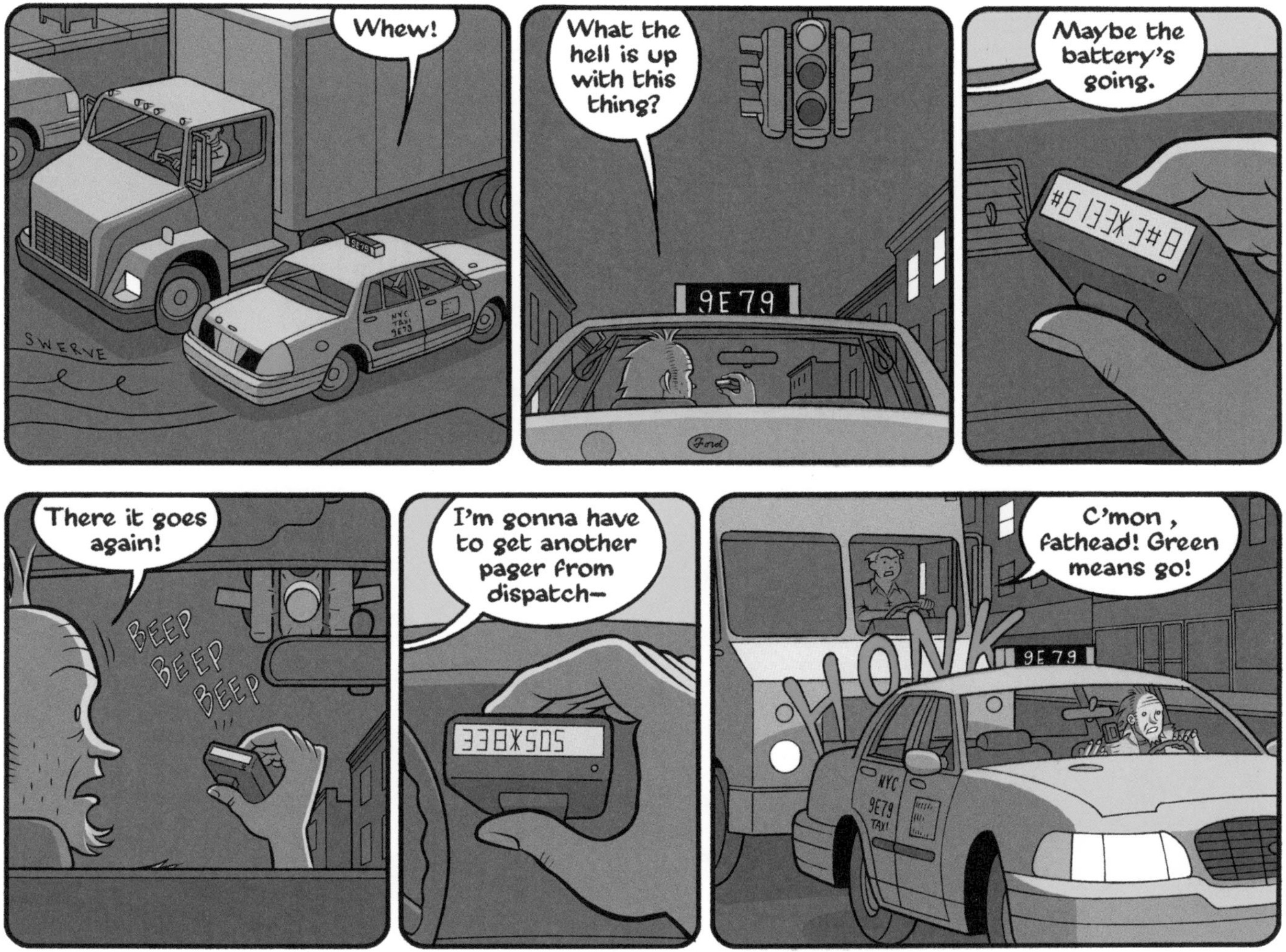
Whew!
SWERVE
What the hell is up with this thing?
Maybe the battery's going.
There it goes again!
BEEP BEEP BEEP
I'm gonna have to get another pager from dispatch—
C'mon, fathead! Green means go!
HONK

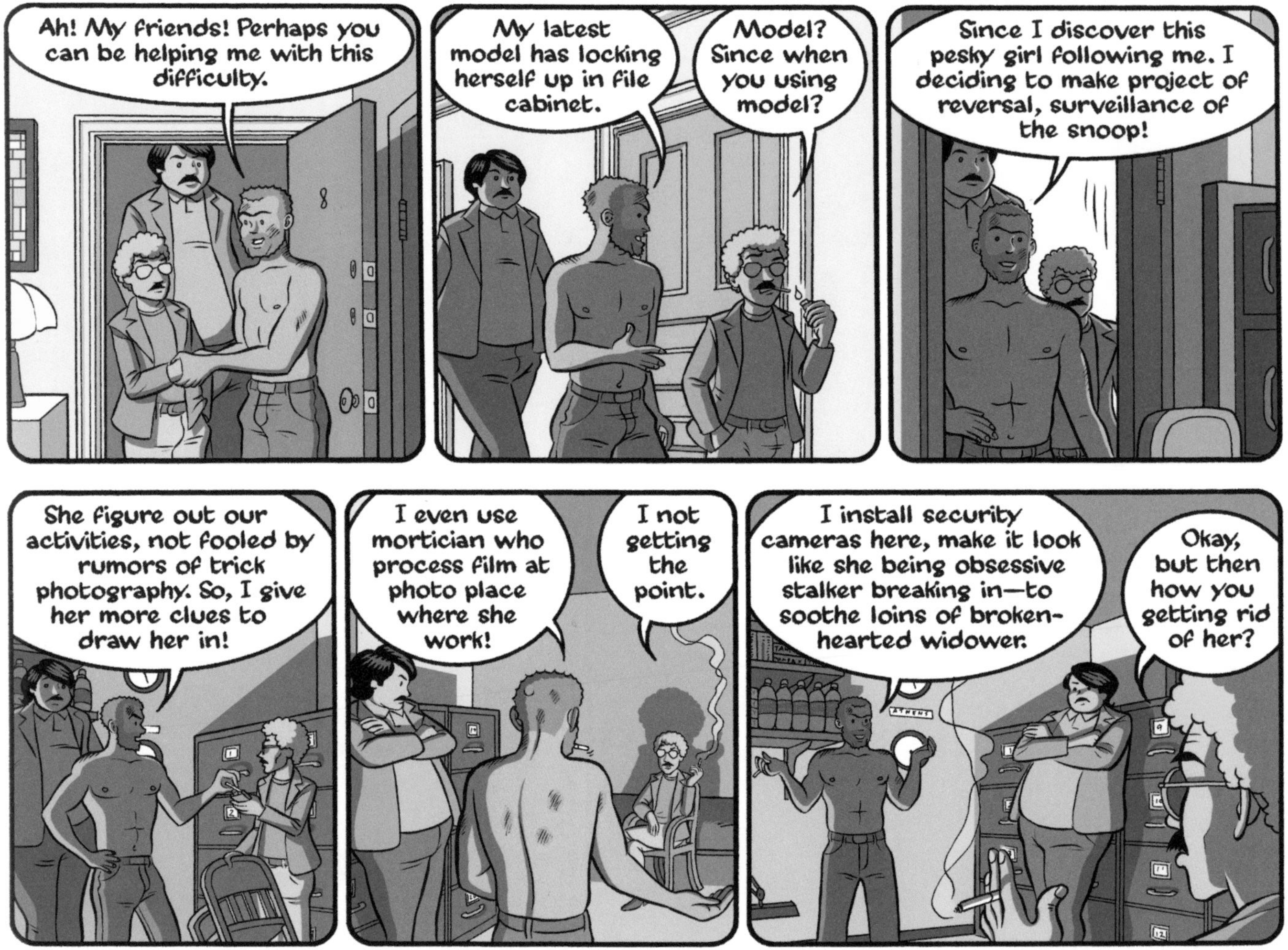
Ah! My friends! Perhaps you can be helping me with this difficulty.
My latest model has locking herself up in file cabinet.
Model? Since when you using model?
Since I discover this pesky girl following me. I deciding to make project of reversal, surveillance of the snoop!
She figure out our activities, not fooled by rumors of trick photography. So, I give her more clues to draw her in!
I even use mortician who process film at photo place where she work!
I not getting the point.
I install security cameras here, make it look like she being obsessive stalker breaking in—to soothe loins of broken-hearted widower.
Okay, but then how you getting rid of her?

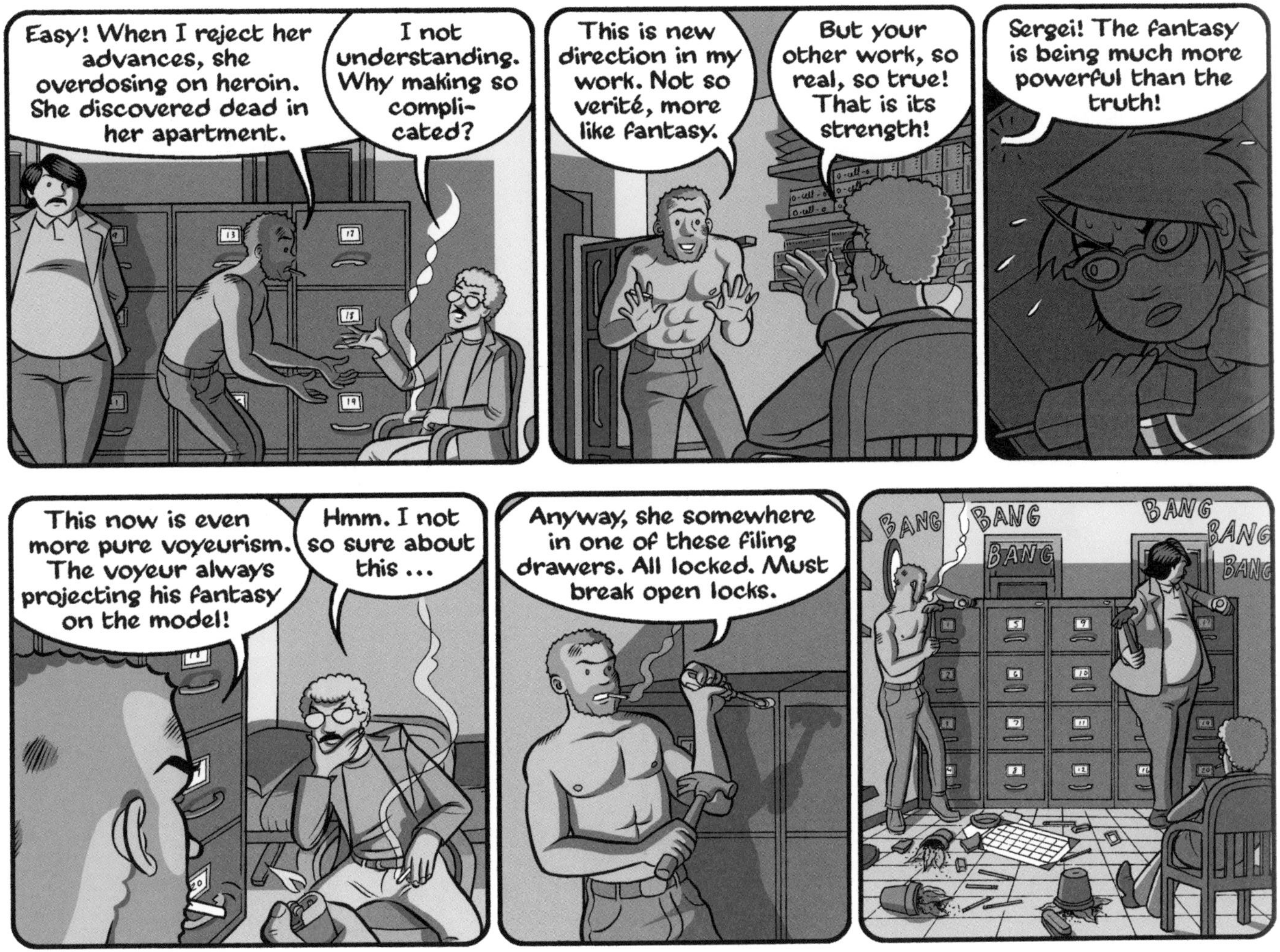
Easy! When I reject her advances, she overdosing on heroin. She discovered dead in her apartment.
I not understanding. Why making so compli-cated?
This is new direction in my work. Not so verité, more like fantasy.
But your other work, so real, so true! That is its strength!
Sergei! The fantasy is being much more powerful than the truth!
This now is even more pure voyeurism. The voyeur always projecting his fantasy on the model!
Hmm. I not so sure about this ...
Anyway, she somewhere in one of these filing drawers. All locked. Must break open locks.
BANG
BANG
BANG
BANG
BANG
BANG

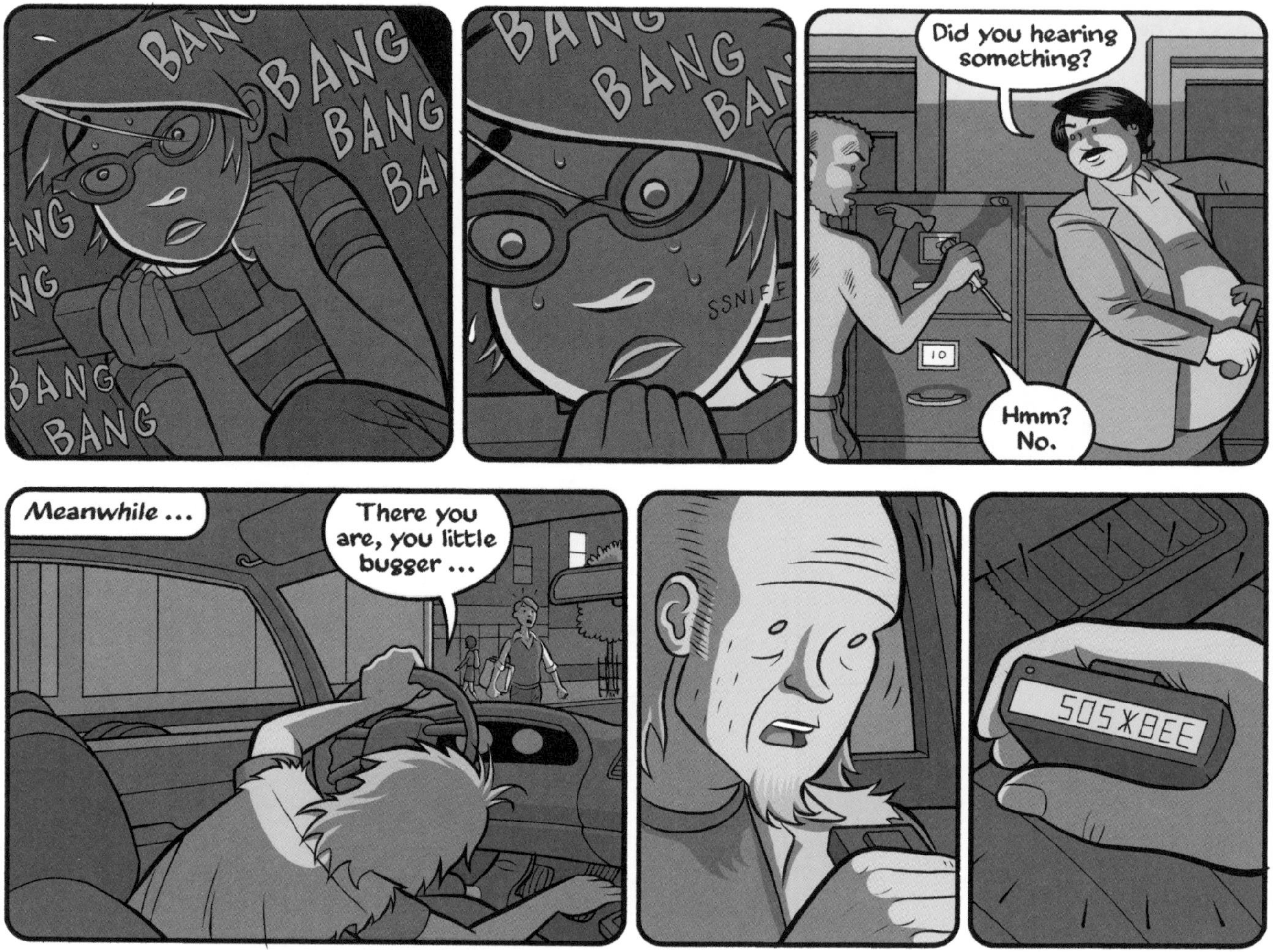
BANG
BANG
BANG
BANG
BANG
BANG
Did you hearing something?
Hmm? No.
Meanwhile ...
There you are, you little bugger ...
SOS*BEE

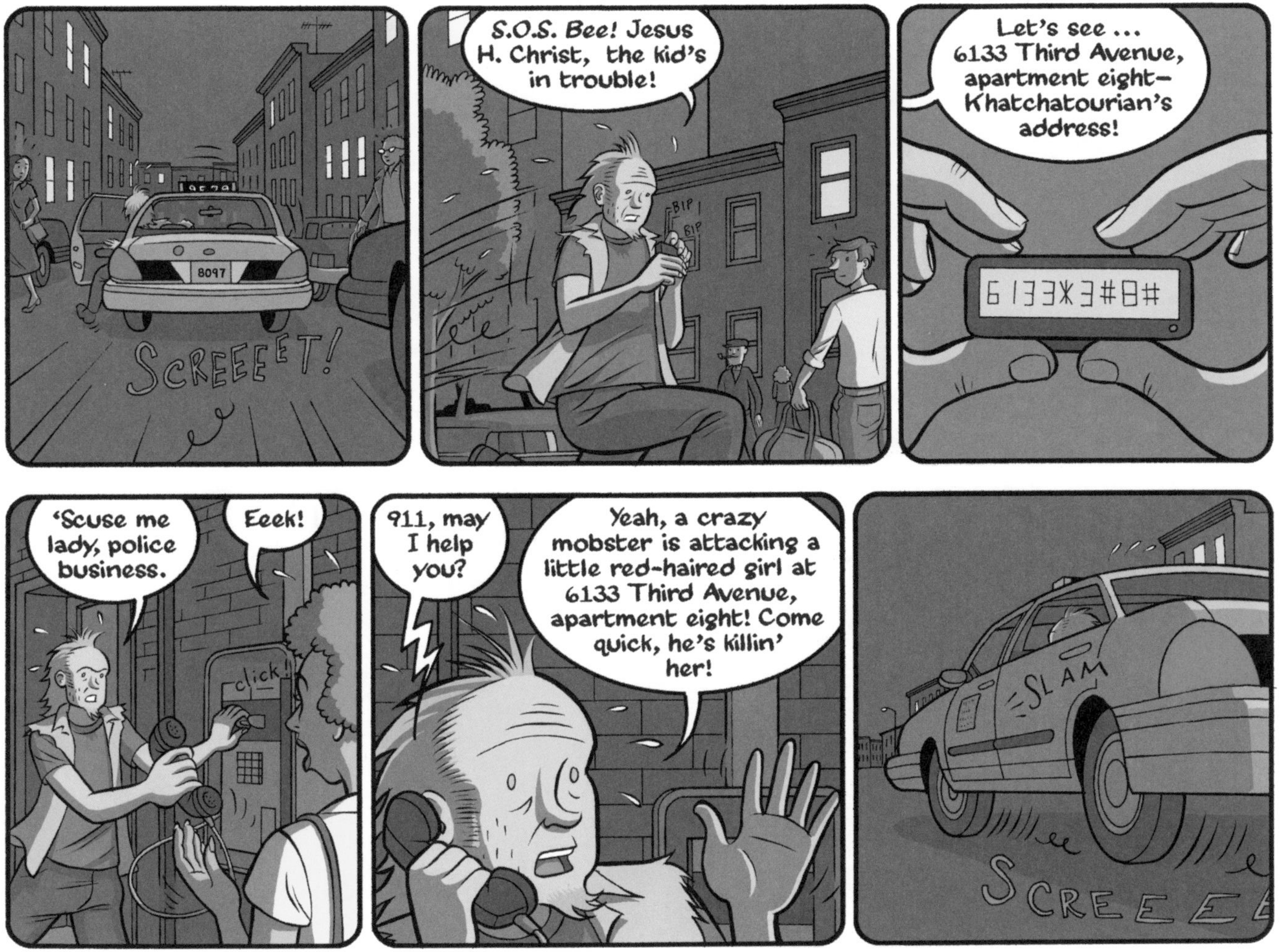
SCREEEET!
S.O.S. Bee! Jesus H. Christ, the kid's in trouble!
BIP BIP
Let's see ... 6133 Third Avenue, apartment eight– Khatchatourian's address!
6133*3#8#
'Scuse me lady, police business.
Eeek!
click!
911, may I help you?
Yeah, a crazy mobster is attacking a little red-haired girl at 6133 Third Avenue, apartment eight! Come quick, he's killin' her!
SLAM

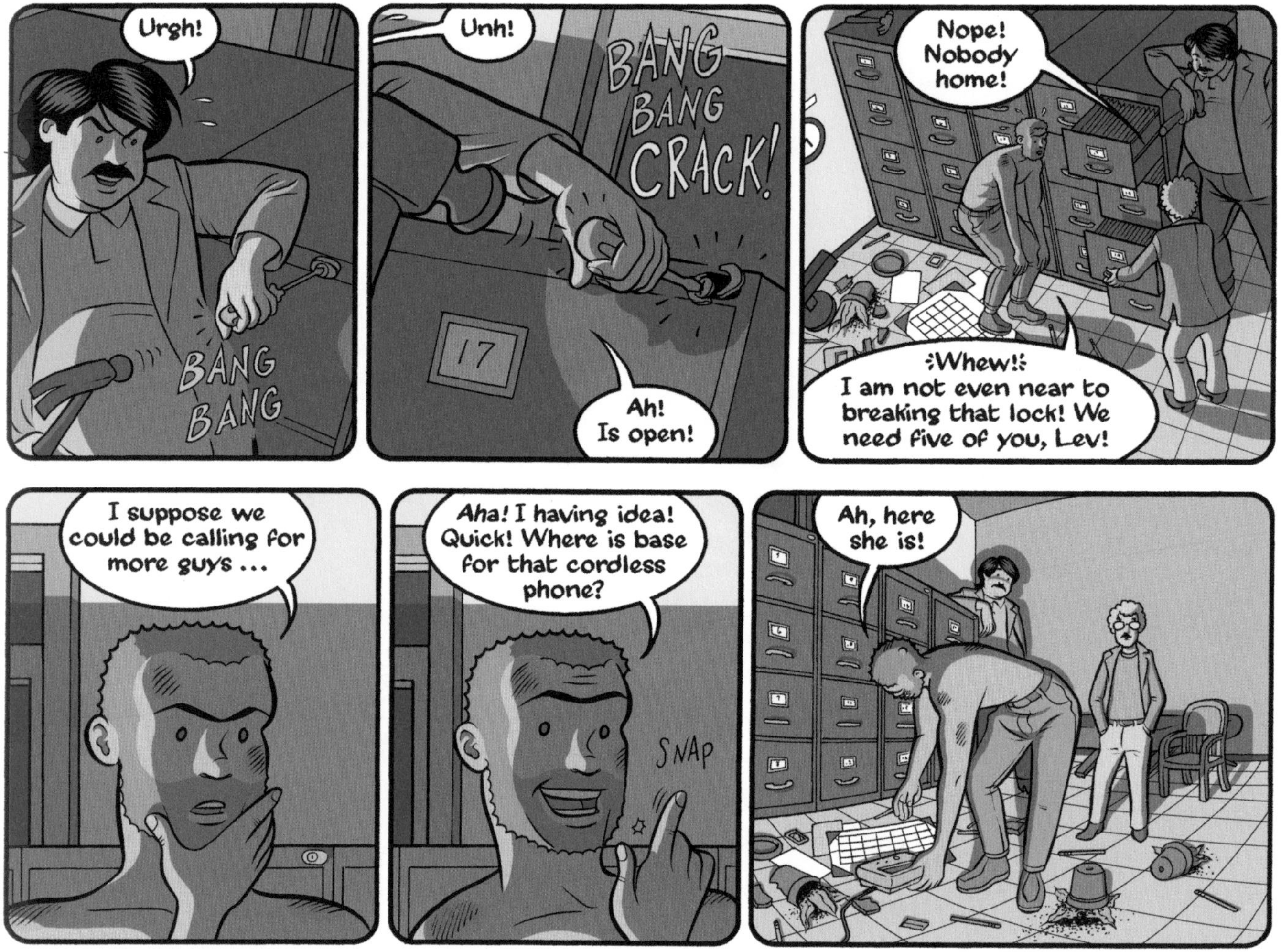
Urgh!
BANG BANG
Unh!
BANG BANG CRACK!
17
Ah! Is open!
Nope! Nobody home!
Whew!! I am not even near to breaking that lock! We need five of you, Lev!
I suppose we could be calling for more guys . . .
Aha! I having idea! Quick! Where is base for that cordless phone?
SNAP
Ah, here she is!

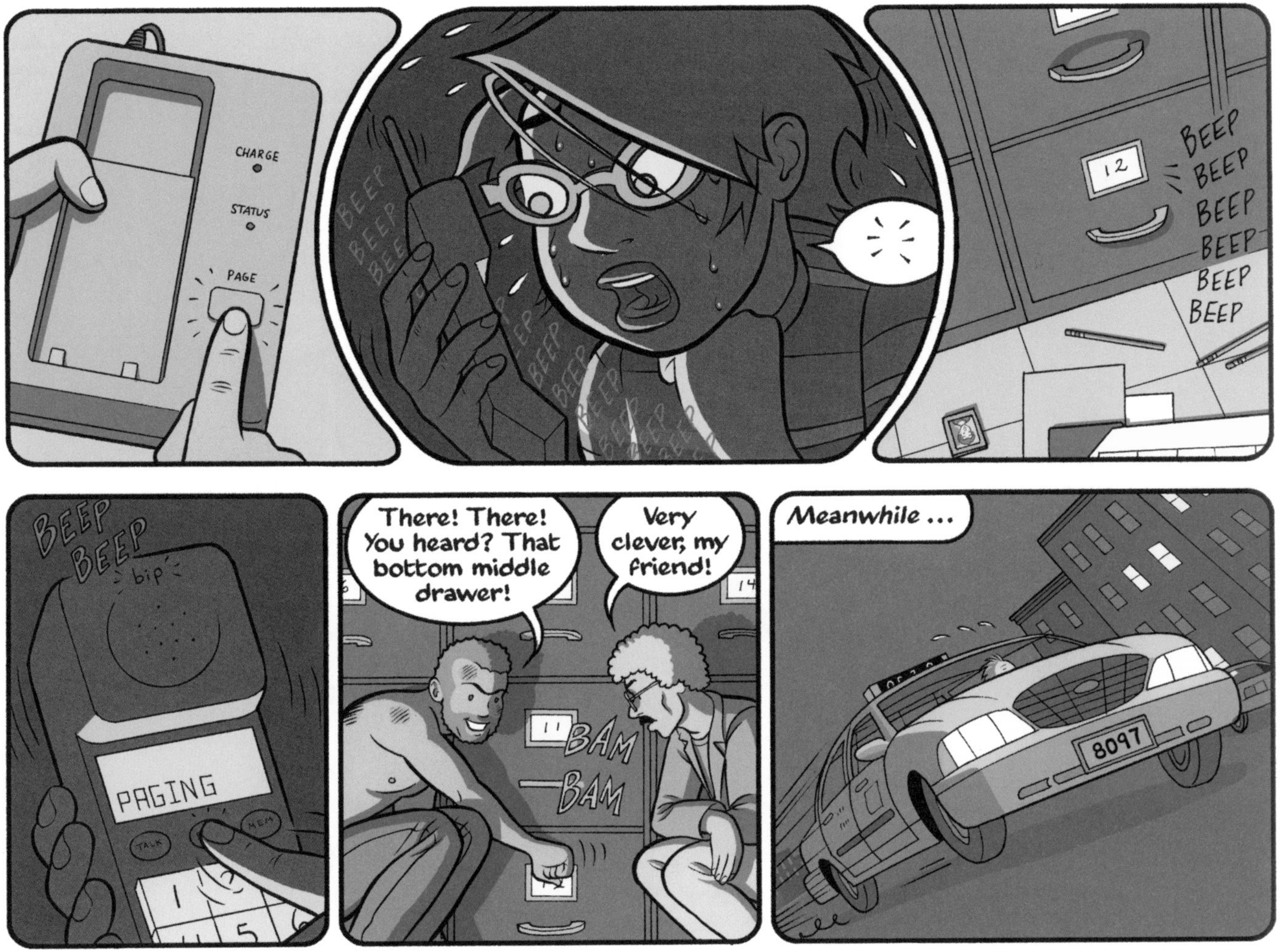
CHARGE
STATUS
PAGE
BEEP BEEP BEEP
12
BEEP BEEP BEEP BEEP BEEP BEEP
BEEP BEEP
bip
PAGING
TALK
MEM
There! There! You heard? That bottom middle drawer!
Very clever, my friend!
11
BAM BAM
Meanwhile ...
8097

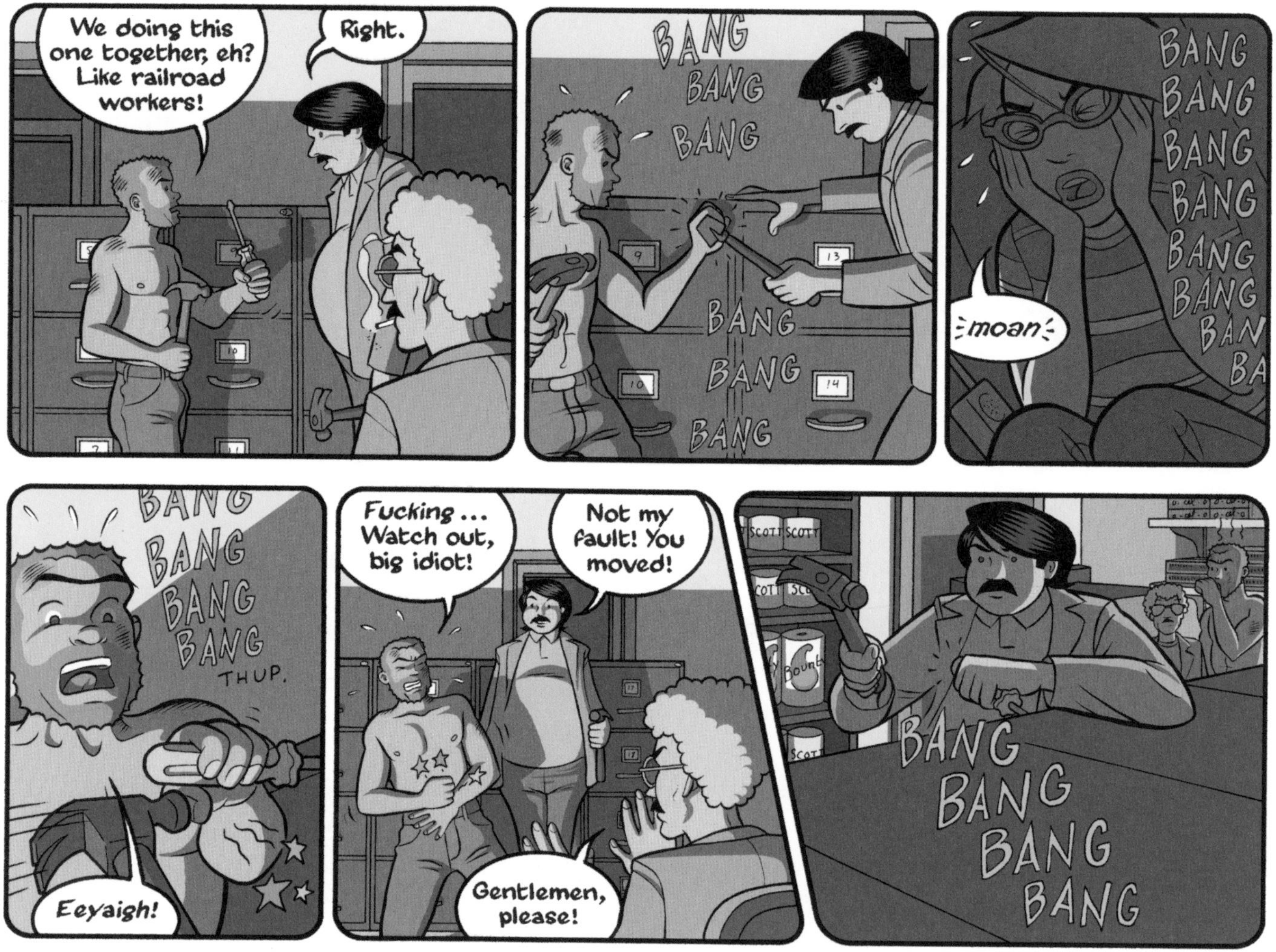
We doing this one together, eh? Like railroad workers!
Right.
BANG
BANG
BANG
BANG
BANG
BANG
BANG
BANG
BANG
BANG
BANG
BANG
BANG
BAN
BA
moan
BANG
BANG
BANG
BANG
THUP.
Eeyaigh!
Fucking... Watch out, big idiot!
Not my fault! You moved!
Gentlemen, please!
BANG
BANG
BANG
BANG

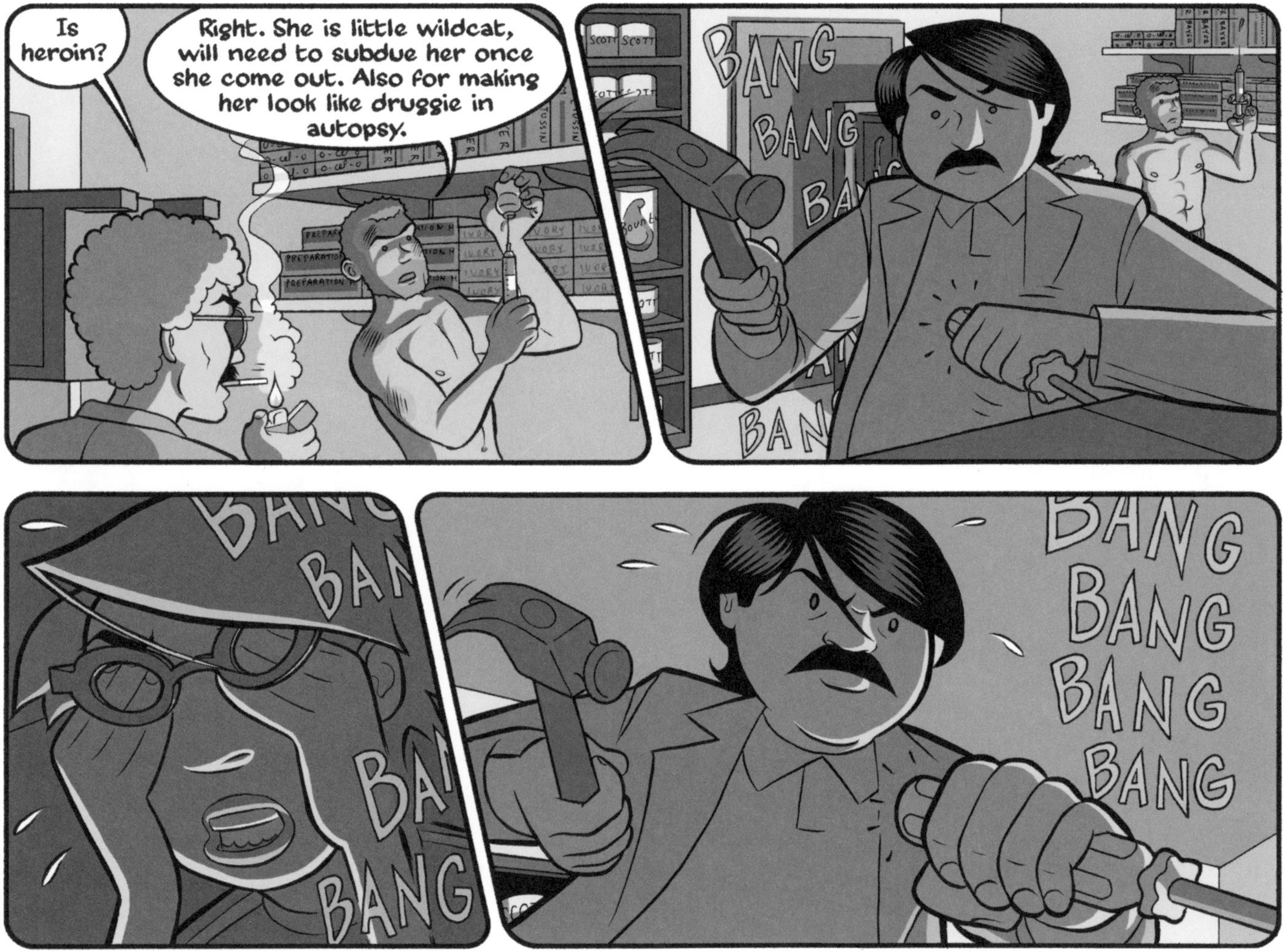
Is heroin?
Right. She is little wildcat, will need to subdue her once she come out. Also for making her look like druggie in autopsy.
BANG
BANG
BANG
BANG
BANG
BANG
BANG
BANG
BANG
BANG
BANG
BANG

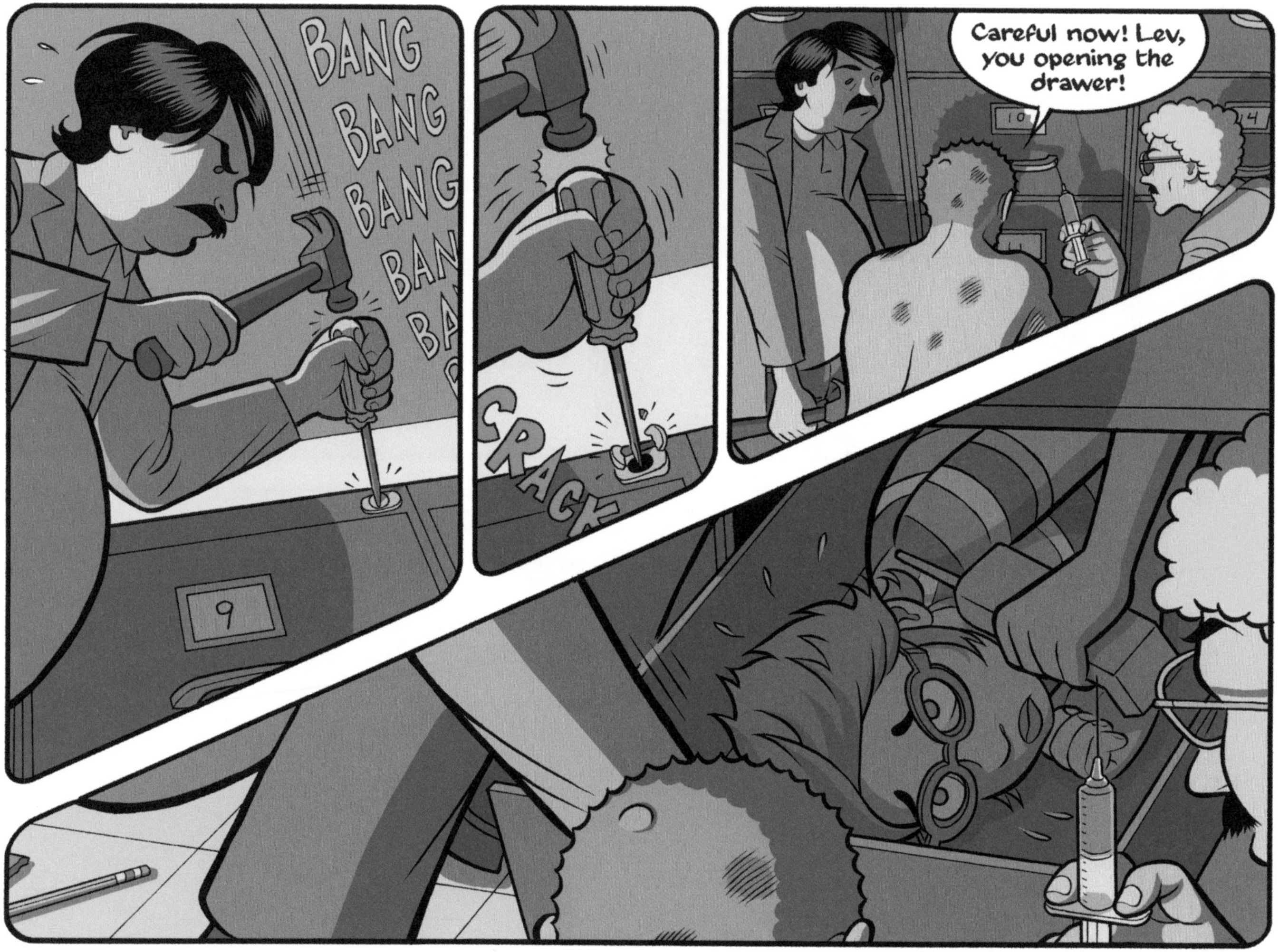
BANG
BANG
BANG
CRACK
Careful now! Lev, you opening the drawer!

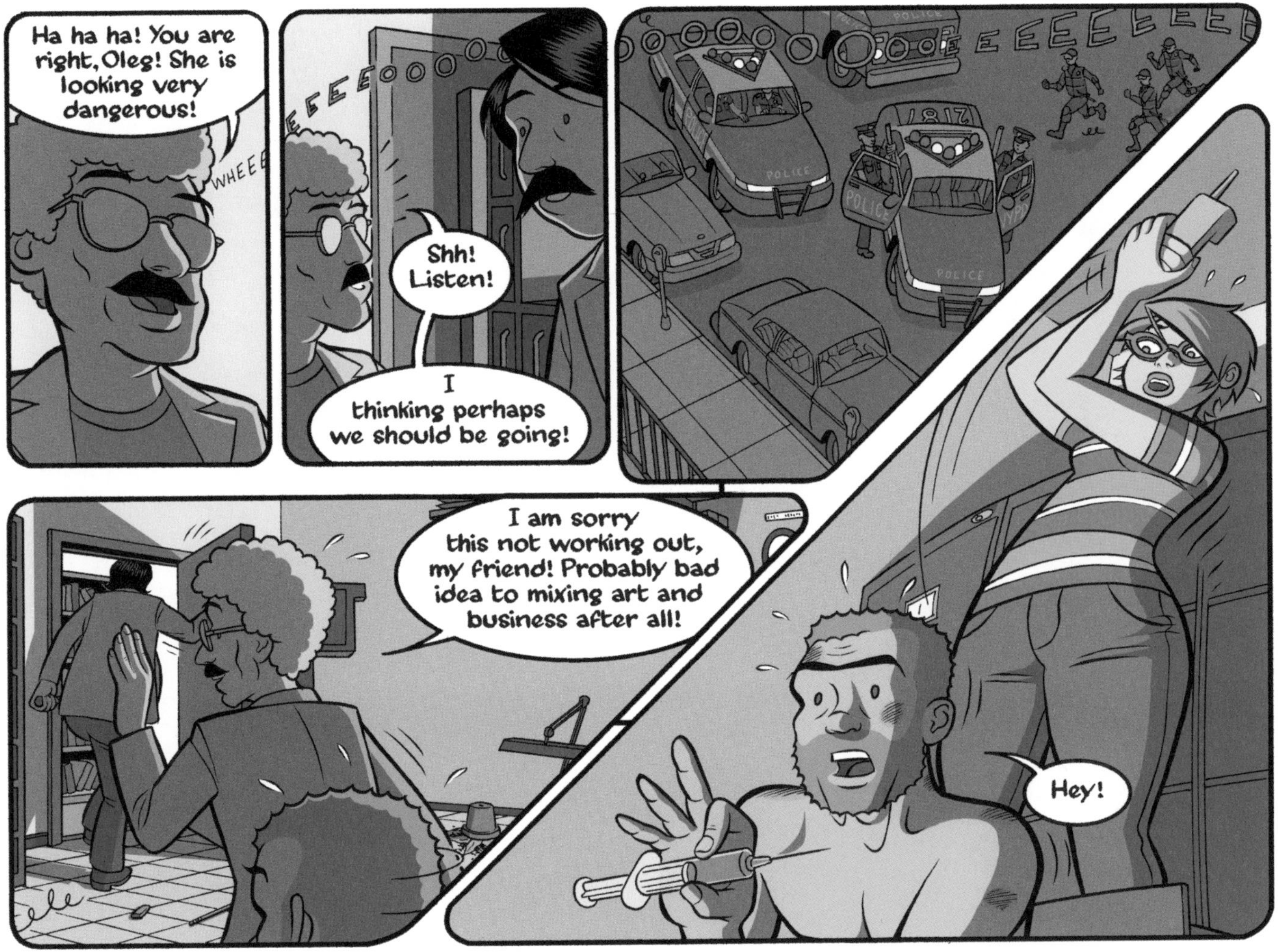
Ha ha ha! You are right, Oleg! She is looking very dangerous!
WHEEE
EEEEEOOOOO
Shh! Listen!
I thinking perhaps we should be going!
POLICE
1817
I am sorry this not working out, my friend! Probably bad idea to mixing art and business after all!
Hey!

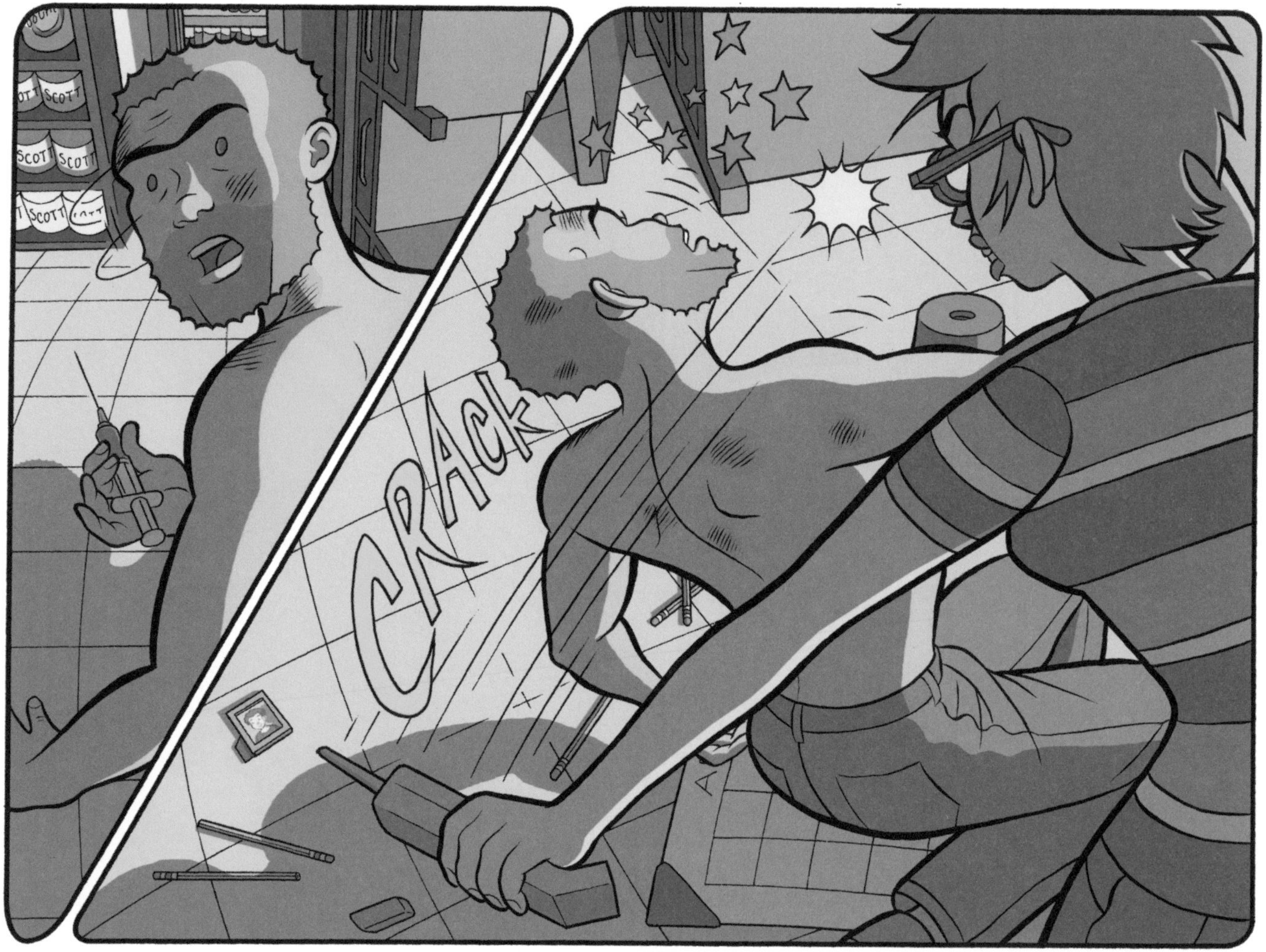
SCOTT
SCOTT
SCOTT
SCOTT
SCOTT
CRACK

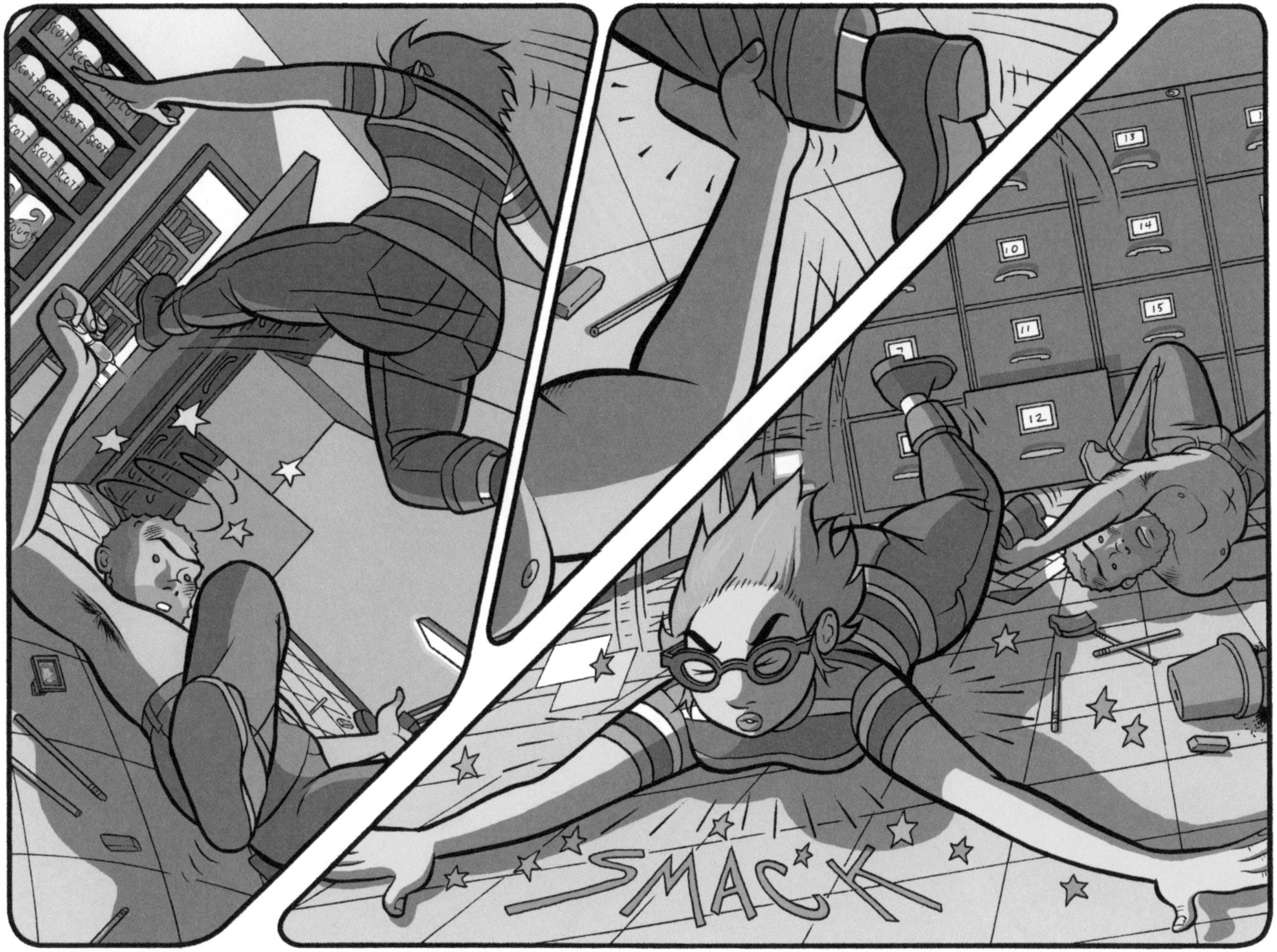
SMACK

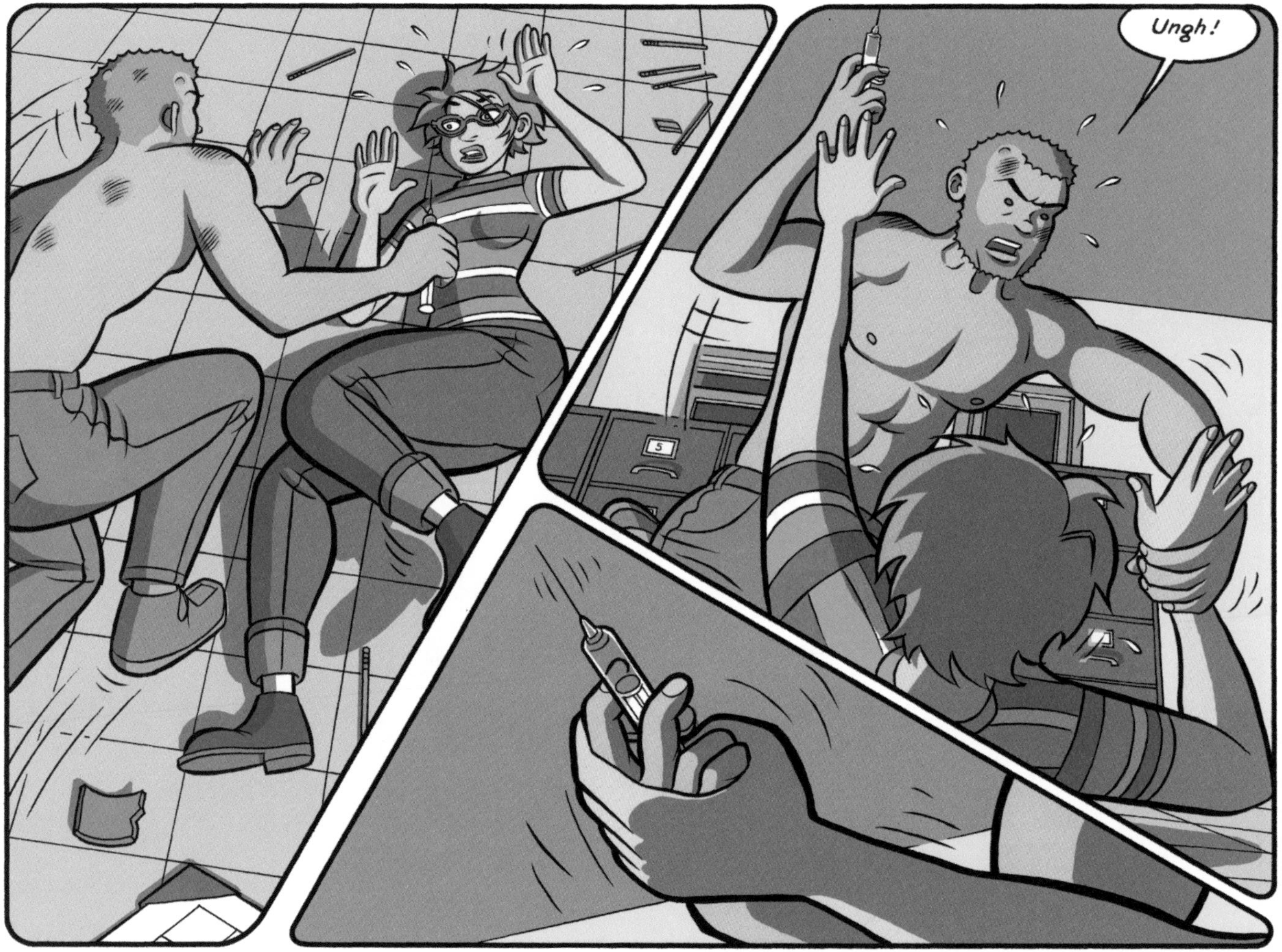
Ungh!
5

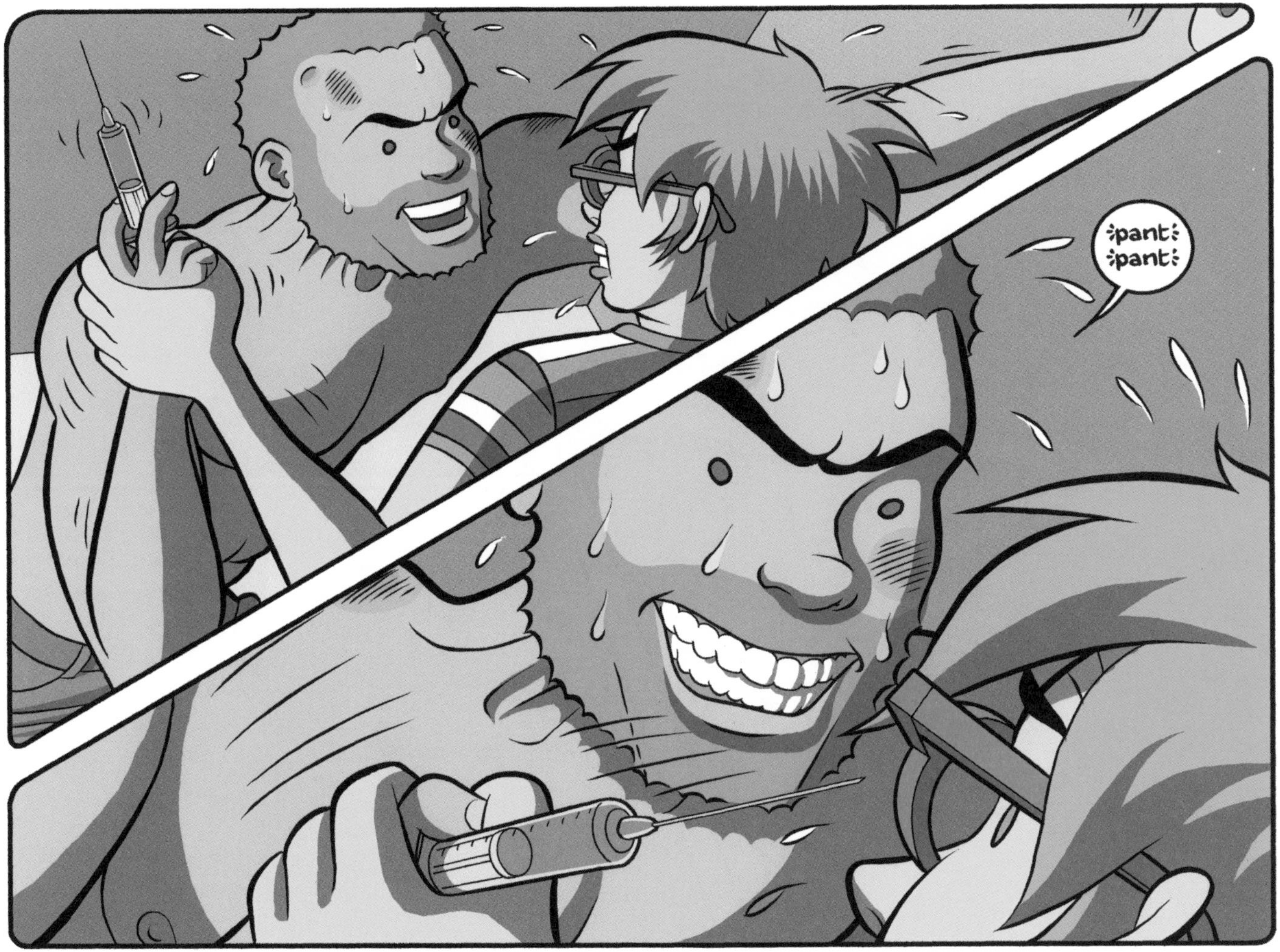
pant pant

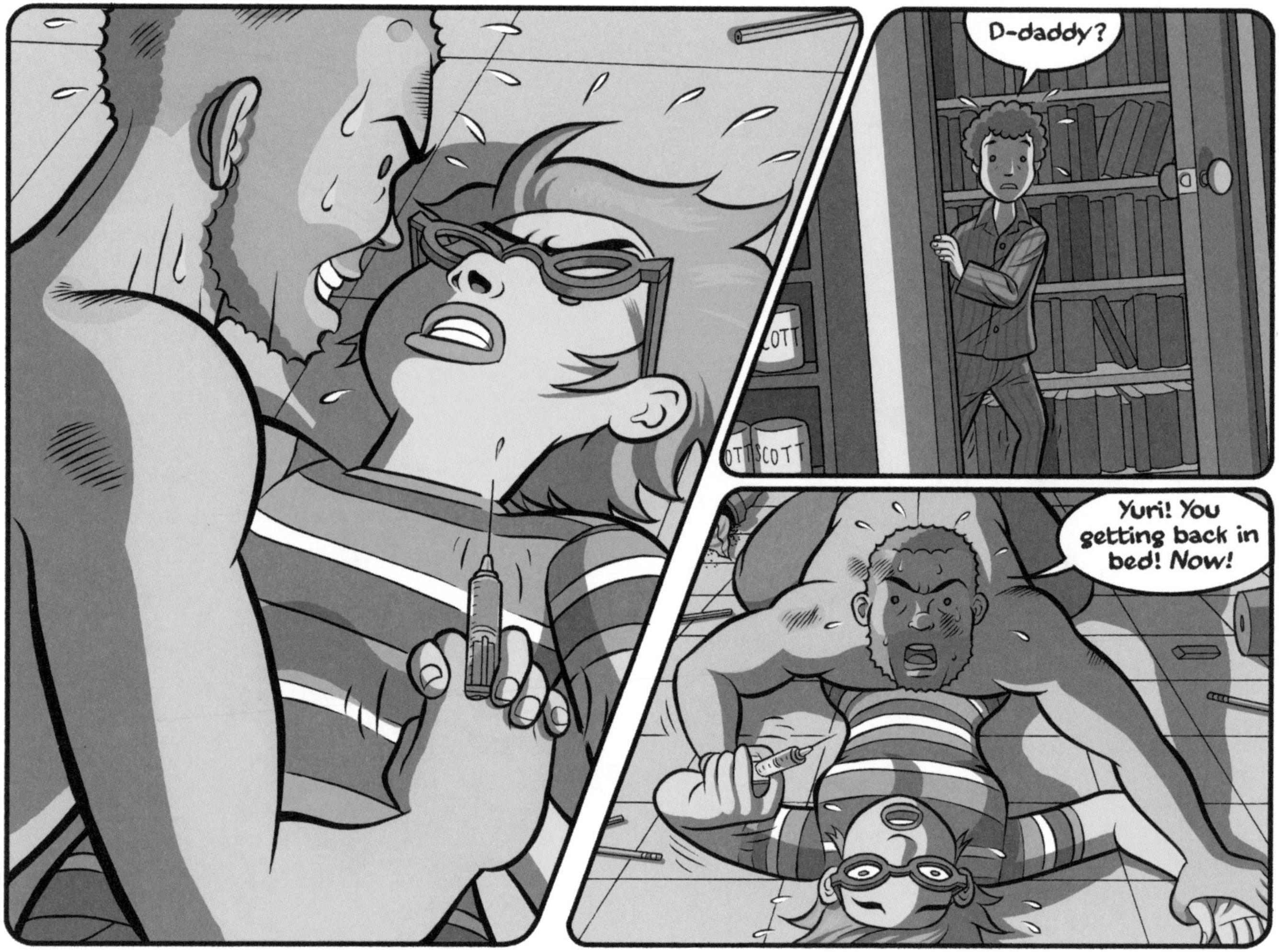
D-daddy?
Yuri! You getting back in bed! *Now!*

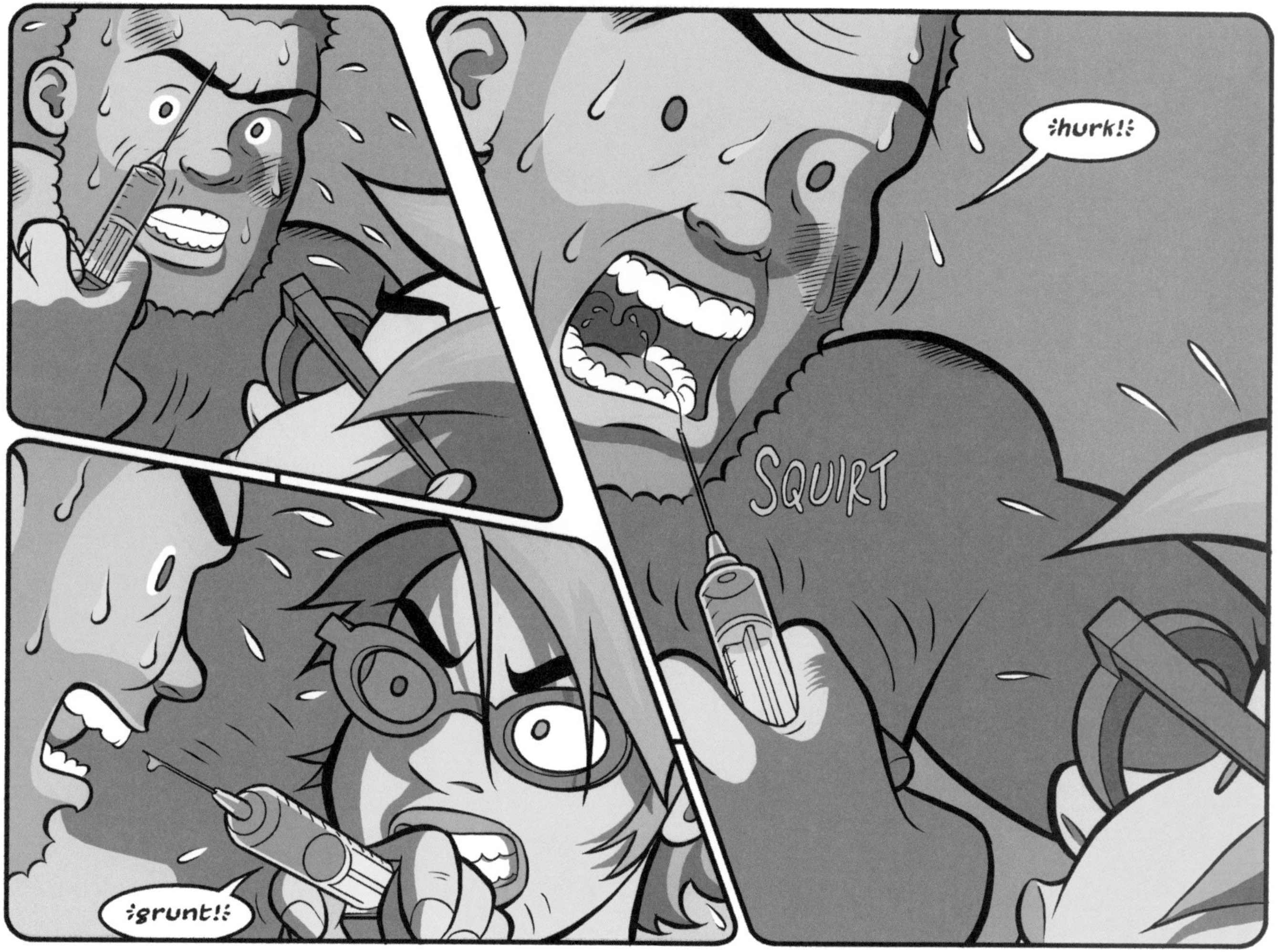
grunt!
hurk!
SQUIRT

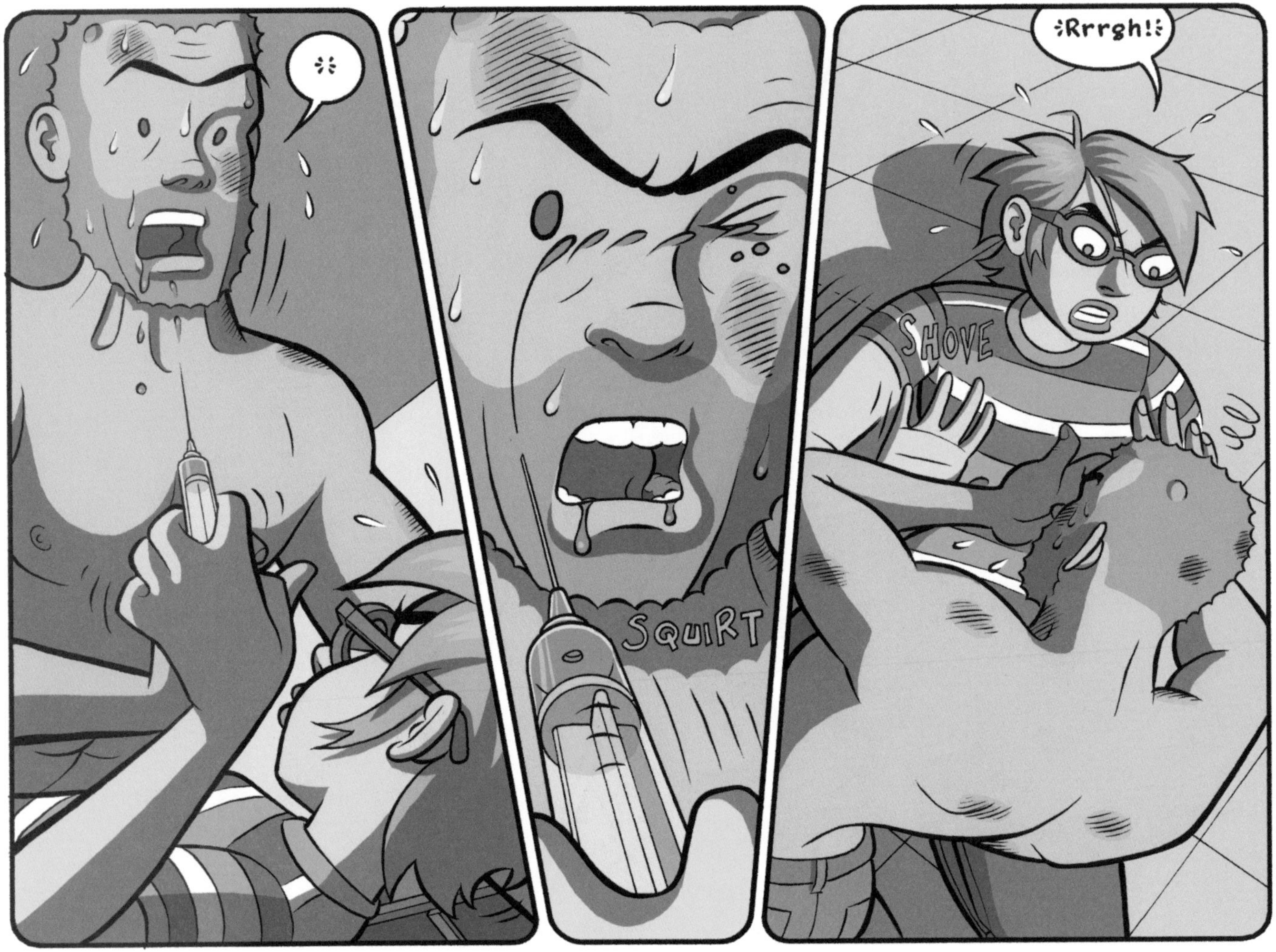
SQUIRT
Rrrgh!
SHOVE

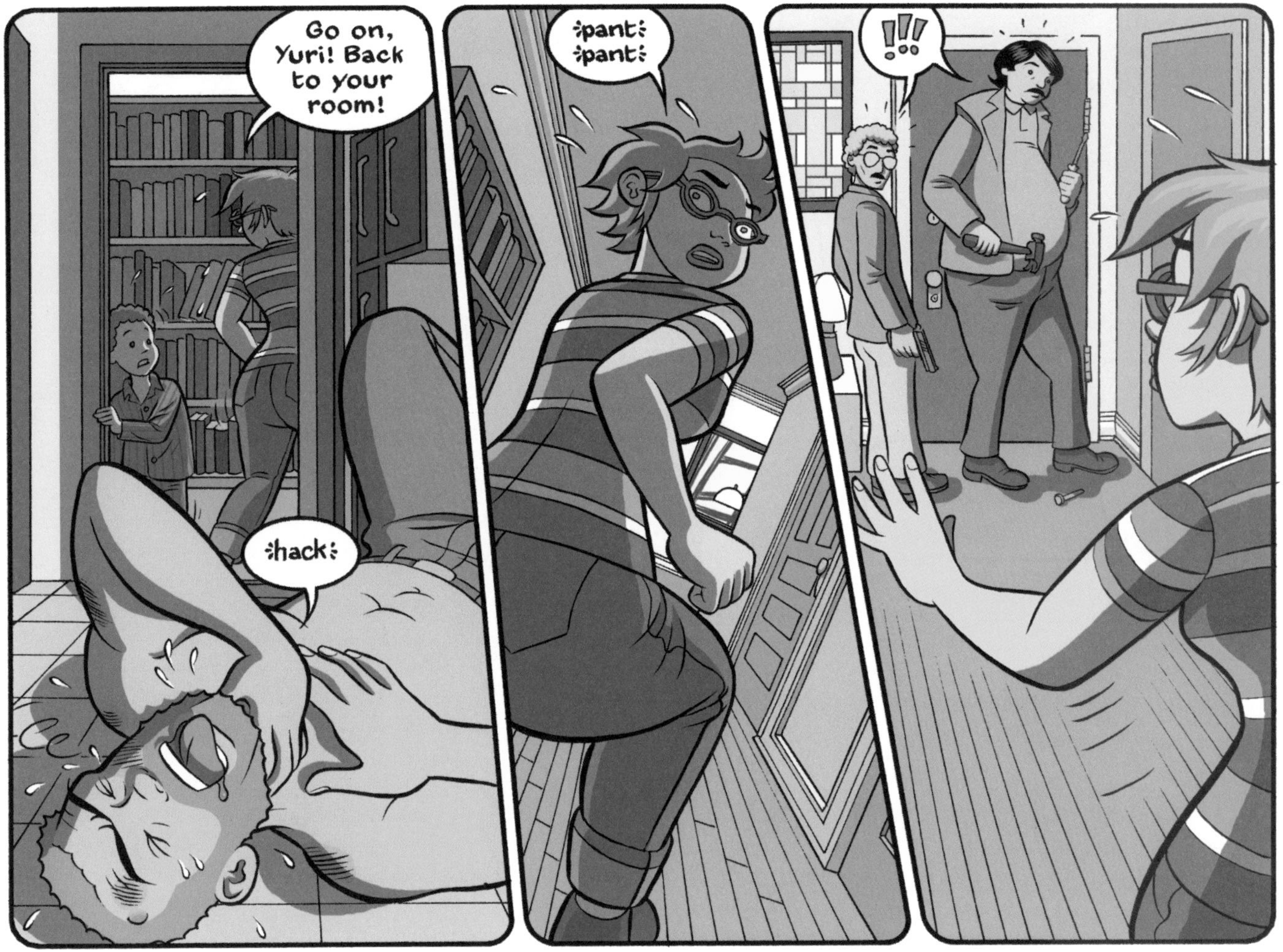
Go on, Yuri! Back to your room!
:hack:
:pant: :pant:
!!!

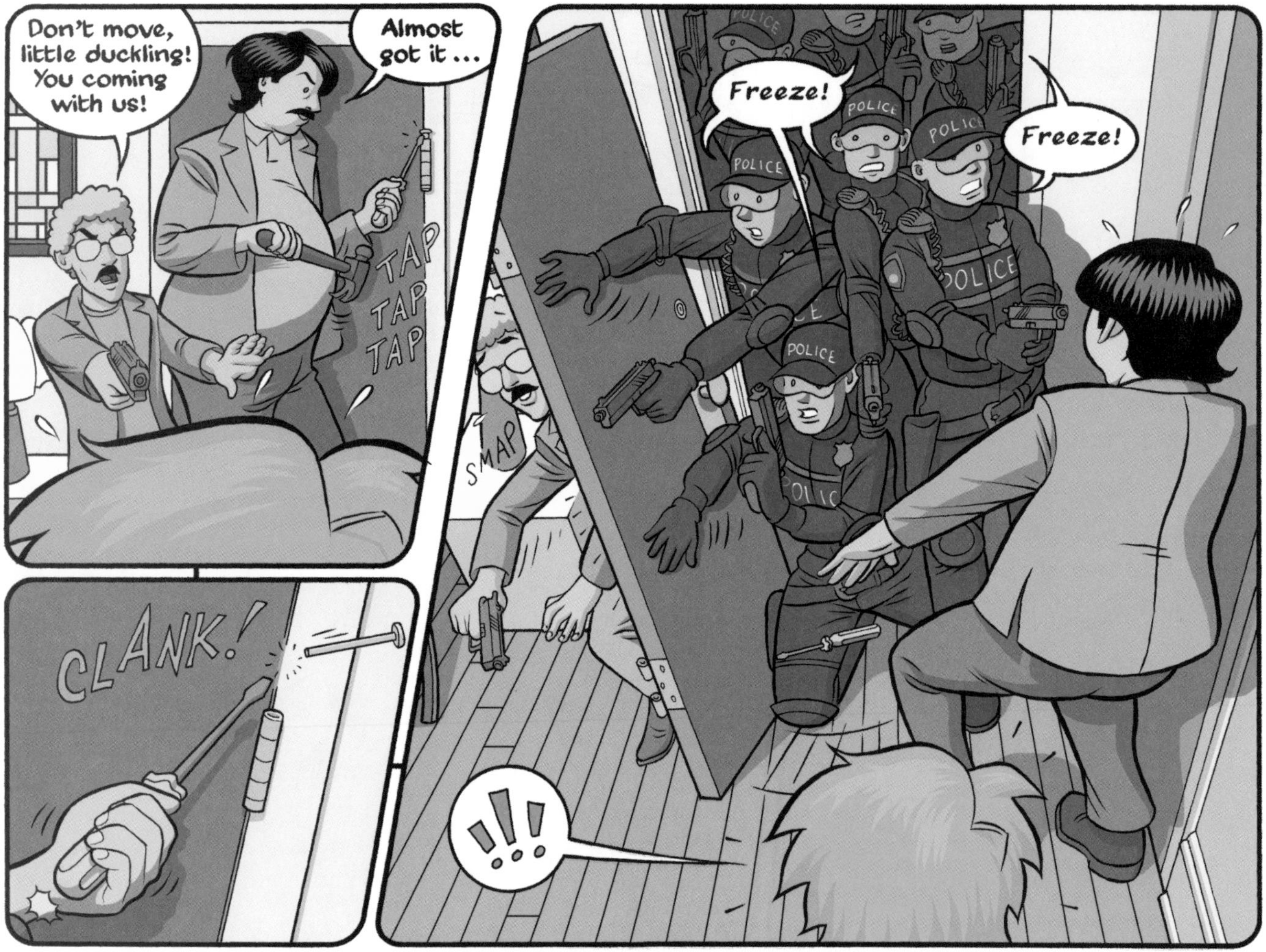
Don't move, little duckling! You coming with us!
Almost got it ...
TAP TAP TAP TAP
CLANK!
Freeze!
Freeze!
SMAP
!!!

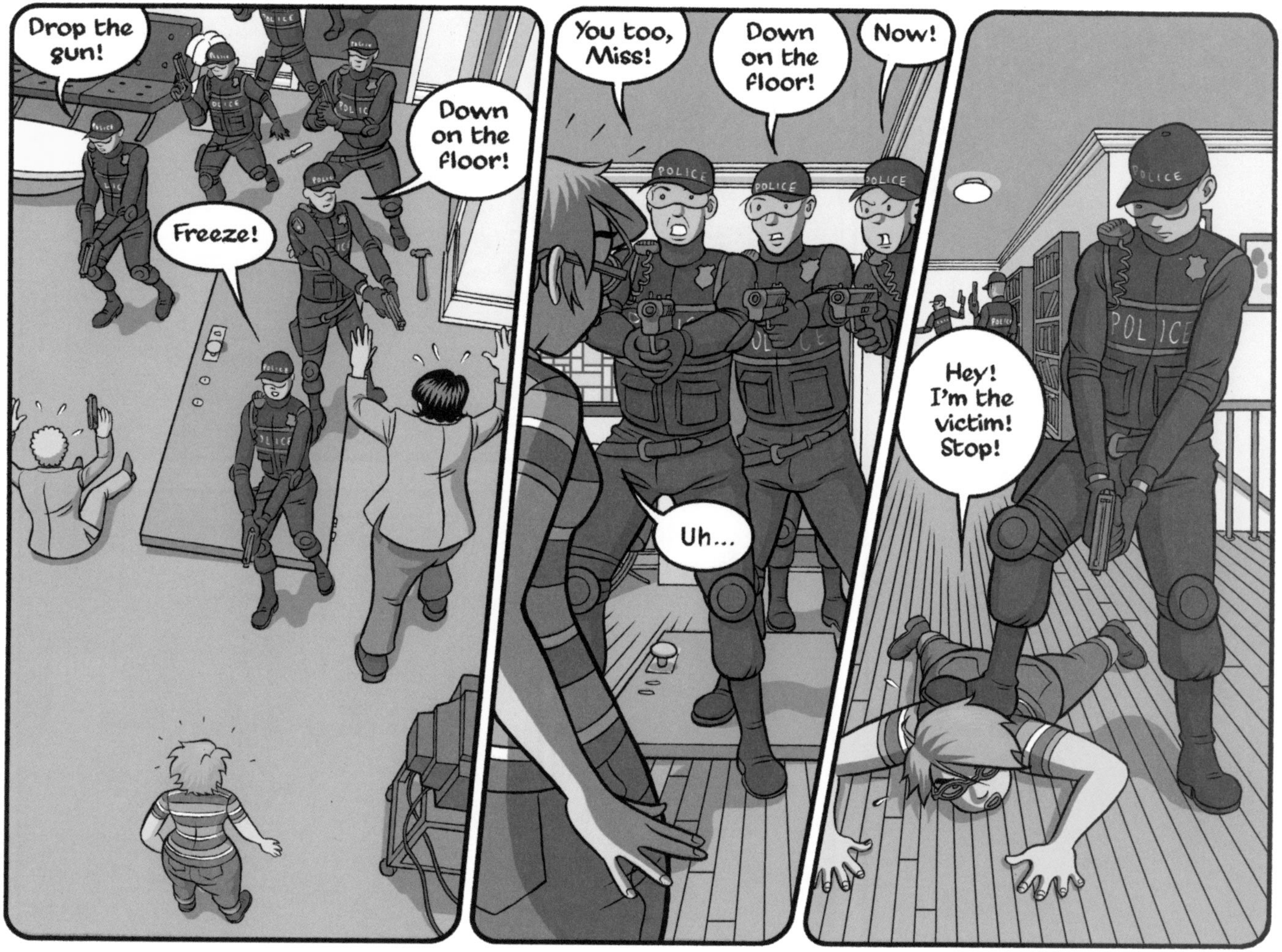
Drop the gun!
Down on the floor!
Freeze!
You too, Miss!
Down on the floor!
Now!
Uh...
Hey! I'm the victim! Stop!

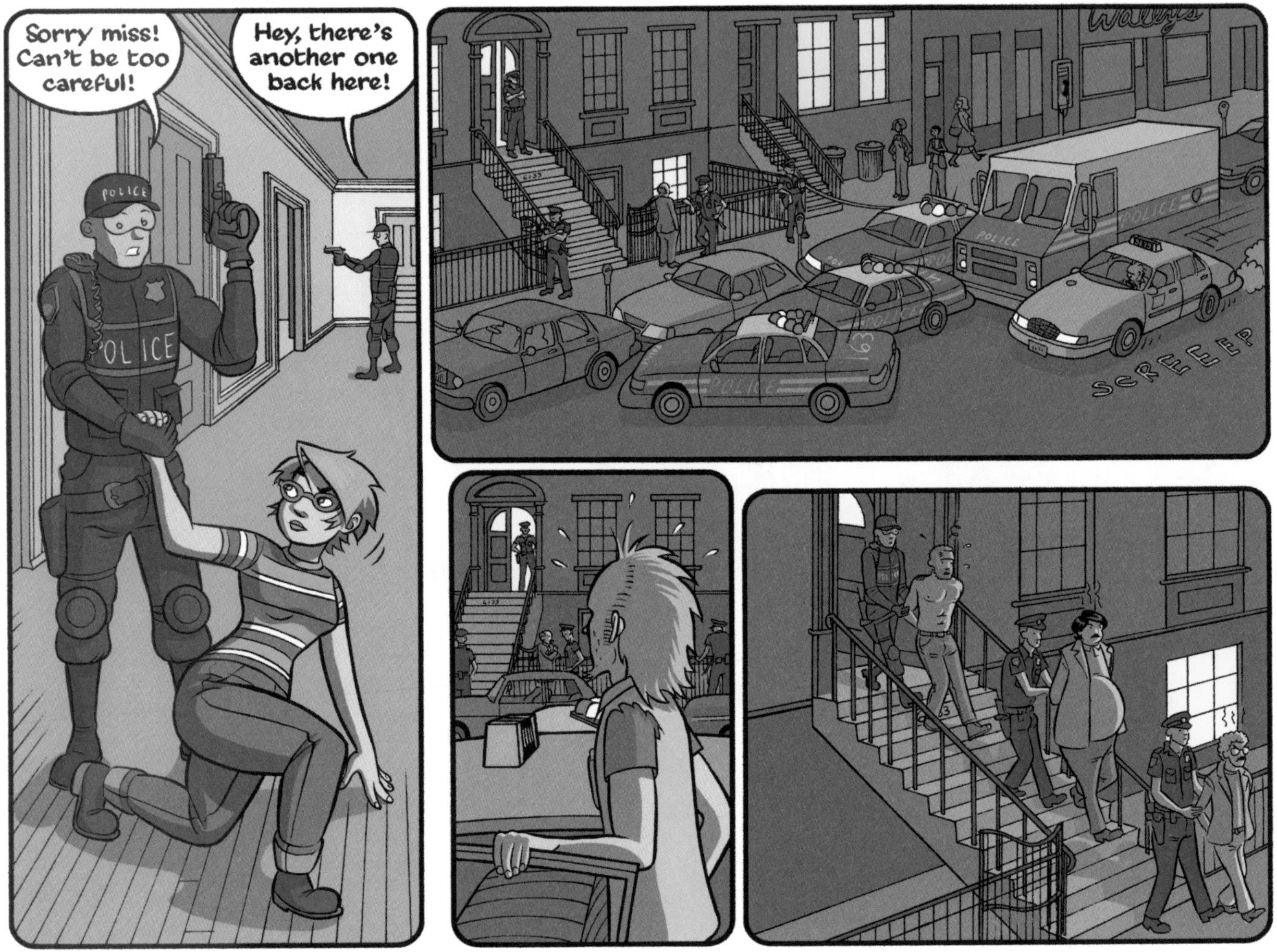
Sorry miss! Can't be too careful!
Hey, there's another one back here!
SCREEEP

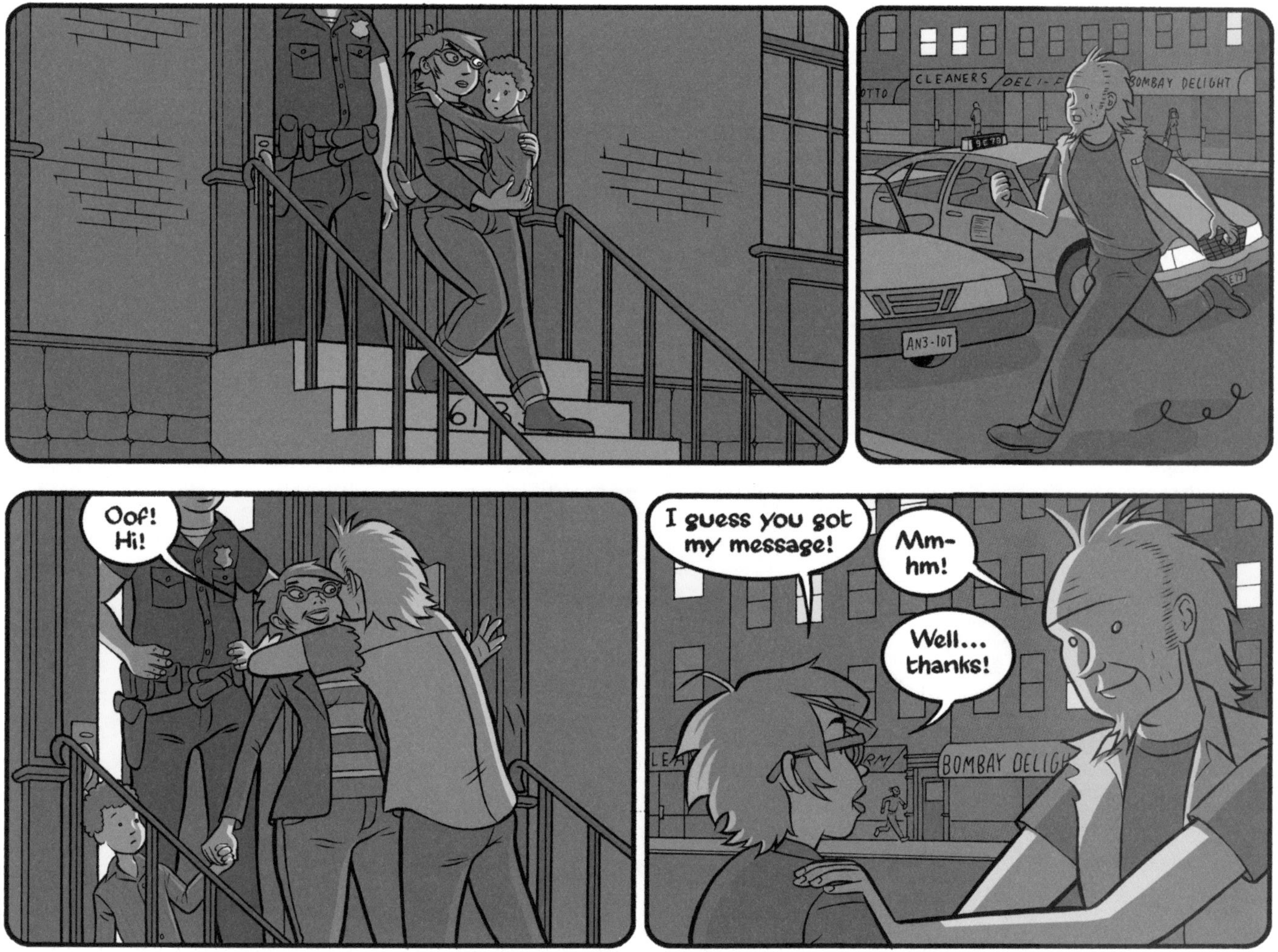
CLEANERS
DELI-F
BOMBAY DELIGHT
AN3-10T
Oof! Hi!
I guess you got my message!
Mm-hm!
Well... thanks!
BOMBAY DELIG

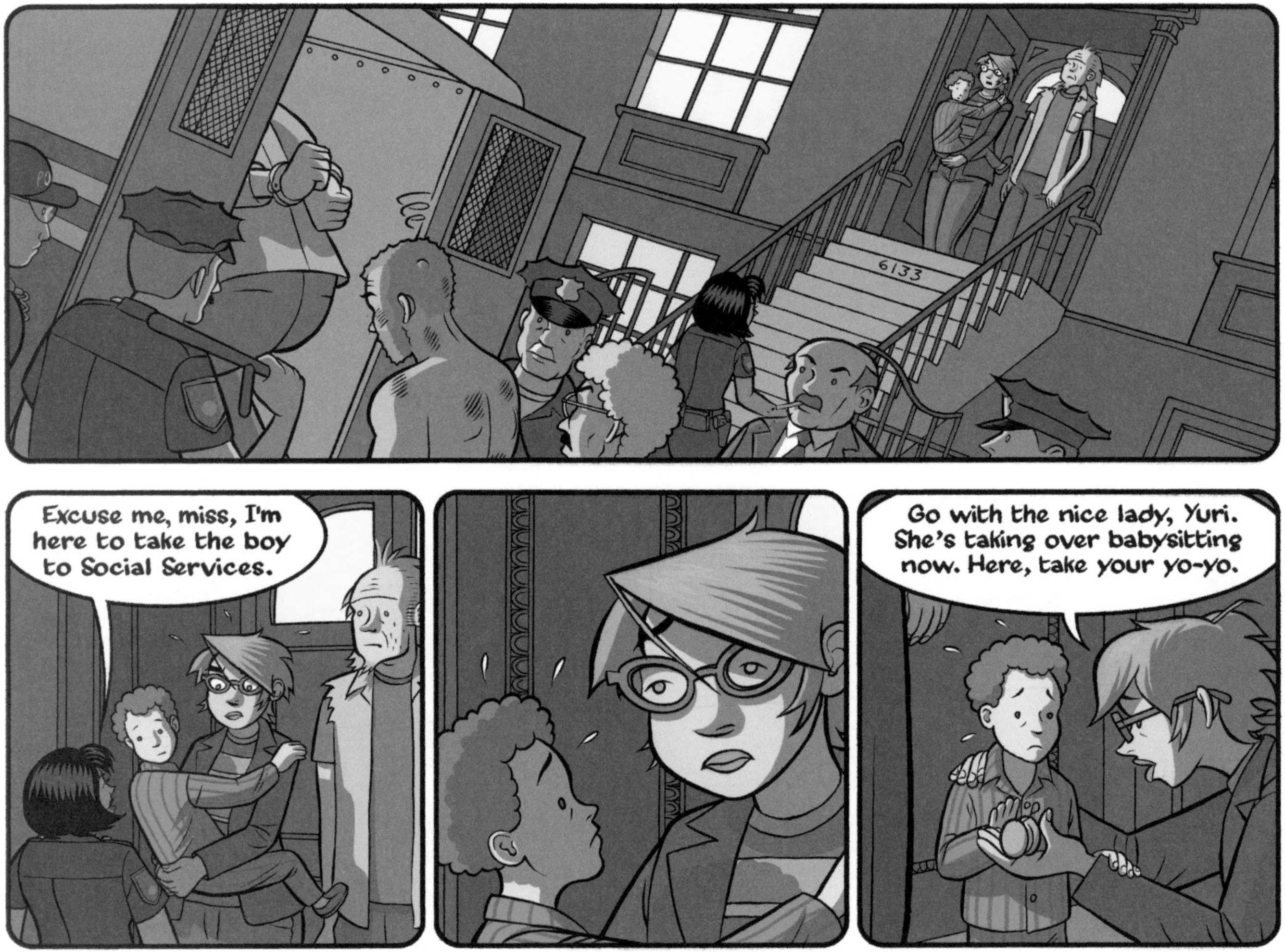
6133
Excuse me, miss, I'm here to take the boy to Social Services.
Go with the nice lady, Yuri. She's taking over babysitting now. Here, take your yo-yo.

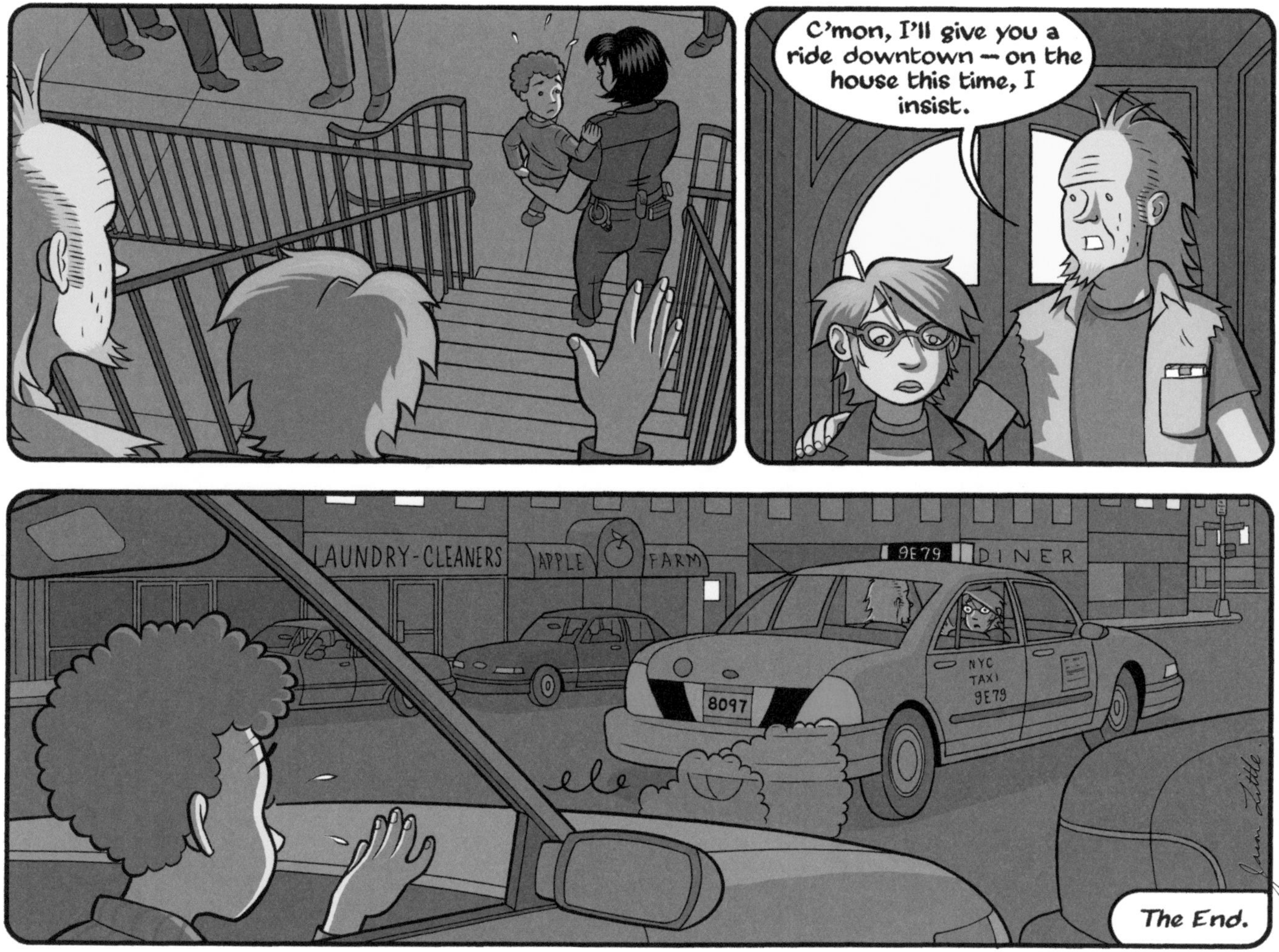
C'mon, I'll give you a ride downtown — on the house this time, I insist.
LAUNDRY-CLEANERS
APPLE FARM
9E79
DINER
NYC TAXI 9E79
8097
The End.

GRATITVDE

Profoundest thanks are extended to my assistants:

    Background inks and color: Raina Telgemeier and
      Ed Chichik;
    background inks: Harold Edge;
    color: Alexander Rothman, Vanessa Bertozzi,
      Cristina "Tintin" Pantoja, and Ellen Lindner.

Titanic thanks are presented to Myla Goldberg.

Mammoth thanks are extended to Wendy Schmalz.

Huge thanks go to Deborah Cowell, Roxy Wu, Chuck
Watson, Edmond Hallas, Jessie Caird, Julia Coblentz,
Nancy Flynn, Scott Russo, and Luisa Francavilla.

Giant thanks are extended to Michael, Adrienne &
Diana Little; Julia Tuznik Veeson; Mark, Ellen & Saryn
Goldberg; Nicholas Bertozzi; Daupo; Dean Haspiel;
Matt Madden; Josh Neufeld; Tim Kreider; Jeffrey
Mason; Stefan Economou; Tom Hart; Leela Corman;
Lance Tooks; Emily Ryan Lerner; Lisa Rosenthal;
Allison Wagreich; Shauna Toh; Vladimir Sakhnov; and
Alan & Sarah Pollard.

Jason Little grew up in Binghamton, New
York. He lives in Brooklyn with his wife,
novelist Myla Goldberg.